MYSTERIES OF THE WORLD

MYSTERIES OF THE WORLD

General Editor Christopher Pick

CHARTWELL
BOOKS INC.

Published by Chartwell Books Inc.
A division of Books Sales Inc.
110 Enterprise Avenue
Secaucus, New Jersey 07094

© 1979 Lyric Books Limited
Depósito legal   TO · 554 : 79
ISBN 0 7111 0003 9
Impreso en Artes Gráficas Toledo
Printed in Spain

CONTENTS

FOREWORD

Ian Wilson

A quick glance at the chapter headings of this book reveals such a variety of the bizarre and unexplained that one may at first be overwhelmed by its breadth. Yet to look no further would be to adopt precisely that academic snobbishness which has caused too many serious but offbeat areas of enquiry not to be given the full measure of authoritative, qualified research they deserve.

Stonehenge, carefully discussed in this book in the chapter by Shirley Toulson, is a typical case in point. A few years ago the evidence became virtually irrefutable that Stonehenge and other similar stone circles throughout N. W. Europe have been built both to incredibly sophisticated astronomical alignments, and to an internationally co-ordinated unit of measure, the so-called 'megalithic yard'. Amateur enthusiasts reacted to this news with often wildly speculative theories that do little credit to the new evidence. Professional prehistorians by contrast have too often simply buried their heads in the sand, ignoring new fascinating questions as to the nature of early British society that demand serious consideration and recognition.

While we may never know the minds behind the megaliths, other mysteries discussed in this book are much more capable of eventual solution, some even imminently so.

The Turin Shroud, for instance, although still shunned by professional historians, has attracted almost every other field of academic interest, particularly following its exposition and subsequent testing during 1978. Definitive findings from this testing, likely to be very supportive of its authenticity, are expected as early as 1980.

The Loch Ness monster, ostensibly a subject far removed from the Shroud, could similarly undergo a dramatic breakthrough in the not too distant future. As Tim Dinsdale makes clear in his excellent chapter there is increasing photographic and sonar evidence for the presence of huge plesiosaur-like creatures in the loch. And why not? As we know the coelocanth survived as a species, despite having been thought long extinct. Why not the plesiosaur?

Atlantis may seem the most bizarre territory of all, yet as Colin Ridler shows, there is now widely acknowledged substance to Plato's story. It may be an anti-climax than instead of a fabled lost continent, Atlantis may have been a somewhat more diminutive Minoan island destroyed by an earthquake in the 2nd millenium BC. But at least it is vindication of the view that legends are rarely invented out of nothing. There is invariably a kernel of truth upon which somewhat taller stories grow.

The world of mysteries is then a fascinating one, but one must beware of some of its wonders. In writing this foreword I would like to make it clear that I am partial neither to the Ufologists nor the exponents of the Bermuda triangle.

The ultimate test of the value of any mystery is not so much the relative bizarreness of the story as the objectivity of the approach and the quality of the evidence presented, and far too many UFO accounts fall on precisely those points.

I would end on the note on which I began. It behoves none of us to be too dismissive of concepts that seem at first sight too outlandish to be credible. To the learned men of the 15th century the earth was obviously flat. It took Columbus to prove them wrong. Of the mysteries touched on in this book, and others relating to the whole nature of man and his role in the Universe, it is best to acknowledge, with Hamlet, our own humility: "There are more things in heaven and earth, Horatio, than are dreamt of in your philosophy..."

Ian Wilson
Author of the bestselling book
The Turin Shroud

Endpapers: **stone statues on Easter Island (Zentral Farbbild Agentur);** *Half-title page:* **gold mask, Iquitos (Michael Holford Library);** *Title pages:* **Sphinx at Giza (Spectrum Colour Library);** *Contents pages:* **wall painting of Akhenaton, predecessor of Tutankhamun, (W. McQuitty);** *Left:* **monastery ruins, Tintagel (Spectrum Colour Library).**

MYSTERIOUS ORIGINS

THE MYTH OF ATLANTIS

The wondrous city of Atlantis holds a fascination that endures to this day. Did it ever actually exist, or is the story related by Plato a subtle combination of fact and fantasy?

Most of us, if we cared to admit it, would like to believe that there could exist, or once did exist, an ideal society, where the affairs of men were ordered by just laws, and peace and prosperity reigned eternally. Sir Thomas More's *Utopia* of 1516 has given its name to the genre of fictionalized accounts of such societies, the derivation of the word 'Utopia' from the Greek for 'nowhere' revealing how much faith More himself had in the realization of his particular dream. But nearly 1900 years earlier a Greek philosopher had already written an account of a 'Utopian' society which, he implied, had actually existed far back in the distant past. This philosopher was Plato and the great but extinct civilization that of Atlantis.

Atlantis has attracted the attention of cranks, mystics, scientists, historians and many others, from ancient times to the present. Utopianism has always been one strand in its enduring fascination, but Plato scores over Sir Thomas More in having given his ideal state both a definite geographic location (in the Atlantic, opposite the Straits of Gibraltar) and a fixed time in history (down to about 11,500 years ago, when it was mysteriously swallowed up in the ocean). Thus Atlantis qualifies not only as a Utopia but as a *lost* Utopia, whose remnants may yet lie undiscovered at the bottom of the sea. It appeals to our innate curiosity about vanished civilizations, a curiosity which prompted Heinrich Schliemann to search for and find Troy in 1871 and Sir Arthur Evans thirty years later to dig up ancient Knossos in Crete and rediscover the Minoan civilization. I choose these examples advisedly, because little more than a century ago, before these pioneering excavations, scholars treated Homer's Trojan Wars and the legend of King Minos and the Minotaur as pure myths, with no more basis in historical reality than Plato's Atlantis or stories about the Olympian gods. Yet if we now sift the Homeric sagas for evidence of what actually went on in the Trojan Wars and uncover labyrinths and decorated walls confirming the existence of a Minoan bull-cult – why should we dismiss out of hand Plato's account of the lost Atlantis?

I shall attempt to assess how much truth there may be behind the story. But first we should ask what the story itself tells us.

The one and only independent source for ancient Atlantis comes in two philosophical

The Egyptians may have identified volcanic eruptions on the island of Thera *(above and below)* **with nearby Crete.**

dialogues called *Timaeus* and *Critias*, written by Plato in about 355 BC, when he was in his early seventies. The dialogues are named after the main speakers in each (Critias was Plato's great-grandfather). Together with one Hermocrates (whom Plato originally intended to speak in a third dialogue), Timaeus and Critias are discussing the 'ideal society' with Socrates, Plato's old teacher. In the *Timaeus*, Socrates recalls an earlier conversation in which he had outlined his vision of the perfect state, and he asks whether any of the others can now bring his vision to life. It is at this point that Critias steps in and gives us the basic story of Atlantis.

The tale, he tells us, 'is a strange one', which he had heard from his grandfather, who himself had heard it from a close friend of *his* father's, the Athenian statesman Solon. Solon had once visited Egypt, where a priest from a place called Saïs recounted the following story.

Nine thousand years before there had existed a great

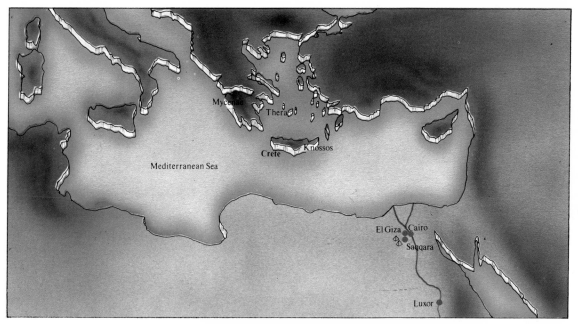

Athenian state, 'pre-eminent in war and conspicuously the best governed in every way', the forerunner of Solon's Athens. 'Our records tell', the priest goes on:

'how your city checked a great power which arrogantly advanced from its base in the Atlantic ocean to attack the cities of Europe and Asia. For in those days . . . there was an island opposite the strait which you call . . . the Pillars of Heracles [Straits of Gibraltar], an island larger than Libya [North Africa] and Asia combined. . . . On this island of Atlantis had arisen a powerful and remarkable dynasty of kings, who ruled the whole island, and many other islands as well and parts of the continent; in addition it controlled . . . Libya up to the borders of Egypt and Europe as far as Tyrrhenia [Northern Italy]. This dynasty, gathering its whole power together, attempted to enslave, at a single stroke, your country and ours and all the territory within the strait. It was then, Solon, that the power and courage . . . of your city became clear for all men to see. . . . She led an alliance of the Greeks, and then when they deserted her and she was forced to fight alone . . . she overcame the invaders and celebrated a victory. . . . At a later time there were earthquakes and floods of extra-

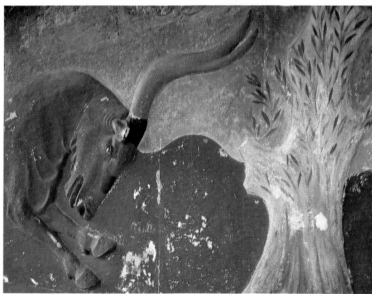

Three frescoes at Knossos, Crete: the bull *(above)*, **whose cult was common to Minoan Crete and Atlantis; the blue bird** *(below right)* **and Cretans in procession** *(right)*.

ordinary violence, and in a single dreadful day and night all your fighting men were swallowed up by the earth, and the island of Atlantis was similarly swallowed up by the sea and vanished; this is why the sea in that area is to this day impassable to navigation, which is hindered by mud just below the surface, the remains of the sunken island.'

In the succeeding dialogue, the *Critias*, Plato goes into greater detail about this 'antediluvian' Athens and Atlantis. Long ago the gods divided up the Earth among themselves. Athene, the goddess of wisdom, acquired Greece and founded

a great Athenian state (Plato's description of it need not concern us here, though bear in mind that it is Athens, representing Socrates' ideal society, that is the real hero of the story; Atlantis is only introduced as a foil to emphasize the Athenian achievement). Poseidon, the sea god, received Atlantis as his share in the division of the world. He made love to one of the island's inhabitants, a girl called Cleito, and produced ten sons by her. Each of these sons was made absolute ruler of his own part of the island, subject only to the will of the overall king, Atlas (hence the name *Atlantis*, 'island of Atlas', and *Atlantic*,

'sea of Atlas'). The island was very large, as we have seen, and rich in minerals, including orichalc ('in those days the most valuable metal except gold'; in fact, an invention of Plato's) and all kinds of animals, including elephants. On its southern coast was an enormous irrigated plain, some 370 km (230 miles) wide by 550 km (340 miles) long. Separating the plain from the sea was the capital city, Atlantis.

The great metropolis was perfectly circular, about 22 km (14 miles) in diameter. At its centre lay an island acropolis, 800 metres ($\frac{1}{2}$ mile) across,

where Poseidon had first dwelt with Cleito. Here there was a royal palace with hot and cold baths, a shrine sacred to Poseidon and Cleito and a temple to Poseidon alone, 'somewhat outlandish in appearance' but 'covered all over' with gold, silver and orichalc. Inside the temple were colossal gold statues of the god 'standing in a chariot drawn by six winged horses'. Surrounding the acropolis were three concentric rings of water and two of land, interconnected by tunnels and bridges. The ring-islands boasted temples, gardens, gymnasia and barracks, as well as a race-course for horses. A series of walls enclosed the city, protecting the inhabitants and the large number of merchant ships and triremes (which could enter via a canal from the sea).

The ten Atlantean kings assembled every fifth or sixth year at the temple of Poseidon for consultations and to pass judgment on wrongdoers. Before reaching a verdict they each had to capture a bull in the temple, 'using clubs and nooses but no metal weapon', and then to sacrifice it.

For many generations the Atlanteans maintained the same

high moral standards as their Athenian contemporaries. But eventually they became over-ambitious and greedy, and Zeus decided to punish them. . . .

Here, for no apparent reason, Plato breaks off his dialogue in mid-sentence. The progress of the Atlanto-Athenian war, apart from the bare outline given in the *Timaeus*, is left to our imagination. It needs to be stressed that this is all we really *know* about Atlantis. The rest – whether it be mystical insight or learned treatise – is speculation. And there have been plenty of people willing to hazard a guess in answer to

the unspoken question Plato has left behind: did Atlantis ever exist? At the last count over five thousand books had been written on the subject.

Speculation began in the generation after Plato and has continued ever since, except for a brief lull between the sixth and eleventh centuries AD, when intellectual life was at a low ebb generally. Aristotle, Plato's pupil, treated the story as a complete fiction, as did Strabo, the famous geographer, but Crantor, Plato's first editor, together with the credulous writers of the later Roman Empire, accepted it as history.

Other classical authors sat on the fence: Pliny the Elder, writing in AD 77, mentions in his *Natural History* a land that may have been swept completely away 'where the Atlantic Ocean is now – if we believe Plato'. Plutarch, in his *Life of Solon*, refers to 'the story or fable of Atlantis'.

Fuel was added to the controversy with the Renaissance expansion of exploration and discovery of America. As voyagers found more and more lands to the West, populated by folk speaking strange tongues, greater credence was given to Plato's account of an island con-

tinent in the west. A Spaniard, Francesco López de Gómara, even made the suggestion in 1553 that America should be renamed Atlantis – despite the fact that Atlantis was supposed to have sunk. The idea remained popular for several centuries and was adopted by Sir Francis Bacon in his Utopian novel, *The New Atlantis*, about a South Sea island inhabited by émigrés from the original Atlantis in the Americas.

But the book that can claim to have initiated the whole modern Atlantis movement is Ignatius Donnelly's *Atlantis: the Antediluvian World*. First published in 1882, it went through at least fifty printings,

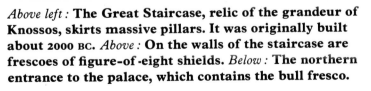

Above left : **The Great Staircase, relic of the grandeur of Knossos, skirts massive pillars. It was originally built about 2000 BC.** *Above :* **On the walls of the staircase are frescoes of figure-of-eight shields.** *Below :* **The northern entrance to the palace, which contains the bull fresco.**

the last in 1963. Donnelly was a compelling character: a former member of the US Congress, he read voraciously and absorbed information uncritically, to be regurgitated piecemeal for the enlightenment of his readers. His main thesis, backed up by a magpie-collection of 'facts', was that Atlantis had indeed existed in the Atlantic, as Plato said, but that it had been a land bridge

between Europe and America and the source of all civilization – as was 'proven' by correspondences between New and Old World cultures. Quite apart from being an unwarranted elaboration of Plato's story, Donnelly's book abounds in misinformation and irrational argument. (For example, why were such fundamentals as wheeled vehicles and draught animals lacking in the New World but not in the Old when the two were supposed to have so much in common?)

It required a more level-headed follower, Lewis Spence, to try to set Donnelly's suppositions on a better scientific footing. Spence's *The Problem*

of Atlantis, published in 1924, and his two later books on the subject attempted to prove geologically that there had been a large land mass occupying most of the North Atlantic in Late Tertiary times, which subsequently broke into two islands, 'Antillia' in the far west and Atlantis off the coast of Spain. Atlantis, before it sank in about 10,000 BC, was linked with the creators of Palaeolithic

cave art in France and Spain, who themselves contributed to the rise of European civilization, including that of Egypt. Antillia, which, Spence maintained, is still visible today in fragmented form as the West Indies, was the stepping-stone by which the 'Atlantis culture-complex' reached America and influenced Mayan civilization.

Now in Spence's day there was a certain amount of support from geologists for his sunken land mass theory. The origin of the so-called 'mid-Atlantic Ridge', which runs from Iceland to the South Atlantic and lies at an average depth of one mile beneath the surface, was then in dispute. Unfortunately for the theory, modern geologists are today in no doubt that, far from being a remnant of a sunken continent, the ridge is being thrown up from deep inside the earth's mantle and is one of the youngest geological features known. So Spence's ideas about Antillia and the whole 'Atlantis culture-complex' must be discarded.

Indeed Donnelly, Spence and the rest have led us rather far from Plato and the original Atlantis. We could be distracted further by those who have sought the lost continent in Brazil, the Bahamas, Spain, Mexico, Ceylon, Iran, Iraq or the Sahara (to name only a few), but it would be more profitable to ask: what does serious modern scholarship make of it all?

If one sets aside for the moment the arguments of those who maintain that the Atlantis tale is a *complete* fiction, then one is left with what is much the most widely held current academic view – that Atlantis and its destruction is in part a memory of Minoan Crete and Thera.

At first glance this may seem to be as far removed from Plato as anything Donnelly or Spence suggested. Didn't the *Timaeus* locate Atlantis in the Atlantic, 'opposite the Pillars of Heracles'? How, then, does Crete qualify as a possible Atlantis?

The theory is an ingenious one, first put forward by K. T. Frost in a *Times* article in 1909 – and elaborated by others since, especially J. V. Luce in *The End of Atlantis* (1969). It hinges on the interpretation of basic elements in the story *from an Egyptian point of view*. Solon, who apparently first told the tale to one of Plato's ancestors, did in fact visit Egypt in about 590 BC, as we know from independent sources. Therefore it is not unlikely that he really did hear from some priests a garbled account of a once-great isle 'to the west' and far back in the past. (Unlike the Greeks, the Egyptians had quite reliable records stretching back two thousand years into the Bronze Age.) However, whereas to Plato or even Solon 'the west' would have meant the western Mediterranean and beyond, to the chroniclers of Bronze Age Egypt, whose records Solon was being told of, 'the west' was a little-known region in the general direction of Crete (or 'Keftiu' as the Egyptians called it). During the Bronze Age, Crete was the centre of the brilliant Minoan civilization, whose sea-based empire encompassed much of

the southern Aegean, with trading links to the east and south. It is not surprising, therefore, that the Egyptians of that time recorded something of the power and prestige of Keftiu-Crete – nor should we wonder that these records ceased in about 1400 BC, when the Minoan civilization itself suffered an abrupt and mysterious eclipse.

The Egyptian priests of 590 BC were, then, recounting to Solon a story of Minoan Crete which – so the argument runs – Solon did not recognize as such because he did not associate the name 'Keftiu' with the Crete he knew (the connection only became possible with Evans' rediscovery of the Minoans in 1900), and the Egyptians' knowledge of Mediterranean geography was too hazy to be of much help. Instead, Solon may have understood enough of the word 'Keftiu', derived from a root meaning 'pillar', to associate it with his own Greek mythology of Atlas, who kept 'the pillars which hold the sky round about', as Homer's *Odyssey* has it. Hence the name *Atlantis*, 'island of Atlas', as we have seen. The transference of the legend from the Egyptian

'west' (Crete and the Aegean) to the Greek 'far west' (beyond the Straits of Gibraltar) follows on logically from this translation of Keftiu into Atlantis.

The whole of this argument may seem bewilderingly complicated. Yet there are some intriguing similarities between Plato's Atlantis and Minoan Crete. The *Timaeus* states that from Atlantis travellers could 'reach the other islands, and from them the whole opposite continent', which is an accurate description of Crete in relation to the Cyclades and mainland Greece *from an*

Egyptian point of view. More significantly, the account given in the *Critias* of the Atlantean bull-hunt, 'using clubs and nooses but no metal weapon', is not unlike the bull-games of the Minoans, who fought unarmed.

But the original Minoan hypothesis, as put forward by Frost in 1909, suffered from a major flaw, in that it could not account satisfactorily for the abrupt disappearance of Atlantis 'in a single dreadful day and night', as the *Timaeus* phrases it. The solution to the problem was first proposed in 1939 by the late Spyridon

Far left : **The drainage system in the palace at Knossos.** *Left :* **Pithoi jars were used for storing oil.** *Above :* **The ancient paved road that leads from Knossos to its port.** *Below :* **Poseidon, the god that Plato said lived in Atlantis.**

Marinatos, who argued that the sudden and gigantic volcanic explosion on the island of Thera (Santorini) in the fifteenth century BC caused widespread devastation and the downfall of Minoan Crete, only 160 km (100 miles) to the south. Subsequent research has indicated just how disastrous this natural catastrophe must have been. To begin with (on the analogy of the well-documented Krakatoa eruption in the East Indies of 1883) there would have been a tremendous explosion on Thera, in which much of the island simply disappeared. Aerial vibrations will have cracked the walls of houses in Crete, causing severe damage and fires. Then there would have been a fearful fall of volcanic ash, covering central and eastern Crete to depths of 20 centimetres (8 inches) and more, which ruined vegetation and rendered much of the country uninhabitable. Colossal tidal waves may have struck parts of the northern coast and, together with the earthquakes which hurled buildings to the ground, may simply have brought Minoan civilization to a standstill.

Not all archaeologists are convinced that the Thera eruption was the prime cause of the Minoan demise – invasion by the Mycenaeans from mainland Greece is another explanation – but from our point of view this does not matter. It is enough that it was *one* major cause, which may have seemed to the Egyptians like *the* major cause, for the parallel with the abrupt disappearance of Atlantis to fit. And how could the Egyptians have known about this disaster? In 1883 people in Western Australia heard the Krakatoa explosion 4800 km (3000 miles) away, so the ancient Egyptians, closer to Thera than that, would certainly have been aware of the eruption there. Travellers and traders from 'the west' would also have recounted tales of the disappearance of a major island, and this would have become associated in the Egyptian mind with the sudden cessation of Minoan contacts – an association which was passed on to Solon some eight hundred years later and which he (or Plato) then wove into the narrative of Atlantis.

So, finally, we come back to our original question, how much historical truth can we see behind Plato's story? The equation of Atlantis with Minoan Crete and Thera is plausible, but how do we really know that Plato didn't just make it all up? Well of course the honest answer is that we don't really know. What we are discussing is the *possibility* or *probability* that there is a kernel of truth, and here the parallels seem impressive between the historical island empire 'in the west' which disappeared largely (or partly) because of a violent natural catastrophe and Plato's account of Atlantis.

But it would be foolish to hunt for detailed correspondences between Minoan Crete and Atlantis. Plato did not intend to write a proper 'history' of Atlantis or antediluvian Athens (the real hero of the story, let it be remembered), nor could he have done so using a thousand-year-old tale handed down partly by word of mouth. His main concern was the philosophical juxtaposition of Socrates' vision of an ideal state with Critias' 'actual' example from the past. (Though just how 'actual' Plato intended it to be may be wondered at when we recall the entirely mythical division of the world, Atlantis being Poseidon's share, and the imaginary metal orichalc.) Instead we should view the story of Atlantis as a piece of 'historical science fiction', in which elements from the present and elements from the past were mingled in Plato's mind with ideas about the perfect state and were projected back far enough into the past to seem awesome and remote. In this light, the tale is neither history nor fiction but a subtle combination of the two.

THE PYRAMIDS OF EGYPT

The pyramids of ancient Egypt have inspired mystery and awe throughout history. How were they built? Was a master race responsible? And what was the purpose of these structures?

Lone survivors of the Seven Wonders of the Ancient World, the three pyramids at Giza are dwarf-like when viewed from high-lying parts of Cairo, often completely hidden by dust storms or heat-haze. From the closer lush greenery of the cultivation they appear to squat on the desert upland, larger but still to be measured on a human scale. It is not until the Great Pyramid begins to loom ever higher above the tarmac road at Giza that its vastness overwhelms. Built in about 2550 BC for the pharaoh Khufu (known to the Greeks as Cheops), the Great Pyramid is still 138 metres (451 feet) high and was originally about 9 metres (30 feet) higher; its sides, each almost precisely 230 metres (756 feet) long, are composed of 203 courses of limestone blocks, 2,300,000 in all, some of which weigh 15.2 tonnes (15 tons). It has been calculated that there is enough room within the area of its base to contain the cathedrals of Florence and Milan, St Peter's, Rome, as well as St Paul's Cathedral and Westminster Abbey in London. During his Egyptian campaign, Napoleon was inspired to calculate that the stone used in the Great Pyramid and its two neighbouring pyramids would be sufficient to build a wall right round France 3 metres (10 feet) high and 300 mm (1 foot) thick.

The Great Pyramid is not, however, the oldest pyramid. That honour falls to the Step Pyramid, built over a hundred years earlier at Saqqara, to the

Left: **sunset over the Giza pyramids, and** *(above)* **a felucca on the Nile at Luxor, site of ancient Thebes.**

south, for King Djoser. As its name implies, it is formed from six square platforms of decreasing dimensions built one on top of the other. Even the first true pyramid, with smooth sides and pointed top, was built not by Khufu but by his father Sneferu. Moreover, the remaining pharaohs of the Old Kingdom, for the next 350 years, continued to build pyramids, albeit increasingly small ones, as did those of the Twelfth Dynasty two hundred years later, although theirs were of brick. Even late in Dynastic history pyramids were being built in the Sudan by non-Egyptian pharaohs. But never again was a pyramid as vast. When the Greek historian Herodotus, writing in about 450 BC, related that its construction took twenty years and the building of its causeway another ten, he cannot have been far from the truth.

It should be remembered too that pyramids did not stand in isolation at the desert's edge: a pyramid was only one part of a funerary complex which also included subsidiary queens' pyramids, a pyramid temple and a causeway linking it to a valley temple which stood on the banks of the Nile or a canal. After the valley temple had been used during the mummification of the dead king its sole function was to stand as a magnificent entrance to the covered causeway that led to the pyramid temple where rituals for the dead king would be carried out by priests as long as his name was remembered.

After the Step Pyramid, Egypt's first monumental stone structure, had been built, successive pharaohs attempted even larger pyramids, but none were completed. The next completed pyramid at Meidum, is attributed to Huni, last king of the Third Dynasty, but was actually finished by Khufu's father Sneferu. The unfinished appearance of this pyramid has recently attracted much attention, leading a distinguished Oxford physicist to propose that its unsound construction led to its collapse shortly after it had been completed, thus altering the plan of subsequent pyramids. But the accretion method of pyramid-building, in which several tall, narrow steps of diminishing height lean against a central tall, rectangular core with sloping sides, was still used in Fifth Dynasty pyramids. Moreover, the Meidum pyramid had still not collapsed over a thousand years later, as the comments left by visitors on its pyramid temple walls testify.

Sneferu built two pyramids of his own, one at south Dahshur called the 'Bent' pyramid (because the angle of its sides suddenly decreases about half-way up its height) and another at north Dahshur. This is the first true pyramid; the courses of stone were filled in with casing blocks and a capstone was added to give the familiar smooth sides and pointed top of a pyramid. It may seem odd that one man should have had two pyramids; in fact, one of them was probably a dummy tomb or cenotaph, and the practice of having two tombs, albeit not pyramids, goes back to the beginning of the First Dynasty.

Thus when the Great Pyramid was built its only novelty was its size. Like all the preceding and subsequent pyramids it was begun during the pharaoh's lifetime, and his courtiers and high officials started to lay out their tombs in streets around it so that they would be near their ruler in death as in life. Sometimes an untimely death caused changes in the building plan: the change in angle of the 'Bent' pyramid helped to speed its completion; the stone pyramid and valley temples of the third pyramid at

Excavations of the pyramid temple of King Teti at Saqqara. The limestone casing has been stripped from the two pyramids. To the south-west stands the Step Pyramid of King Djoser, Egypt's earliest pyramid.

Giza were hastily completed in mud-brick, probably by the dead king's successor. Certainly the state of Egypt's economy and the personal power of a king affected the scale of pyramid-building. Although the small pyramids of the weak Sixth Dynasty pharaohs were little more than mounds of rubble kept in shape by a 'skin' of stone casing blocks, it was one of these pyramids that gave its name to Memphis, one of the greatest cities of the ancient world.

Although the Great Pyramid is but one of the more than seventy pyramids that flank the Nile valley, it has inspired more speculation and misinterpreta-

tion than any other monument, ancient or modern. Because of its nearness to Cairo and to the Mediterranean shore of Egypt and, of course, because of its size, it (and its two neighbours) was not merely one of the first ancient monuments to be seen by foreign visitors to Egypt, it also left a lasting impression. Strange theories about the purpose of the Giza pyramids go back as far as the Middle Ages, when they were equated with the granaries built by Joseph to contain the harvests of the seven good years. Even the Greek historian Herodotus, who knew that pyramids were tombs, nonetheless related a scurrilous story to explain the

building of one of the three subsidiary queens' pyramids, to the east of the Great Pyramid. According to him Cheops (Khufu) sent his daughter to a brothel to help to finance the construction of the Great Pyramid; in order to perpetuate her own memory, she demanded a building block from each of her customers. The fruits of her labours were used to build her pyramid – and the length of each of its sides is 45 metres (150 feet).

The first of the modern pyramidologists (or pyramidiots, as they have been more aptly termed) was an Englishman, John Adams, who believed that the Egyptians

Above left : **the Great Sphinx at Giza and part of the valley temple of the Second Pyramid flanking the pyramid of Khafre.** *Above :* **the reconstructed entrance, with two-pillared porch, of a nobleman's mastaba tomb, south-east of the Great Pyramid.** *Left :* **view over the streets of mastaba tombs of noblemen and princes which lie to the north-west of the Second Pyramid.**

were not sufficiently advanced to have built the pyramids themselves and that a master-race had been responsible. The tradition reported by Herodotus and Diodorus Siculus, another historian, that the pyramid-building pharaohs were hated by the Egyptians seemed to confirm the theory. In fact, Adams' ideas are clearly based on a misinterpretation of a passage by the historian

Manetho about the Hyksos, foreign rulers of Egypt who reigned a thousand years after the Fourth Dynasty pyramids were built. The modern version of the master-race theory is surely the recent suggestion that beings from outer space built the pyramids – an idea unthinkable a mere fifty years ago when space travel existed only in fiction.

In fact, popular ideas about

23

how the pyramids were built have always involved thousands of slaves, usually of Hebrew origin, sweating under the taskmaster's lash to move massive blocks of stone over roads oiled by the blood of old women and children. Had this indeed been the system, so many pyramids could not have been built on such a scale over so long a time. During the great pyramid-building age of the Old Kingdom (Third to Sixth Dynasties) Egypt was an agricultural community, its population largely consisted of peasant farmers whose sole skill lay in making the black soil of Egypt teem with crops. Until the early part of the twentieth century the Nile used to overflow its banks every year in a natural flood known as the Inundation which turned Egypt into a vast lake stretching from the eastern desert escarpment to that in the west, only outcrops of high-lying land remaining above the water. Thus for three or four months each year the farmers and their families starved while they waited for the waters to recede so that they might plough and plant the fertile soil.

At this time all the pyramid sites were on the west bank of the Nile, up on the desert's edge, running in a narrow line about 72 km (45 miles) long from Abu Roash in the north to Meidum in the south. There was always a body of permanent workers, stone-cutters, polishers, plasterers, architects, carpenters and labourers, working throughout the year at the pyramid site. From the quarries at Tura on the opposite bank (behind the site of future Cairo) came fine quality limestone used for casing blocks and relief carving; from the quarries at Aswan, far to the south, came granite for sarcophagi, plugs, statues, portcullises and some casing blocks. There, too, permanent bodies of stone-cutters worked preparing blocks ready for transport to the pyramid site.

During the Inundation, large numbers of idle farmers were impressed to work at the

pyramid site or in the quarries. They were housed in barracks, well fed and well clothed; in return they provided muscle-power to pull quarried blocks down to the flooded river's edge, ferry them across to the opposite bank (or down the Nile, as the case might be) and then drag them up to the pyramid site and into place in the pyramid. Even taking this large influx of unskilled labourers into account, it has been calculated that no more than 100,000 men were ever employed at any one time.

The benefit of this system was that the farmers did not starve while they were unable to work the land and there was

Top: **the desolate Valley of the Queens at Thebes; the entrances to the tombs are carefully concealed among the rocks.** *Above*: **the three pyramids on the Giza plateau.** *Right*: **descending corridor in the tomb of Queen Nefertari at Thebes; the ceiling is covered in stars imitating the night sky, as were the ceilings in pyramids.**

no widespread internal unrest. Moreover, the king promised an afterlife to those who before had merely hoped. At the beginning of the Old Kingdom the pharaoh was a god on earth; to touch his person meant certain death, so only his relations could hold the highest offices in the land and render him personal service. It was during the reigns of these god-kings that the greatest pyramids were built; as the personal prestige of their successors declined so did the size of their pyramids and the desire of their nobles to be buried around them. During the Third, Fourth and Fifth Dynasties only the king was certain of an afterlife,

together with those nobles whom he favoured. They alone were embalmed and buried in splendid stone-built mastabas, embellished with funerary equipment presented by the king, and endowed with lands and servants to provide perpetual offerings of food and drink for the deceased. The vast bulk of the population, however, especially the peasant farmers, was not embalmed or interred in a fine tomb; they were merely rolled into a hole in the sand with a few amulets. To those who worked on his pyramid the pharaoh offered an afterlife of service, and so one might say that the pyramids were built by men inspired by

nine-tenths food in the belly and by one-tenth religious zeal!

There is no direct evidence from ancient Egypt to show how the pyramids were built, but there is to show how large stone masses were moved; the remains of ramps and examples of the tools and equipment used have also survived. There can be no doubt that ramps were employed in building pyramids, but there is some dispute as to whether the ramps ran back from one face, being extended as the height of the pyramid increased so that the gradient of the ramp did not alter, or whether the ramps, beginning at each of the four corners of the pyramid, snaked back and forth across each face. The first method seems to be more probable. Some of the stone blocks used in the Great Pyramid weigh 15.2 tonnes (15 tons), yet the Egyptians had no mechanical means of moving them; contrary to the fanciful suggestions of some of the Greek historians they had neither capstan nor windlass, sheers or pulley. What they did have was unlimited manpower and time. A scene in a tomb at Beni Hassan, dated five hundred years after the great age of pyramid-building, shows a sled bearing a huge alabaster seated statue, calculated as weighing 60.9 tonnes (60 tons), being moved on wooden rollers with some sort of lubricant, by an army of men pulling on ropes to a rhythmical chant. There can be no doubt that this was the method used to move pyramid building stones. Levers (which have rarely survived) and sled-like rockers were employed to manoeuvre blocks from one level to another and into position.

Sometimes an outcropping mass of rock was used as the nucleus of a pyramid (as in the case of the Great Pyramid) so that fewer blocks had to be cut for the filling. Chambers and passages were built into the mass of the pyramid as its height rose. In the case of the

Above : **demons of the Underworld from Tuthmosis III's tomb.** *Right :* **astronomical ceiling in Seti I's burial chamber.** *Opposite above left, and below :* **Osiris, king of the dead in the Underworld and Anubis, jackal-god of embalming, from the nobleman Sennedjem's tomb.** *Opposite above right :* **Queen Nefertari making offerings in her tomb.**

Great Pyramid, Khufu's granite sarcophagus in the so-called King's Chamber had to be set in position while the pyramid was being built, since it was too great to have been introduced through the passages after the pyramid was completed. When the pyramid reached its intended height it consisted of up to two hundred courses of masonry steps varying in height from about 600 mm (2 feet) to 1.4 metres (4½ feet) encased in smooth-sided blocks of fine-quality limestone (or even granite for the lowest courses) crowned by a pointed capstone.

In the middle of the nineteenth century, there was a marked increase in interest in ancient Egypt and the mass of detailed information provided in numerous new publications was turned to their own uses by adherents of the new mania, Pyramidology. One of the most distinguished of the Pyramidologists was C. Piazzi Smyth, the Scottish Astronomer Royal, who based his intricate calculations on the Pyramid

Inch, a measurement entirely of his own fabrication. The Pyramid Inch, according to him, corresponded to the twenty-fifth part of the sacred cubit, which itself measured 625.635 mm (25.025 inches). There is no basis for such a measurement, and the royal cubit used by the pyramid-builders measured approximately 510 mm (20.5 inches). At this time it was fashionable to seek connections between the Bible and Great Britain; there were also strong feelings against the moves towards metrication in measurement. The British Pyramid Inch was of use to both movements. Piazzi Smyth's zeal allowed him to gloss over the weakest part of his theory, that other pyramids

exist whose measurements do not produce the same value for the Pyramid Inch as the Great Pyramid. These he called imitation pyramids, claiming that the Great Pyramid was the oldest – which has been shown to be far from the truth. As often happens, Piazzi Smyth's eminence as an astronomer was instantly transferred in the public mind to his theories about the pyramids, and his theories gained many adherents, though not among his fellow scholars.

Once Piazzi Smyth had suggested that the Egyptians had secret knowledge only just rediscovered, other Pyramidologists in search of the lost wisdom of Ancient Egypt took to the field. Using their own

values for the Pyramid Inch, they claimed that because the Egyptians employed it and the Pyramid Cubit they must have had knowledge of the polar circumference of the earth, which can be divided exactly by these fabricated measurements (depending on which set of figures you use). In fact the Egyptians had no idea of the existence of the earth's diameter – they believed that the earth was a flat dish. Unconfounded, Piazzi Smyth explained that the Egyptians had built the Great Pyramid guided by Divine Inspiration and had incorporated this information unaware of what they were doing.

The natural development from the theory of Divine

Inspiration and Lost Wisdom was the belief that the Great Pyramid not only records all world history (or rather the history of Christian Europe) up to the present time but that it also forecasts the future. If it should seem strange that a monument as foreign as the Great Pyramid should have any significance for the predominantly Anglo-Saxon adherents of this theory, it should also be remembered that they believed themselves to be descendants of the Lost Tribes of Israel which are concealed somewhere in Great Britain. All kinds of cataclysms and world wars and even the destruction of the earth are said to have been prophesied by the measurements of the internal chambers and corridors of the Great Pyramid. Whenever the precise dates for such events have come and gone without such calamities, the date has been re-read and placed further in the future, still to no effect so far, though the latest date for the destruction of the earth is 1979.

Yet the Great Pyramid has all the features common to all pyramids dating from the Old Kingdom; faces aligned as nearly as possible to the four cardinal points; the entrance in the north face, some distance

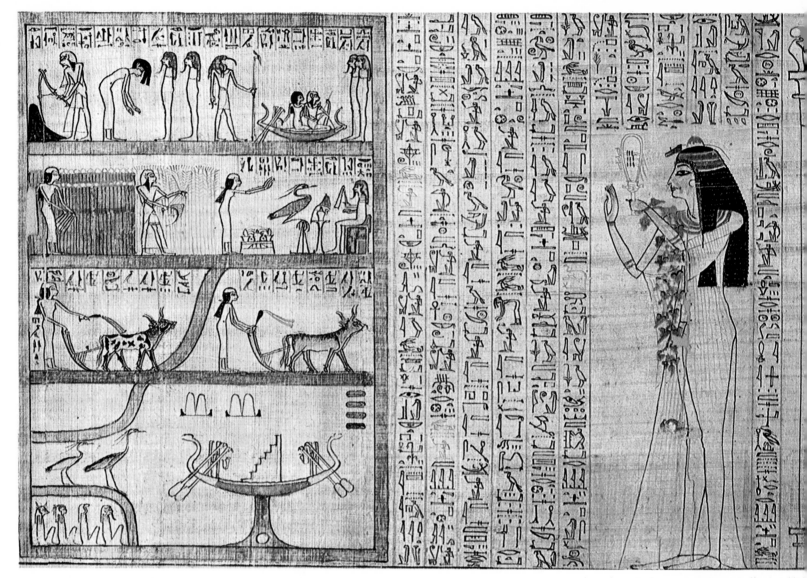

above the ground and off-centre, and within, corridors and galleries, blocked after burial by portcullises and plugs, leading eventually to a burial chamber containing the stone sarcophagus in which the pharaoh's body was interred. Other pyramids, however, do show exceptional features: the 'Bent' pyramid has, uniquely, two separate entrances, one in the north face, the other in the west, each leading to separate corbel-vaulted rooms; the second pyramid at Giza also has two separate entrances, but both are in the north face and their corridors merge and lead to a single burial chamber; the internal arrangements of the third pyramid at Giza also show a change of plan during building. Thus the changes of plan clearly shown in the internal arrangements of the Great Pyramid should cause no surprise. Two of its three separate burial

chambers were abandoned; the one which was finally used is at the top of the Grand Gallery and contains Khufu's now empty granite sarcophagus. Yet the second abandoned burial chamber is still incorrectly called the 'Queen's Chamber', although queens at this time were buried not with their husband in his pyramid but in subsidiary pyramids of their own. The Great Pyramid, however, does have two unique features. The five separate compartments (the fifth with a pointed roof) above the 'King's Chamber', Khufu's final burial place, seem to have been intended to prevent the roof of the burial chamber collapsing under the great weight above it. Less easy to explain are the two rectangular shafts which run from the King's Chamber, one from the north wall, the other from the south, through the mass of the pyramid to pierce

the outer casing. However, two more unfinished shafts have been found within the second pyramid, and their measurements seem to confirm that these mis-named air-shafts were merely dummy entrance and exit corridors.

Today the Pyramidologists of Europe are led by the British Institute of Pyramidology, which claims that the Great Pyramid embodies in stone exactly what the Bible embodies in writing. They seek Divine Wisdom and a more spiritual life by studying it. Indeed all Pyramidologists of this century have stressed that the Messianic message of the Great Pyramid brings hope and spiritual uplift in a world governed by science and scepticism. Yet some Pyramidologists also believe that the Great Pyramid embodies in stone not the Bible but the Egyptian Book of the Dead, which is in

fact a collection of spells and rituals to enable the deceased to surmount all obstacles and reach the Other World successfully. A few of the spells in the Book of the Dead can indeed be traced back to originals in the Pyramid Texts, a series of spells written on the inner walls of pyramids, but the earliest of these did not appear until two hundred years after the Great Pyramid was built.

Moreover, the earliest Book of the Dead papyrus was written eight hundred years later. Nevertheless, W. Marsham Adams considered that the Book of the Dead contains all the lost wisdom of Egypt. The initiate to Egypt's wisdom would move through the corridors and chambers of the Great Pyramid, which symbolically represent the divisions of the Underworld, as listed in the Book of the Dead, re-enacting man's gradual emergence from

Papyrus vignettes from the Book of the Dead showing the priestess Anhai carrying out agricultural tasks in the Other World and worshipping Osiris, Isis and Nephthys.

ignorance and evil to a pure spiritual state. Unfortunately he used as proof of his theory a version of the Book of the Dead which was written another eight hundred years later than the earliest copy.

More outlandish theories about the Great Pyramid's purpose have included suggestions that it was a huge horoscope, a landing mark for flying saucers, an observatory or even a gigantic water-pump! The water-pump idea apparently worked so well in model form (in spite of the fact that the original stands in the desert) that a US patent was taken out on it.

That the pyramids were tombs cannot be doubted: the first pyramid was merely six mastabas stacked one on top of the other, and the mastaba had been a tomb for king and nobility alike since the start of the Dynastic Period, in about 3100 BC. The word is Arabic for 'bench', which describes the mastaba's rectangular superstructure with sloping walls as it stood in the open desert. The true pyramid was a step pyramid of many courses finished with casing blocks and cap-stone to give it smooth sides and pointed top. All pyramids contain burial chambers, either within or beneath their mass. That such an obvious burial place, crammed with a pharaoh's grave goods (the Egyptians did take everything with them), would attract tomb-robbers meant that from the very beginning the entrance was hidden; during the Twelfth Dynasty the entrance to a pyramid was often concealed some distance away from it. Inside, the corridors were blocked after interment with stone portcullises and plugs; Twelfth Dynasty pyramids also contained ingenious blind alleys and doubling-back systems. Yet pyramids seem to have died out as a royal tomb not only because they were impracticable, and because religious beliefs changed slightly, but because they needed so much open ground. For the pharaohs of the New Kingdom at Thebes the only open land was agricultural, and so they began the practice of excavating subterranean rock-cut tombs in the barren hills of the Valley of the Kings, leaving no visible sign of their location. The final indignity came when, just as all those funerary rituals and beliefs which had once been exclusive to the king were taken over by commoners, the pyramid, the once exclusively-royal tomb, was reduced to a small triangular limestone pyramidion which capped the tall, pyramid-shaped mud-brick roof of any private New Kingdom tomb chapel.

Why did the kings of Egypt suddenly decide that instead of being buried beneath a rectangular mastaba they should be buried under a stepped structure which eventually became a true pyramid? The origin of the step pyramid may lie in a curious stepped mound that occurs in some royal First Dynasty tombs within the structure of the mastaba and over the shaft leading to the burial chamber. This in turn may have been influenced by a passage in the Pyramid Texts. Although they only occur for the first time in the pyramid of Wenis, last king of the Fifth Dynasty in about 2345 BC, their content clearly goes back to Egypt's prehistory. Pyramid Text No. 267 says that a staircase to the sky is set up for the king to ascend to heaven; Spell 619 says almost the same thing. It is not difficult to see a stepped pyramid as a staircase.

But another origin must be sought for the true pyramid with its smooth sides. It has been noticed that when the sun's rays break through cloud at Giza their angle is exactly that of the Great Pyramid. Moreover, the Pyramid Texts speak of the king lifting himself to heaven by the rays of the sun and even of his treading them. One of the foremost symbols of sun-worship in Egypt was the ben-ben, a pyramidal stone. A true pyramid is merely an enlarged ben-ben. Perhaps the idea that the true Pyramid has its origins in the sun's rays is not so fanciful. The final confirmation that both types of pyramid were thought of as means of reaching heaven is surely to be seen in the Egyptian word for pyramid – mr – which apparently means 'place of ascent'. Yet even the word 'pyramid' itself, which is, of course, Greek and not the original Egyptian, was pressed into service by F. W. Chapman, who claimed that Pi Ra Mo Id meant 'the great sun-god' and sought to show that the Great Pyramid was a monument to π, the 3.1416 ratio.

Over four and a half thousand years after it was built, the Great Pyramid continues to arouse speculation; within the last three years the word 'pyramid power' has been coined to explain curious phenomena. As long as it stands, the Great Pyramid will continue to attract interest and so effectively achieve for Khufu, who built it, what every Egyptian wanted, the survival and recollection of his name.

STONEHENGE

The most complex ancient temple of Europe is situated on Salisbury Plain, England. Who built it and to what plan? How were the stones brought to the site and set in position? For centuries scholars have pondered these questions. Now astroarchaeology suggests plausible answers.

Stonehenge is one of the most visited tourist sites in Great Britain and the most famous prehistoric monument in northern Europe. In fact so many visitors are attracted to this group of stones on Salisbury Plain, two kilometres ($1\frac{1}{4}$ miles) to the north of the village of Amesbury, that the circle has now had to be fenced off in order to preserve it. Yet the monument still remains clouded in mystery.

Thanks to modern archaeological techniques, we can now be pretty certain as to when it was built; and we can be pretty confident that we know how it was constructed. But we are still left to speculate about why it was put up at such immense cost in time and labour and why it should have been sited where it is, although several fairly

convincing theories on the first of these points have recently been put forward by such eminent scientists as Sir Frederick Hoyle and Professor Alexander Thom of the University of Oxford.

To start with what we know. The circle of stones which we call Stonehenge was built in three phases, phase one being separated from phase three by about a thousand years. About ten years ago scholars put the date of the construction of the first stage at between 1900 and 1700 BC, but recently more refined techniques of radio-carbon dating have placed it back in time to about 2500 BC, that is at the end of the Neolithic age. At that time men were gradually turning from hunting to farming, but they still lived in small scattered groups, apparently had no way of com-

municating or recording by written signs and were still ignorant of the wheel. No wonder that for centuries modern man regarded these people as little more than primitive savages. We know better now. When the Spanish came to Peru in the fifteenth century AD, they found that the Incas, another unlettered people with no knowledge · of the wheel, had created a highly complex civilization marked by monuments of immense grandeur. What we now know of that civilization helps us to appreciate the skill and creativity of the Wessex people who built Stonehenge.

In its first phase, Stonehenge consisted of a circular earthwork, made up of an outer ditch, the earth from which was used to construct a bank about 6 metres (20 feet) wide

Opposite : **Stonehenge, showing the remaining arches of the sarsen circle, as seen from the inside.** *Top :* **Men-a-tol, a holed stone from the Bronze Age, is near Morvah in Cornwall.**

and 1.8 metres (6 feet) high. The diameter of the circle was 95 metres (320 feet). The circle of the earthwork was broken in the north-east in the direction of the midsummer sunrise; and a great stone (now known as the Heel Stone and possibly consisting originally of a massive timber post) was erected on that alignment, about 85 metres (280 feet) from the centre of the circle. In many ways this first building must have resembled the earthworks that form a part of many other stone or wooden sacred circles, such as Arbor Low in Derbyshire and the Cheesewrings in Cornwall, built in Britain during Neolithic

times, most of which are considerably more ancient than Stonehenge.

The great bank of the original building at Stonehenge has now eroded to a height of only half a metre (1½ feet), but it is from the broken shards of antler picks which must have been used in its construction and then have been thrown away into the bottom of the ditch that the site has been dated; and it is from the depth of that ditch that the original measurements were calculated. Just inside this circular bank we find the first mystery of Stonehenge: 56 holes placed at fairly regular intervals from each other and forming a circle around the in-

terior of the earthwork. These holes, which apparently never held stones or timbers, are named after their discoverer, the seventeenth-century anti-quary John Aubrey, who first noticed them as patterns of depressions in the ground. Subsequent excavations have shown that they were pits used for some ritual purpose, possibly involving human sacrifice, for some of them contained the remains of cremations.

It could be that the rituals enacted there resembled those that scholars believe took place in the earlier long barrows, such as the great chamber tomb at West Kennett near Avebury, to the north-west of

Above: **The Cheesewring on Bodmin Moor, Cornwall, was probably used for religious purposes.** *Top right:* **Pentre Ifan cromlech in Wales.** *Above right:* **Stoney Littleton long barrow, Somerset.** *Right:* **Arbor Low, Derbyshire.**

Stonehenge. These barrows, which were built about 4000 BC, are judged to have been in use for about a thousand years; and because comparatively few human remains have been found within them it is thought that they were used more for ritual meeting-places than for normal burials. Very likely the rites that were performed in

32

the long barrows were intended to increase the fertility of the soil. Similar rituals, occasionally involving human sacrifice, may have taken place within the great bank of Stonehenge. It is important to remember that these rituals had nothing to do with the ceremonies of the Druids, who did not come to Britain until the first millennium BC and who could have had nothing to do with the erection of Stonehenge, though they may later have used it for purposes of their own. In any case the Aubrey holes may well have been originally dug for a purpose far more scientific than that of sympathetic magic with or without human victims; I

shall come back to these holes again at the end of this chapter, when I come to consider the explanation that Sir Frederick Hoyle gives for their function as part of a lunar observatory.

The second phase of the building of Stonehenge took place at the beginning of the second millennium BC. It also has its mystery. Bluestones, which had once formed a sacred circle in the Prescelly mountains of Dyfed, were transported to the site. The technology involved in moving the stones over such a distance is amazing (I will describe how it was thought this was done later), but the real problem is why their presence was considered so essential that such a feat of transportation had to be undertaken. When the bluestones were brought to the site of Stonehenge they were put up in a double circle within the centre of the earthwork. And at some time during this second phase of the building an avenue of stones was erected leading to the Heel Stone and marking the entrance to the whole monument.

Apart from the Aubrey holes and the incorporation of the distant bluestones, the circular earthwork at Stonehenge still does not seem to have been

Stonehenge is a relic with impressive visual impact. *Above:* **The arches of the outer circle seen from inside.** *Above right:* **Two trilithons of the inner horseshoe and remaining bluestones.** *Right:* **The temple as seen from the outer earthworks.**

very different from the many other sacred sites in Britain erected in Neolithic times. It even shares basic measurements and proportions with many of them, particularly with the Ring of Brodgar near Stromness in the Orkney Islands. The similarities are so striking that Professor Alexander Thom, after carefully surveying about three hundred such sites throughout north-west Europe and visiting many more, believes that the Neolithic megalith builders worked to a common unit of measurement, 2.72 feet (0.6 metres), which he called the 'megalithic yard'.

But in the third phase of the building at Stonehenge, started in about 1500 BC, the monument was given the quality that makes it unique. At that time the people who lived in this part of southern England had reached a high level of sophisti-cation, so that historians have labelled a civilization for them and have called it the Wessex Culture. From artefacts found in their graves it is clear that these people were engaged in some sort of trade with the Mediterranean; and on one of the Stonehenge stones the carving of a dagger has been discerned, which closely resembles one found in a grave at Mycenae in Greece. This has led many scholars to speculate that a

Greek architect was involved in this last stage of the building of this ancient British monument.

The last stage took a century to complete and is itself divided into three phases. In the first stage the double circle of volcanic bluestones was dismantled and sarsen stones (locally known as grey wethers because of their resemblance to grazing sheep) were brought to the site from the Marlborough Downs, 32 km (20 miles) to the north. They were shaped into fairly regular rectangles, one side being left rough and the other polished. Then thirty of them were put up to form a circle, the polished surfaces facing inwards, with their tops joined by lintel stones to form a continuous upper ring. Five of these are still in position.

From an examination of the grooves in the remaining stones it is clear that whoever put them up had a sophisticated knowledge of carpentry and an ability to transfer those techniques to the medium of stone. Each lintel was put in place by a double joint consisting of a mortise and tenon and a mortise and groove. Inside the sarsen circles five massive trilithons, standing about 7.5 metres (25 feet) high, with the lintels fixed in a similar manner, were erected to form a horseshoe, whose open end faced the northeast. A recumbent stone, now known as the Altar Stone, lies in the centre of this horseshoe. Like the bluestones, it comes from Dyfed, but unlike them it is formed of micaceous sandstone and not volcanic rock.

During this stage of the building, the four Station Stones were put into place, at the

outer edge of the circle. Scholars now consider that these had a key function to perform in any astronomical observations made from Stonehenge. We can only be sure of the exact position of one of these stones. It stood by the outer bank between two of the Aubrey holes in the east; a stump of stone still stands there. Immediately opposite it, on the western edge of the circle, a fallen stone marks the approximate position of another. The whereabouts of the stones that we would expect to find in the north and south of the circle is uncertain, but it is believed that they probably stood on the mounds (once thought to have been barrows) at opposite sides of the circle, just within the earth bank.

This done, it seems that a very grand design was started, which had to be scrapped before it was completed, possibly because of lack of resources or labour. Two large concentric circles of holes (now known as the Y and Z holes) were dug outside the ring of sarsens; and presumably they were intended to hold further stones. But they do not appear ever to have been used.

In the last stage of all, the bluestones were replaced. They were set where some of them still stand today, one group being used to define a circle between the ring of sarsens and the trilithon horseshoe; and the others (twelve of which can still be found) to make a central lesser horseshoe within the greater one. So, sometime about the middle of the second millennium BC, Stonehenge was completed.

For years scholars puzzled as to how the immense technical problems confronting its builders could have been overcome. There were four apparently insurmountable difficulties: the transportation of the bluestones and the Altar Stone from Dyfed to Stonehenge, a distance of some 215 km (135 miles), at a time when there were no wheeled vehicles or pack animals; the bringing of the great sarsens, each one weighing at least 26 tonnes (26 tons), over 32 km (20 miles) across the downs from the north; the positioning of them into an erect circle; and finally, hardest of all, the raising of the lintels.

Various ideas, not excluding fanciful notions that the stones had magical properties and could move themselves, were put forward to explain how all this was achieved. It was in the early 1950s that the archaeologist Richard Atkinson was given an opportunity to see how his theories could be worked

Left and above : **Double stone circle and stone rows at Merrivale, Dartmoor.** *Top :* **Rollright stones on the border of Oxfordshire and Warwickshire form a Neolithic circle known as the King's Men.**

out in practice. With the help of his own colleagues and those of Paul Johnstone of BBC television, and with additional labour provided by senior boys from Bryanston and Canford Schools, he showed how it was possible to get the bluestones to the site. This experiment formed part of a television documentary broadcast in 1954.

Richard Atkinson believed

that the bluestones must have been brought most of the way to Wiltshire by water. The question was what sort of a craft could have been used. The available alternatives would have been a raft or a dug-out canoe, for a skin-lined boat such as the wicker Welsh coracle would clearly never have been strong enough to carry the weight of the stone. Although a sturdy raft would have great advantages over a boat in a rough sea, one that was large enough to carry the stone would be difficult to manoeuvre in an emergency and useless in inland waters. So it is most likely that a dug-out canoe was used, and Atkinson worked out that it

would be quite reasonable to assume that one could be hollowed out from a single tree trunk, so that the craft would have a length of 10.5 metres (35 feet), a beam of 1.2 metres (4 feet) and a depth of 0.6 metres (2 feet). Its walls would be about 75 mm (3 inches) thick. Such a craft should be capable of carrying a weight of 3900 kg (8700 lb) with a displacement of half its depth, according to his reckoning, and from that he argued that two such boats lashed side by side would be able to support the Stonehenge Altar Stone and a crew of at least ten men and still have a freeboard of 0.3 metres (1 foot).

But he realized that, if two boats were used, the weight of the load would be concentrated on the central half of each vessel, and that could easily cause the sides of the individual canoes to spread and buckle or even break the back of the composite vessel. So he believed that it was across three canoes, possibly only 7 metres (24 feet) long, with the boulder resting on bearers extending the whole width of the vessel, that the Altar Stone was brought to Stonehenge.

To show how this could be done, Atkinson and his friends

built three canoes of elm boarding measuring 3.5 metres (12 feet) by 0.6 metres (2 feet 3 inches) by 0.4 metres (1 foot 6 inches) and fixed them together by four cross beams, which eventually supported a replica of one of the bluestones, made in reinforced concrete. The only thing not satisfactorily explained is how the Neolithic builders of Stonehenge could have lowered the stone on to the craft without sinking it. In the experiment, the problem of keeping an even distribution of weight was solved by using a mobile crane. Once loaded, the vessel was manned by a crew of four Bryanston boys, bringing the total load up to some 1630 kg (3600 lb) and giving a draught of 225 mm (9 inches). The boys punted the linked canoes so easily up and down the stretch of the River Avon by Salisbury that Atkinson believed that the craft could have been handled by one man.

This still leaves us with the problem of how the stones were transported overland. Atkinson reckoned that even with full use being made of the waterways, the stones would still have had to be dragged some 38 km (24 miles) by sledge throughout the course of the journey. To test how this was done he built a sledge of 150 mm (6 inch) timbers, 2.7 metres (9 feet) long and 1.2 metres (4 feet) wide. With the replica bluestone lashed to it, it weighed some 1580 kg (3500 lb).

This sledge was hauled over the downs immediately south of Stonehenge up a gradient of 1 in 15 by a party of thirty-two senior boys from Canford School. They were arranged in ranks of four and used a single hauling rope, though as Neolithic man would not have had access to any vegetable fibres tough enough for this job he would have had to use a plaited leather thong. The Canford boys did not find the task an easy one; but when wooden rollers were inserted under the runners of the sledge, it was possible for fourteen boys to

haul the load fairly comfortably. Although this saving in manpower seems considerable, Atkinson reckoned that at least a dozen extra pairs of hands would have been needed to manoeuvre the rollers and to operate guide ropes to steer the sledge. The great Altar Stone must, of course, have required a larger sledge and more men to haul it. On Atkinson's calculations that sixteen men were needed for every tonne weight to be moved, it would have taken 110 to shift the great sandstone boulder.

The removal of the sarsen stones poses an even greater problem, for the heaviest of these weighs about 50.8 tonnes (50 tons), and the complete set was seven times heavier than the estimated weight of all the bluestones. Atkinson worked out that because much larger rollers would have to be used to move such a load, twenty-two men would be needed per tonne of stone and that the average rate of movement would be 0.8 km ($\frac{1}{2}$ a mile) a day. This means that over a thousand men would have had to be engaged to shift most of the stones, and their journey to Stonehenge, which must have included at least one steepish hill, must have taken at least seven weeks. Then one has to allow a further two weeks for the men to make the return journey to Marlborough and to load up again and presumably to have some days' rest. On this basis it must have taken almost 1500 men at least five and a half years of continuous work to bring the eighty-one sarsens to the site.

When you consider how hard people at this time had to work to get enough to eat, the difficulty of providing so many men with food over such a long period must have been prodigious. So one of the main questions to be raised in considering the possible purposes of the building is whether the value of any suggested function could have justified this cost and effort. However, we must remember that man has always

Right : **The stones at Avebury, one of the largest sacred monuments in Europe.** *Below right :* **The man-made Silbury Hill, sited near the Avebury circle and probably pre-dating it. Its exact purpose is unknown, and there is no evidence that it was used for burials.**

been driven to such mammoth tasks. Medieval cathedrals and supersonic aircraft were just as costly in their different ways.

To return to the two remaining technical problems: the placing of the stones in an upright position and the raising of the lintels. Once more Atkinson is the authority. He describes the carefully dug holes in which the stones were placed, each one being about 0.3 metres (1 foot) wider all round than the base of the stone. Three sides of each hole are vertical, and the fourth slopes from surface to base at an angle of 45 degrees. On the side opposite the ramp, wooden stakes were set in place to prevent the chalk being crushed as the stone sank into position. Archaeologists have found that this was already an ancient practice. Traces of similar stakes have been found to show that they were used when the Heel Stone was put in position during the first phase of the building and in the erection of the neighbouring earlier stone circle at Avebury.

Exactly how the stones were erected must be a matter of speculation, but Atkinson, who experimented with scale

models, suggests the most obvious way for the work to have been accomplished. The base of the stone must first have been aligned with the ramp side of the hole and the stone itself raised on rollers as high above the ground as possible. As the stone was dragged over the leading roller, it would overbalance into the hole and come to rest against the ramp.

Now came the hard task of hauling it into a vertical position by ropes attached to the apex. It is possible that, in order to make the job a little easier, some sort of leverage system may have been used, so that the initial pull would have been at right angles to the length of the rope rather than at 45 degrees. Atkinson experimented with such a device and found that a stone of 26 tonnes (26 tons) would require a pull of 4.5 tonnes (4½ tons), so he calculated that the hauling would have had to be done by 180 men each exerting a pull of 25 kg (56 lb).

The last part of this task, adjusting the stones to a truly vertical position and filling in the holes, must have seemed like relaxation. But we are left with two minor problems. Were the

stones levelled without a plumb-line, and if so, how? And why were the stone holes packed with pieces of rock from Chilmark, 18 km (11 miles) away?

The final technical problem was raising the lintels. Atkinson argues that the tenons and mortices must have been prepared first, the mortices being sunk in the underside of the lintels and the measurements being matched very carefully. That this was the method adopted is made more likely from the evidence of one stone where the measurement seems to have gone awry to the extent of some 225 mm (9 inches), so that a second mortice had to be sunk.

There are three theories about how the lintels were raised into position. The first, which involves the use of earth ramps, is based on the methods that seem to have been used in the erection of the Pyramids and the colossal stone statues of Egypt; according to Atkinson it has some similarity with the way barrels of beer are rolled on to a brewer's lorry. In the case of Stonehenge, a ramp would have had to be piled up against the two up-

rights on which the lintel was to be placed. The amount of labour needed for this method would be enormous: either simultaneous ramps would have had to be erected or the ramp would have had to be dug away and rebuilt for each lintel. What makes this possibility unlikely (although it doesn't discredit the theory completely) is the fact that there is no sign anywhere around the site of such activity having taken place.

If ramps on this scale had been built and dismantled, one would expect to find at least some traces of the operation, such as a filled-in quarry somewhere in the neighbourhood. There is no evidence of this sort.

It is just possible that a heavy timber frame was used instead of an earthen ramp. Atkinson constructed a working model of such a piece of scaffolding and

demonstrated it during the television broadcast. It can now be seen in the Salisbury Museum. Yet he was not happy about this theory either, for to build a wooden scaffolding heavy enough to support the lintel stones deep post holes would have had to be sunk in the ground, and no traces of these have been found.

The theory which he favours involves an almost incredible amount of slow persistent labour, but it does give a satisfactory explanation as to why we can find no traces of this enormous feat of engineering. The idea is that the stone was raised into position in gradual stages, being levered about a foot or so further off the ground at each stage. At each raising, heavy squared timber would be inserted under the stone and left there while a solid timber platform (composed of several layers of planks placed at right angles to each other) was built under and around it. This platform would have to be strong enough to support the next raising of the stone, and the subsequent platforms that would have to be built, until the lower edge of the lintel came level with the top of the upright stones. This must have been a very delicate as well as a very heavy operation, and no one, as far as I know, has yet calculated how many men would have been needed for such a project or how long it would have taken, though it would be a fairly simple matter for a mathematician or an engineer to do, in the light of Atkinson's ratio of manpower to stone weight.

However, the answer could tell us nothing about why this enormous amount of labour should have been expended. To arrive at some satisfactory ideas about that, it will be necessary briefly to trace the story of beliefs about the purpose of Stonehenge from the seventeenth century to the present day. The earliest notions were either that the place had been erected (under the direction of the wizard, Merlin) as a great sepulchre for that noble Roman Briton, Ambrosius Aurelius, uncle to King Arthur, or that it had even more supernatural origins, having been created, or possibly even made of, giants. The latter idea, which in some superstitions and tales of folk lore still persists, is based on a belief that the great stones are alive or at least are composed of petrified living creatures.

Fortunately King James I wanted to work out a more

likely explanation for the existence of Stonehenge and the many other stone circles throughout Britain. In 1620 he sent the architect Inigo Jones to look at the monument and Jones gave his firm opinion that the henge had originally been erected as a temple, confirming that belief by naming the Altar Stone. Some fifty years later, when John Aubrey came to investigate the site, he completely accepted its religious significance and linked it with Celtic Druidism, the religion which the Roman conquerors described as flourishing in Britain in the first century AD. The idea persisted until the beginning of this century, when the real age of Stonehenge was ascertained. We now know that although it is very unlikely that the Druids made use of the temple, and of many other henge monuments throughout Britain, they were all set up many centuries before incoming waves of Iron Age Celts brought the Druid priests to these islands.

Hardly anything is known of the religion of the Neolithic and Bronze Age peoples who built Stonehenge and Avebury, but it is reasonable to assume that their worship was closely connected with the natural forces on which they depended for survival. To say that they were sun-worshippers is to suggest that their cult was a crude and simple one; but the current practice of regarding the henges and monuments as observatories for monitoring the course of the moon and the stars as well as the sun means that their mathematical knowledge, at any rate, was extremely sophisticated.

We have already noted that the Heel Stone of Stonehenge is aligned almost directly on to the midsummer sunrise; and it was from that fact that the first investigators started to calculate the predictions and observations which could be made from the orientation of the other stones in the monument. These investigations were started in 1901, when Sir Norman

Lockyer, a brilliant amateur astronomer, set himself the task of calculating the date of Stonehenge by computing the rate at which the earth's position changes in relation to the sun throughout the centuries and so, working backwards from the slightly oblique angle at which the midsummer sunrise now appears over the Heel Stone, discovering when it would have shown directly above it. Subsequent radio-carbon datings of the stone come very close to the approximate date that he arrived at. Although Lockyer's work at Stonehenge and at various other megalithic sites throughout Britain was treated with a certain amount of cynicism, not to say scorn, he

started a tradition of investigation which has flourished in the last twenty-five years and which is gradually evolving into the respectable, but fascinating, science of astro-archaeology.

In the 1950s and 1960s, the two methods of investigating Stonehenge, by archaeological excavations and by the observations of astronomy, developed rapidly but separately; and it is only in the 1970s that they have come close together. In the 1950s, new excavations on the site, led by Professors Richard Atkinson and Stuart Piggott and by Dr J. F. S. Stone, produced the evidence for the construction of the monument which I have outlined in the first part of this

chapter. Then, in 1966, the American Gerald Hawkins published his book *Stonehenge Decoded*, which helped to intensify the already existing interest in the orientation of the stones in relation to the processions of the heavenly bodies. Professor Alexander Thom, as I have already noted, took this interest a stage further. An engineer by training, he applied the knowledge of that discipline to his investigations of some six hundred stone circles, including Stonehenge. Although only a professional mathematician could possibly understand the full implications of his observations, we can all appreciate the significance of his discovery that all the monu-

Above left : **Rudstone monolith, Yorkshire.** *Top :* **The Devil's Arrows, three Yorkshire stones near Boroughbridge.** *Top right :* **The Rollright stones.** *Above :* **One of the long stone avenues of Carnac, Brittany.**

ments he investigated owed their proportions to multiples of a single measurement, the 'megalithic yard'. This work has led him to become a Fellow of the Society of Antiquaries, to which body he was recommended by Professor Atkinson. And so the two disciplines of archaeology and astronomy have come together.

The latest development is Sir Fred Hoyle's book, *On Stonehenge,* published in 1978. He extends our understanding of Stonehenge as an observatory by putting forward the theory that the fifty-six mysterious Aubrey holes (corresponding in number to the weeks in a year of lunar months) were used as a very refined peg-board (or

early computer) by which eclipses of the sun and moon could be predicted and recorded.

Hoyle even argues that the very complex mathematics involved in these calculations could be the basis of a theology that is current today in the doctrine of a triune God. He proves that the astronomers at Stonehenge, using the Aubrey holes as guides, must have based their calculations on the

movements of the sun (god), the moon (goddess) and an invisible third factor composed of the nodes of the moon's orbit of the earth. (These nodes are the two points nearest the earth's surface at which the paths of the sun and the moon in the sky intersect.)

His leap from mathematics to theology must be taken as a matter of opinion. What seems indisputable, however, is the fact that in late Neolithic and

Bronze Age times, the practical and religious significances of Stonehenge were inseparable. Man is a creature who operates in space and time, and the first function of the temple of Stonehenge was to help him to orientate himself in those dimensions. By making a building aligned on the heavenly bodies, he could start to make extensions from it (primarily in relation to sun rise and sun set) that would give him directions for moving about the heavily wooded, sometimes swampy and often featureless landscape in which he lived. Furthermore, by noting the positions of the moving heavenly bodies in relation to that of the static stones he could record the annual cycle of the seasons and link it to the sowing and harvesting of crops.

Even so, many questions relating to the bluestones, the siting of Stonehenge and the link with the Orkneys temple are left unanswered. Until further evidence comes to light, there remains only the partial explanation that Stonehenge is a sophisticated extension of the earlier sacred observatory at Avebury and the primitive orientation of other stone circles, causewayed enclosures and long barrows.

SOUTH AMERICAN CIVILIZATIONS

The peoples of ancient America differed widely in culture and mythology. The Spanish conquest of this new world in the early sixteenth century slowly brought to light strange peoples whose lives were filled with fascinating ritual and unusual beliefs, including magic.

The earliest explorers of the New World were men of Europe. Their whole upbringing and culture was that of Christian Europe, and they found it impossible to conceive of any other. The first mystery they encountered was the inhabitants of the New World and their origins. Many a monk, hoping to hear another story about Eden, questioned them. 'But we have always lived here where the Gods made us', was the usual reply.

The white men speculated. Were the Indians really human? The Church stood up for the Indians. They must have descended from Adam, so they too were the children of God and must not be enslaved. Later, scientists worked out that the Indian tribes must have crossed the Bering Straits long ago and slowly marched south. But no ancient stone tools have been found to link Siberia and Alaska. There are plenty of theories of migration across either the North Atlantic or the Pacific. So far Bering Straits is the best theory, but neither it nor any of the others has any single piece of material evidence to attest its truth.

I know of no legend of tribal origins outside America. Truly there can be only the very slightest evidence of the movements of a dozen people or so, one or two families of hunters who came into the continent from time to time, chasing animals for their dinners and the skins to protect them from the cold. At this stage they would have been simple nomads, without any high culture, simple in belief. Their gods were like themselves, but were more magical in power.

Later on, thousands of years later, some of their descendants settled and built themselves shelters. They discovered how to grow food and later built up civilizations of great value. But nowhere did they retain memories of the ancient nomadic times. Everywhere, the Indians answered their questioners 'We were always here' and then recounted their myths. The white man made a lot of wonderful theories but let us look at some of the Indian legends . . . which they also invented.

In Peru, the coastal Indians talked about Viracocha, who came out of the waters, clothed in white and with a long white beard. Up and down he went along the empty coasts. He wondered why they were so flat, and pulled up mighty ranges of mountains and flat-

Opposite : **ruins of the Toltec temple at Tula,** *c.* **900 AD.** *Above :* **a Maya observatory at Uxmal, a building for determining dates exactly for the magical calendar.**

tened the plains between the *altiplano* and the coastal plains. Then he formed people to live in this land. They grew and changed, building great civilizations one after another until at last the Incas came mysteriously out of the eastern forests and built their Empire of the Sun. But Viracocha still watches over his world and protects the people.

Far to the north the gods gathered together and created mankind. They formed the land between the waters. Tezcatlipoca sacrificed his foot when he dragged up the monstrous earth. But the first men were ignorant and dull and did not worship the gods, so the earth was flooded and a new race

we find a third legend from the Muisca of Colombia. It begins with the condemnation of an early race. The gods sent a great flood; ever the waters rose and the tribes climbed the mountain in terror. Many were drowned. Then Bochica the Sun God flew to the mountain and cleft its side, so that the flood ran into it. The last two people changed into golden serpents and slithered down into the lake. The gods created people and the golden serpents returned and told them stories and taught them to worship the gods properly. Every year the Muisca painted their chief with clay and gold dust so that, when he jumped into the lake and washed, the gold dust went

of wooden men was created. They also were tested for some four thousand years, but they failed and when the next catastrophe came two were turned into the ancestors of all the monkeys. The stone men were next given the spark of life, but again they failed to adore the gods. So clay was taken and moulded, and maize was made into paste, and then once again men were made. They were independent of the gods, but most were turned into monkeys. Two, however, were put in a canoe and became the ancestors of mankind. So mankind learned to love maize from which he was created.

In between these two nations

down as an offering to the ancestors and the gods.

We must note that not one of the stories about the creation gives any hint of the migration of the human race. Humans are always in the area in which they still lived. The only migration story is told by the Navajo. Their evolutionary story began under the earth and ascended in four stages to the surface, which is the present land of the Navajo. But still there is no hint of surface migration; it is too much to expect that to have been handed down by ancestors of perhaps a hundred thousand years ago.

The puzzle of their origins

aside, the Indian peoples have left many mysteries, mainly discovered by the white man. On a desert plateau just inland from Nasca, on the southern half of the Peruvian coast, are strange markings made by white stones. These take the forms of straight lines. interspersed by occasional patterns of birds and spiders. It has been suggested that the white lines might be directives for 'flying saucers'. But if saucers did visit that land they would not have needed approach roads but rather squares or circles for vertical landing. So what were these markings? That is partly answered by the archaeologists.

The birds and spiders are in the style of similar creatures embroidered on Nasca style textiles of AD 300 to 500. How they were designed is not known, for they are not visible on the flat ground except as a jumble of lines; one has to fly over them to see their forms. But a Nasca artist might well have walked the ground, taking one pace as one stitch of the embroidery. If he kept to the right directions and the correct number of paces he would reproduce the form of the embroideries.

That theory suggested, we have to ask, what was the meaning of the lines? The straight lines are probably

44

sighting lines to important points on the horizon marked by the motions of some of the fixed stars. The living creatures probably refer to planets, birds to the fast-moving Mars and Venus, the spiders to the slower Jupiter and Saturn. All this may have been part of a complex apparatus for working out a calendar, but as none of the traditions of the Nasca people have survived we must rely on investigations by modern astronomers and guess that they used a calendar like that of the later Incas, which was a mixture of solar and lunar reckonings and seems very confusing, at least to us modern westerners.

Another great mystery is largely of the white man's dreaming. At the beginning of the present century a great German scientist surveyed the ruins of the ancient city of Tiahuanaco at the northern end of Lake Titicaca in Peru. It was right inland on the high plateau. The ruins which were obviously ancient, included great courtyards and the remains of large buildings made with stone sections of wall with open spaces between them (probably once filled with mud brick). There were huge monolithic standing figures in a very distinctive style and a stone gateway, locally called the Gateway of the Sun, another monolithic construction in the same style. The explorer had no help

eleventh century AD. Is it a relic of a Peruvian visitor from the Tiahuanaco empire?

Excavations at many sites have produced pottery and textiles, including strange square hats of a style similar to that of Tiahuanaco. Alas for mystery, they date from the seventh to the early tenth centuries AD. Tiahuanaco was not so very ancient. In fact Montesinos, one of the earlier Europeans to set down the stories of the Indians, recorded a tradition that Tiahuanaco was ruled by *Amautas* (wise men) many generations before the Incas. It controlled a powerful empire in the southern half of Peru, from the highlands to the coast. But though the mystery

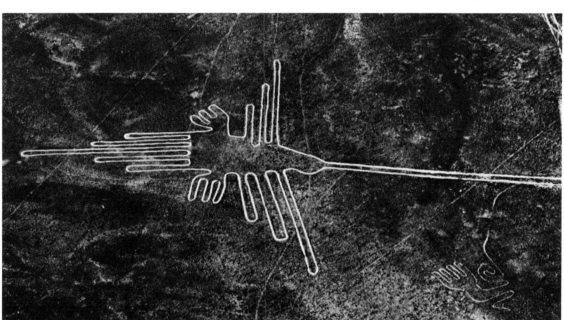

A group of symbolic outline designs from the hills above Nasca, *c*. 400 AD, made of white stone pebbles laid out on the sands. They represent in the Nasca art style a form of sacred maze, a spider, two birds and a spider monkey, and reproduce the designs found in Nasca textiles.

even by sequence dating which dates objects according to the depth at which they are found. It was obviously long pre-Inca and his serious and learned work with its meticulous surveys created a sensation; 'before the Flood' was his conclusion. Many people still believe this. Just as an added confusion, a similar squatting stone statue has been found on Easter Island far out in the Pacific. It is earlier than the local Polynesian giant statues of after the

of date has been solved, there remains much to be done in unravelling its history, finding the meanings of the patterns, and discovering how the people lived. The stone gateway has a central figure with tear marks carved on its cheeks. This illustrates a later Inca myth about the sun weeping gold. All around are winged figures, probably the stars in their courses, but we would really like to know the truth of this ancient Inca story.

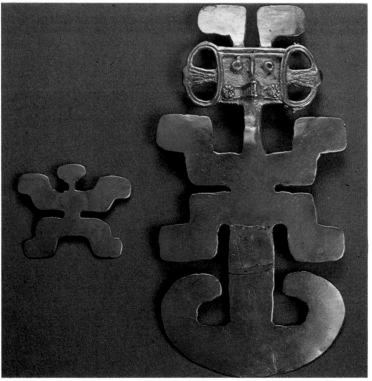

Above left : **a group of ruins at Copan, Honduras, carved entirely from blocks of the local limestone by the Maya in the sixth or seventh centuries** AD. *Left :* **a beaten plaque of tumbaga (a mixture of gold and copper) from the Indians of the Tolima region of Colombia,** *c.* **fourteenth century** AD. *Above right :* **probably tenth century** AD, **stone columns of a temple at Tula showing Toltec warriors, that once formed part of a colonnade, now destroyed.**

Further northwards, in what are now Colombia and Panama, the Indians obtained great quantities of gold by placer mining. But they had no unity. Tribe after tribe is listed, each with strange customs, each rich in gold; most were cannibals. The country was rough, heavily forested and with steep rushing rivers. In the Cauca river valley in Colombia lived the Quimbaya, who mixed gold with copper. They etched away the surface copper and bur-nished the golden outer layer to a high degree. Figures cast hollow, and big breastplates, and masks all glittered gold; technically splendid work. Among the Quimbaya only working people wore cloth skirts. The upper class went quite naked to show that they did not need to dig the fields. They are always depicted bare in the middle, displaying their beauty. Up in the highlands around Bogotá lived the Muisca tribes whose chief, El Dorado,

there was a group of sculptures with hieroglyphs in what later became the Toltec style of central Mexico. One can recognise some of the later Toltec gods carved on them, although each glyph (a symbol meaning a sound) is surrounded by a ring, which was not used later. Some of these glyphs appear again, in central Mexico, and, without the rings, they were used at Tollán the Toltec capital up to about AD 990. It is by this kind of detective work that we can trace the migration of the Toltecs' ancestors. This calendar which even later still was adopted by the Aztecs, is also found in the magical books, one of which, the Codex Vindobonensis, traces history through the reigns of the Toltec kings back to the eighth century. So another question – who were the Toltecs? – is partially solved, and they stand out as a historical people.

In southern Mexico, Guatemala and the northern strip of Honduras dwelt the Maya, a group of people who spoke six closely related languages in various districts. They believed that they had always lived in the same region and had always worshipped the same gods. Their written history probably goes back to the second century AD. They carved the local limestone with a series of glyphs which give us clues as to their dates. But a great part of these inscriptions is only just beginning to be read. Mayan writing comprises symbols for some 750 syllables. The Spanish priest, las Casas, met Mayan priests and got them to write down the calendrical signs. But he made a mistake about the syllables, thinking they were an alphabet, leaving us the means to read dates but not the texts, on which scholars are now making progress. Archaeologists working in the south of the Yucatán peninsula have discovered another civilization, dating from before 1000 BC which used a few elementary glyphs on monuments. These

appear to predate the Mayan glyphs. Perhaps these people, the Olmecs, invented the system. The Olmec sites are remarkable. At one Tres Zapotes, there are a number of beautifully sculptured stone heads which never had bodies. They are huge, one as much as 3 metres (10 feet) high. What did they represent? Gods, planets, chiefs? Not far off, at La Venta, yellow clay had been brought from some miles away and a huge pyramid built. Nearby, a platform some 3 metres (10 feet) deep had been prepared and inside it, obscured for ever from the sight of man, they had hidden a gigantic jaguar mask. It was obviously magic, for the jaguar was an earth monster responsible for earthquakes. Was it a magical protection?

A thousand years later in the same region the Maya built immense stone temples of most complex design, covering them with carvings, including dates. The insides were plastered and painted with pictures in an advanced style. The high culture of the Maya lasted until about AD 900. Then all of a sudden the old towns were deserted. Why? Probably because of some religious prediction. Then the people returned and made offerings in the old temples. But the new temples they built were smaller and simpler and were mostly further north; their artistic talent had deteriorated and never recovered. Later a Toltec chief assumed rulership. Still later Toltec power failed, and the chief Maya families ruled a much simpler civilization until the arrival of the Spaniards in 1540.

A great civilization had perished, its survivors had come back much simpler and poorer. But there is no history of the debacle, just a few tribal legends of little certainty. The people are still there and speak the old languages, but they have divulged nothing of their past history.

The ancient Olmec culture, which is possibly ancestral to

the gilded one, was washed with clay and then rolled in gold dust, which he washed off in lake Guatavita as an offering to the ancestors who in return conferred the blessing of power on him.

Further to the east were great tombs lined with huge stone figures of warrior gods wearing jaguar masks. But of these monuments around San Augustin we know nothing except that they were made about the first century AD. America is full of mysteries awaiting solution, for it has had a long history.

In Panama, the Pacific coast tribes wore ornaments of gold and also dived for pearls. Archaeologists say that their period was in the fourteenth century. A little further north

inland on the borders of Nicaragua lay another mystery – enormous stone balls. They are a complete mystery. They are Indian, but what do they represent? Are they substitute heads? Or are they objects representing a long-lost mythology? Again a mystery without date and with no identifiable contacts with the tribes.

Further north, on the Pacific coast of Honduras and San Salvador some relics attributed to the Pipil tribes have been found. They appear to date from the first to the fourth centuries AD. Inscriptions on them use the Toltec calendar of later times. It appears that the earlier date comes from San Salvador and that the Pipiles moved northwards. At Santa Lucia Cotzumahualpa, a Guatemalan town,

the Maya, influenced all Mexico, as far as the Western Cordillera and northwards into Michoacán. Everywhere these people left art works and the seeds of culture. Everywhere stone carvings have been found, and strange little pottery figures of baby-faced individuals and massive beautiful jade axe blades often with jaguars carved on them; often the jaguar is shown holding sky symbols as if he towered above the sky. Obviously this was an important deity, but what was his name, what rituals were performed in his temples? We know little except that the heavy axes bore some relationship with human sacrifice. Though the Olmecs mixed with the other tribes of Mexico for a thousand years, leaving works of art everywhere, we know litle about them. Even their name, which means 'Rubber People' because their early cities were in the rubber-growing regions, carries no significance. What they called themselves we simply do not know. They were great pioneers with no history, only archaeological remains.

Near the city of Oaxaca around which many of the Zapotecs now live, are the ancient ruins of Monte Albán, the White Mountain. The top of the hill has been cut into a great plateau and many ancient Zapotec temples have been built there. At one end, however, stands an ancient building, partly built over in older times, a pre-Zapotec monument. The great stone slab walls are carved with a series of curious contorted figures, now called Los Danzantes, the dancers. Alas they do not dance! Their eyes are closed in death, and their contorted forms look as if their bodies had been thrown down. In the middle of each is a kind of pattern made from the shredded flesh of the penis, usually of a beautiful but somehow horrible, flower-like form. Who they were is hinted at by glyphs beside some of them – 'monkey', 'jaguar' – but other than that they date from about

Above : **outline carving of one of** *Los Danzantes* **at Monte Alban. The closed eyes indicate, however, that the figure is not dancing but has been sacrificed, and is dead.** *Right :* **general view of the court at Monte Alban, a Zapotec holy place for some fifteen centuries.**

200 BC we know nothing more. To us they are a ghastly monument of sacrifice, but to what gods they were offered remains a mystery.

Later, the Zapotecs ruled the mountain shrine, paraded and danced in the great open space, observed the sun and planets in a special observatory and buried dead chiefs in tombs under temples. The symbol of a zapota tree shows that these were indeed Zapotecs. Over each tomb door is a ledge which once supported a group of beautifully modelled pottery urns representing the Zapotec gods and goddesses. In one of the tombs a conquering Mixtec chief from the nearby tribe was found, a skeleton decorated with a treasure of golden ornaments. Around the body were a number of little heaps of black powder, the remains of silver which had oxidized. We shall probably never know why Monte Albán was deserted.

Down the hill and some fifteen miles along the valley is Mitla, the place of the dead and the last Zapotec capital. It consists of a series of palaces and courtyards. The palaces are built on high plinths and are made up of a series of stone rooms built around courtyards. When the buildings were roofed they were dark and it would have been hard to distinguish the stone mosaic-like decorated walls, painted in white and red, in great patches of geometrical patterns. These were the palaces of the Uija Tao, the Zapotec priest-king, but the meaning of the mosaics is lost probably for ever. Most of the palaces are above subterranean chambers, which according to legend were burial grounds. Once upon a time, it is said, those who despaired of life made a confession to the Uija Tao and then descended into the pitch black of the tomb chambers and there wandered for a few days until they died in the mysterious darkness. That is why the conquering Aztecs called the place Mitla, the underworld of the dead.

The Zapotecs painted the walls of their tombs with great religious pictures of gorgeously dressed priests and gods. The neighbouring Mixtecs, how-

48

ever, who were descended from one branch of the Toltecs, painted true books, long strips of prepared, lime-washed deer skin which folded like a fire screen. On these they painted histories and religious works. The most important of these are the Codex Vindobonensis (now in Vienna) and the Codex Zouche Nuttall in the British Museum. These great works, which are delicately drawn in black outlines filled with colour, cover a period of some seven centuries and list the stories of the Mixtec kings and nobles. As the names and dates are readable they give us a skeleton history of the people. Many mythological items are included, including the making of the Mixtec ancestors, who were born from a tree beside

years old, but the earliest remaining documents go back only to about AD 1350. The earliest of these records were lost because of the unfortunate Mexican habit of burning all the documents found in conquered palaces and temples. Those that survived have perished partly because of age but mostly through the offices of Spanish priests who, horrified by some of the pictures, thought they were works of Satan and must

were made, started in the second century BC as a small pyramidal mound, with, buried in the earth, a number of pottery figures typical of the agricultural people of the time. All of a sudden somebody enlarged the mound considerably, making it into the biggest pyramid ever built by man, over 150 metres (500 feet) high, with sides sloping more broadly than the Egyptian pyramids. Great stairways scaled its four

in Guatemala where they were in contact with the Maya. A very queer thing about this civilization is that it made very little monumental use of writing; only about a dozen hieroglyphs have been identified. Perhaps all their written documents were on skin or paper and have been lost. But we can be sure that such a huge civilization must have kept records. From pottery figurines we can trace the development of fashion from necklaces and nudity to loin cloths and cloaks and skirts and feathered headdresses but not a word can we read, not a name do we know.

Having started high civilization in highland Mexico, developed it to a rich and complex level, soon after AD 700 they suddenly fell and their cities were abandoned. All was lost except the ancient pyramids of Teotihuacan, which remained as a mysterious holy place. Now they are places of pilgrimage to tourists who laboriously climb the ancient pyramids and wonder who were the people who built them.

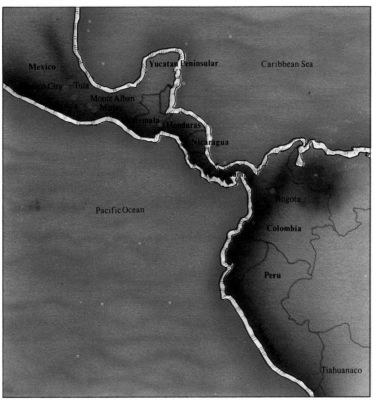

Above : **view of Teotihuacan, built** *c.* **500 AD. Even in ruins, the city was a place of pilgrimage until 1520.** *Far left :* **one of the masks of the serpents of the wind and rain that decorates the temple of Quetzalc. Once they were brightly painted in green and blue. The holy city was dominated by the gigantic Pyramid of Sun** *(left)* **which was surmounted by a statue of the sun, now totally lost.**

a sacred stream at Apoala, in the seventh century AD.

After the mythological beginning, we are told of the Toltec period, and then, after the fall of Tollán, the Toltec capital, of the days of Mixtec greatness before the Aztec conquests of the country. It is an exciting story of ceremonial marriage, wars and sacrifices. Though they mostly chronicle the royal family, some do list town rulers over periods of centuries. They were painted in ink on sheets of cotton cloth. This method of making painted documents is probably well over a thousand

be destroyed. The Maya also had painted books inscribed with Mayan glyphs. The earliest is the Codex Dresdensis, preserved in Dresden, a delicate and beautiful work, which goes back only to the eleventh century. It contains no history, only long and complex ceremonial calendars.

But let us turn to the central plateau of Mexico. There we meet the biggest monuments in the American continent, the great pyramid at Teotihuacan and the even more massive mound at Cholula. Toetihuacan, the place where the gods

sides, and it is said that on top stood a huge statue of the Sun God, of which no fragment now remains.

What made the people undertake such a stupendous task? Why did their little villages turn into a city? Why all of a sudden did they spread their culture over the whole of the civilized part of Mexico? Obviously Teotihuacano power erupted suddenly. We do not know their language, nor even the original name of the people. But they had enormous power and established a secondary centre far away at Kaminaljuyu

Then the Toltecs : who were they? We can trace the migration of their calendar and their writing from Guatemala and Honduras. But tradition in Mexico has it that they came as warlike tribes from the North. Probably both traditions are true, and the Toltec empire was really a confederacy. According to the Mixtec codices it included the ruling family of the Mixtecs, who inherited independence after the fall of the empire in the late tenth century. But the real Toltec problem is the personality of the divine king, the Quetzalcoatl. According to the painted history books he was at once a god and a king, for his name had been borne by nine kings of the Toltecs. But was the god human or spiritual? The stories conflict.

The original Quetzalcoatl seems to have been the wind god. He blew the clouds and held up the sky which held all the water that fell as rain. Then he came to earth as a marvellous divine king and ruled wonderfully. But his goodness angered a jealous god who worked magic against him. He was tempted by the other gods and discovered alcohol, was persuaded to drink; he became drunk. He lost all control, and took a goddess and had intercourse with her, which was not easy, for he had a huge penis. However the goddess tempted him to go further and further. He fell into a drunken stupor and awoke to realize that he had broken the law. Disconsolate, he could not find forgiveness and eventually ran away. He climbed the mountains with a few companions, some cripples and hunchbacks. One by one they suffered accidents and went away from him. He descended to the coasts, lost all his ornaments and cast away his clothing. Then he embarked upon a raft made of serpents' skins. He sailed eastwards towards the sunrise and was burnt up by the rising sun, but his heart blazed up and rose into the sky as the planet Venus.

This wonderful story is based directly on the apparent movements of the planet Venus, its climb into the sky, its apogee and gradual descent, then the darkness followed by its reappearance with the dawn.

The pictures in the codices of the kings who adopted Quetzalcoatl as a title, show the dates of birth, a list of their conquests, and the date they died. It is a skeleton history, but one that seems to be very accurate.

After the fall of the Toltecs, there was a period of civil wars, of invasion from the north as the Indian tribes were disturbed by a terrible drought. Various people tried to establish empires; it was a period of confusion. Whence did the Aztecs come? Their own legend recounts sorrowful wanderings, apparently from quite near Mexico City. But some think that their homeland was in California which fits their Aztec legend of the Seven Caves from which the tribes originated.

The works of three Mexican cultures: *above :* **the pyramid at El Tajin,** *c.* **1300** AD; *right :* **a face on the Temple of the Warriors at Chichen Itza, Yucatan, Maya Toltec,** *c.* **1200** AD. *Opposite :* **the Mayan pyramidal based Temple of the Inscriptions at Palenque,** *c.* **600** AD. **The styles differ, but the basic idea is the pyramid, of which each stage represents a layer of the heavens.**

One Aztec king had all the historical records destroyed and so messed up history by mixing it with propaganda – making things all the more confusing for us.

The Aztec high chief Montezuma II extended Aztec rule from the Atlantic to the Pacific oceans and tried to reconstruct the Toltec Empire, building a small palace in the ruins of ancient Tula to retire to when he needed solitude. About ten years before the Spanish invasion, there was a very curious

incident in Mexico City. Montezuma's young aunt, the Princess Butterfly (Papantzin), was sitting on a garden wall in the palace. She had been playing with the children and suddenly fell down unconscious. The children ran to the Emperor. He came with priests and found her dead. Amid lamentations, for she was a favourite aunt, the body was laid in a stone box in readiness for cremation. Three days later the youngsters were playing and went through the court-

yard, where they pulled up short. There was the lady Papantzin, sitting in the garden, sewing. Scared, they ran to Montezuma, who came with some of his nobles. The Princess called to him and bursting into tears told him of her vision while she had been 'dead'. She had been travelling. On the shore she had seen giant floating houses, and later men from those houses came and fought their way to Mexico City. They were strange creatures with hair on their faces, and some of them rode on big animals like hornless deer. They were

clothed in grey stone (her idea of iron armour) and carried shining wands which they used to cut down the Indians. She saw them advance to Mexico. Montezuma entered her vision and he was captured and killed. Eventually Mexico was destroyed and the strangers ruled the land.

Montezuma was terrified at this prophecy and thought that perhaps his power would pass away. He retired more often to his refuge in Tula. Eventually the Princess's vision came true in the terror of the Conquest. The princess lived to an old age

difficult to traverse, but the tribal warfare and cannibalism deterred travellers. So we have a confusion of evidence of smallish groups of people all highly skilled in the arts and without history. Only archaeological excavations can give us any lead.

But despite all the changes of climate and terrain these many tribes and nations were of one human race. From the naked farmers of the tropical forest to the well wrapped peoples of the highland civilizations they were all physically alike. They had no more

as a great lady under Spanish rule and often told her story. What it meant was always a mystery.

The study of these ancient civilizations helps us to understand the immense differences between the two high cultures of the region. It is said that some Peruvian balsa rafts visited Panama and spread news of their wonderful golden world. The ancient pottery of western Mexico has several parallels with that of Peru, but nothing can be proved. We can trace Maya arts some way southwards in Central America and echoes of symbolic pictures can be traced almost into Panama. The mountains and forested valleys in Panama led to a great cultural division; not only was the area very

variation than the European peoples. All brown-skinned, black-haired mongoloids. They were intellectually alert and developed their own cultures. They all believed that the nearby tribes were enemies and fought vigorously on any occasion. They were capable of high intellectual achievements in mathematics and of great skills in artwork, whether pottery and weaving or stone and gold. Not one of them had any idea of different lands or peoples apart from creation stories of life under the earth. Wherever they attained to high civilization their philosophers and rulers were among the world's best. Nowadays their descendants are stirring and a few are winning the freedom they lost so long ago.

THE STONE STATUES OF EASTER ISLAND

One of the most dramatic landscapes of the world is Easter Island with its famous and strange monoliths. How did they come to be there? Were they made by man or visitors from outer space?

For such a tiny speck of rock miles from civilization, the Oceanian Easter Island has achieved widespread fame, fame which ranks with Loch Ness (and its elusive inhabitant), the stone circle of Stonehenge – and the writings of Erich von Daniken in which it figures largely. Its nearest neighbour, Pitcairn Island, home of *Bounty* mutineers' descendants, lies 1800 km (1000 sea miles) away, and its only taste of mainland life and culture is a yearly visit from a Chilean man o' war. Yet this remote lump of volcanic rock holds a fascination totally disproportionate to its size or sophistication.

Half sunk in the infertile soil and dotted apparently at random all over the island are huge carved statues of mysterious beings, capped with chunks of red stone, some weighing nearly 16.2 tonnes (16

Left and above : **The giant stone statues depicting stylized heads dwarf all living men, native and explorer alike.**

ing zeal. Sadly her scientific records were lost, but she did have this to say: 'the dweller there is ever listening for he knows not what, feeling unconsciously that he is in the antechamber to something yet more vast which is just beyond his ken.' In other words, it's all very mysterious.

It was not until 1955 that a scientific expedition arrived in Easter Island which set the popular imagination on fire and managed to achieve serious archaeological recognition. It was led by the Norwegian explorer and anthropologist, Thor Heyerdahl, hero of the *Kon-Tiki* voyage of discovery which had taken him to other parts of the South Seas in 1947.

tons) and standing up to 9 metres (30 feet) high. Their long faces stare blankly across the island and across the sea, offering no answers but only inviting infinite speculation as to how they got there – and from where; whose mighty hand carved them; and, inevitably, what they *mean*.

For centuries only the sea-birds visited Easter Island, or *Te Pito te Hanua*, which means 'Navel of the World'. Then, on Easter Day 1722 the first European visitor, a Dutchman named Roggeveen, landed among the stone giants. He was greeted by natives of mixed blood and surprising variations of hue, typically dark, small Polynesians standing side by side with 'completely white' natives with red hair.

Next came the Spanish and then the indefatigable Captain Cook, bringing the islanders respectively the ability to say 'Ave Maria, long live Charles III, King of Spain' and intense irritation at being disturbed by curious seafarers. In fact when Cook made his preliminary reconnoitre the aristocracy of the island hid in their many underground caves until Cook's men went down with scurvy and left hurriedly. In 1914 a Mrs Katherine Routledge arrived from England all Edwardian energy and pioneer-

and that the only explanation and that Heyerdahl was laughably wrong became 'obvious' that *Gods?* hit the bookstalls it moment his *Chariots of* von Daniken. From the very man – ex-hotelier Erich the late 1960s up popped the wanted more mysteries and in mysteries had been solved, they didn't want to hear that the But it seems that the public they did. academic world is concerned, of Easter Island. As far as the months to solve the mysteries gave themselves at least six had been made of reed) and *Tiki*, though a seaworthy vessel, normal seagoing vessel (the *Kon-* scholarly crew luxuriated in a This time his distinguished,

for the stone giants on Easter Island was that they were the creation of 'intelligent beings' (spacemen) who had been stranded on Easter Island and had carved a few hundred statues out of boredom. Then a rescue ship arrived and the Beings threw down their make-shift stone axes, jumped aboard and went home. The natives they left behind tried to con-tinue the stone carving but were frustrated by their primitive tools which they flung down in disgust.

Von Daniken points out to those of us who had missed the refinements of his argument that the statues were far too large for mere primitives to have carved, the stone was too hard, there were too few inhabi-tants, no trees to serve as rollers for transporting the statues, and the red 'hats' of stone atop the statues were 'obviously' visual reminders of the helmets the 'intelligent beings' had worn. While the von Daniken school of thought went from strength to strength, Heyerdahl and other academics maintained a

disbelieving silence. In 1976 Ronald Story deliberately pro-voked a confrontation between von Daniken and the facts as scientists saw them in his book *The Space Gods Revealed.* He asked Thor Heyerdahl to answer von Daniken's asser-tions in print for inclusion in the chapter on Easter Island.

Naturally the explorer was scathing about these wild claims, and Heyerdahl draws the readers' attention to his popular book describing his findings on that mysterious island, *Aku-Aku* (a book, in-cidentally, that von Daniken claims to have read). The account deals in detail with the various mysteries on the island and how the Norwegian-funded team found answers to most of them, including answers to the rhetorical questions *Chariots of the Gods?* uses to inflame our imagination. Before such mas-sive arrogance and illogicality Heyerdahl's painstaking work on Easter Island was as nothing. The public, most of whom, it must be said, had probably never heard of *Aku-*

Aku (but whose Sunday news-papers had thoughtfully serial-ized Von Daniken's book), lapped up the spacemen theory. Heyerdahl remarked drily that if spacemen had landed and erected the monoliths why didn't they leave behind any bit of metal or plastic. Instead of these, only stone implements were found, indicating human toil on a vast scale. But why believe in shift-work and human ingenuity when you can have a Close Encounter?

Heyerdahl was no stranger to crackpot theories. Before setting out on his 1955 voyage to Easter Island he had been buttonholed by a quiet man who wished to impart the ancient secret of the stone statues. Break one open, he said, and you'll find a man inside. Simple, just like the pyramids.

In those days Heyerdahl and his team had other things on their minds, however. Archaeologists Dr William Mulloy, Dr Carlyle Smith and Edwin Ferdon helped to make up a distinguished expedition,

Grave-faced monoliths tower over the Easter Island landscape. Some still retain the *pukao* or redstone topknot; others lie half-buried; some stand on plinths in the temple square at Vinapu – but all are made by man.

Ranks of stone giants – impressive witness to the craftsmanship of Easter Island peoples of the past. Many were later vandalized.

the patron of which was no less that Crown Prince Olav. Also on board the *Anakena* were frogmen and photographers whose skills are supremely useful on any thorough and serious expedition of this kind. One supposes that von Daniken's inspiration more than made up for his lack of scholarship, back-up team or knowledge of the island. However academic the explorers, they were not immune to the peculiar magic, almost mystical in its intensity, which permeates the very air of Easter Island. Thor Heyerdahl is a sensitive man and often a poetic writer. On page twenty-four of *Aku-Aku* he waxes lyrical about this atmosphere – and in so doing can be said to make the only mistake in the book: 'It was as though we had anchored with a hovering space-ship off the shore of an extinct world, where once had lived beings of a kind other than those on our earth. . . .'

A reader with a vivid imagination and impatient of the rest of the book, perhaps a visionary without a cause, could well have found his fate (and fortune) on page twenty-four.

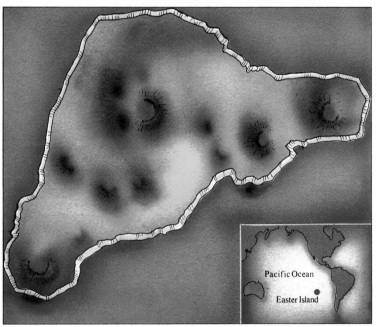

The natives were friendly, overtly Catholic – and much impressed by their present Father Sebastian, a robust and kindly pastor – but still practising pagan ways and indulging in age-old superstitions. They believed that all Islanders had an *aku-aku* which was a sort of pagan guardian angel. Some *aku-akus* worked stronger magic than others, bestowing upon the fortunate *mana* or supernatural powers.

One's *aku-aku* whispered secrets, was invisible and had power over time and space; the mayor's own *aku-aku* could travel to Chile and back in two minutes. During his visit, Heyerdahl managed to impress upon the natives the power of his own *aku-aku* through a mixture of role-playing and often desperate ingenuity.

Because the natives came to believe that he had *mana*, Heyerdahl was gradually shown the island's secrets. Some of the mysteries were explained very quickly once the natives had been won over. For example, the mysterious red stone 'hats' on top of the statues were always referred to by the islanders as *pukao*, which means 'top-knot'. And some of the islanders still had bright red hair, so the red-stone blocks were not so mysterious after all.

Then there was the major problem of the *moai* (statues), many of them apparently overthrown in a hurry, and the stone implements used in the statue quarries which also seemed to have been cast aside in a panic. Gradually Heyerdahl pieced together a likely explanation for the statues and the state they were left in, by listening carefully to the legends told him by his native friends, especially the red-haired mayor's family.

It was widely known on the island that there were two sorts of islander, the *hanau eepe* or 'long-ears' and the *hanau momoko* or 'short-ears'. The long-ears were the direct descendants of the ruling race whose long features were clearly depicted in the statues. All the *mana* was concentrated in the long-ear descendants; theirs was the key to the island's secrets. They knew, for example, what the *rongo-rongo* (or hitherto unexplained script found on the island) meant. Only the long-ear descendants had caves full of stone carvings (of which Heyerdahl became the recipient, many, many times) – and only the long-ears knew about the statues.

When Heyerdahl had asked the mayor, Atan, how the statues had been transported from the quarries to their present sites he had answered glibly, 'they walked.' When it became plain that Señor Kon-Tiki was impatient with such an answer, Atan's honesty was disarming. Well, he said, this

height. The great god Quetzal-coatl is believed to be one of these beings – and this legend was seized upon by modern Mormons to 'prove' that the risen Jesus (white-skinned and red-haired) visited the New World, as recorded in *The Book of Mormon*.

When the invader/explorer Francisco Pizarro arrived in Peru he discovered that the ruling Inca family were taller, whiter and had redder hair than

The bleak landscape of Easter Island was once thickly wooded, and stones still abound. With these simple resources the 'long-ears' undertook the building of these huge sculptures.

is the legend and it wouldn't do to upset the old people who believe it. But who knows whether the *moai* 'walked' with the help of *miro manga erua* (wooden sleds)?

It was apparent that in past times the island had been thickly wooded. The trees had been used up and then the remainder had been consumed in the great conflagration when the short-ears invaded the settlement of the long-ears. There had only been one survivor of the fire, Ororoina, whose direct descendant was the mayor.

Further questioning added flesh to the skeleton story. For a time the long-ears had ruled the short-ears, who slaved for them in their set task of ridding the island of superfluous stone in order to cultivate the land more readily. Then the short-

ears rebelled and in the civil war that ensued many of the stone statues, set up to honour deceased kings, were flung down.

Carbon dating of excavated areas mentioned as the last-ditch battleground of the long-ears revealed that the last statues had been carved as late as 1680, that the short-ears were latecomers to Easter Island, arriving about ten generations before Heyerdahl, and that there had indeed been a massive conflagration about the same time as the 'statue-overthrowing time' (which is still very real to the natives). But about the time before the civil war there were no legends and, as far as the present islanders are concerned, no need for them.

Who were the long-ears?

Even now a tiny proportion of the island people have curiously milk-white skin and glossy, flame red hair like, according to legend, the long-eared ruling class. In many parts of South America there are also stories of bearded, red-haired gods or superior visitors of unusual

their subjects. The Inca Indians told him they were *viracochas*, or a divine race apart, very like the European invaders – which is why Pizarro found little opposition initially from the natives, who naively supposed him and his men to be the gods returned.

But all this did not explain

who the long-ears were, although it seemed to prove beyond dispute that they had existed and made their influence felt with the raising of humanoid monoliths from Mexico to the deeply-hidden jungles of South America.

Heyerdahl took blood samples of the Easter Island long-ears and sent them to the Commonwealth Serum Laboratories in Melbourne for analysis. Dr Simmons there

proved that they had no relationship whatsoever with the Polynesians or 'original' American Indians. The only speculation the scientific Heyerdahl allows himself is that the 'divine race of long-ears' could have drifted on strong reed boats from Malaysia and could possibly have been Nordic way back in the mists of time (one must discount anything so romantic as mere chauvinism on the Norwegian explorer's part!).

As a genuine, pure-blooded long-ear, the Easter Island mayor agreed to show the visitors how to raise a fallen giant statue, using the old knowledge. The whole secret was an ingenious form of leverage, as Edwin Ferdon later explained in an interview with Ronald Story. Using only three strong poles and a growing mound of boulders, twelve men took only eighteen days to raise a statue weighing between 25-30 tonnes (25-30 tons). (De-

tailed diagrams are given in *Archaeology & Physical Anthropology in Oceania* vol. 5, no. 1 [April 1970], drawings by William Malloy.)

So raising the statues is possible without power tools, but what about carving them in the first place? The indefatigable long-ear mayor knew how to do that, too, but naturally it was a longer and more arduous business. Von Daniken describes the rock as 'steel hard', but in fact it was volcanic ash which the islanders wetted continuously to soften it as they carved, carving the same piece out one after the other to make it easier. It was obviously a fine art and one which has not entirely died out.

So Heyerdahl's expedition in 1955 answered every one of von Daniken's questions posed in 1969 with one exception: in *Chariots of the Gods?* he called Easter Island 'Land of the Bird Men' – the bird men being synonymous with extraterrestrials. But Edwin Ferdon made a special study of the bird man legend while on Heyerdahl's expedition. Apparently there was an annual ceremony to celebrate the sooty tern's coming to the island. Men chosen to represent the island chiefs, or the chiefs themselves, dived 270 metres (900 feet) from a cliff into the sea in an attempt to be the first to collect an egg from the bird colony. The one who did (having survived this incredibly dangerous dive) accrued much *mana* or supernatural power over others. Surely astronauts would value their equipment, not to mention their lives, too much to go leaping, lemming-like, over cliffs?

One of the more respectable fringe theories about Easter Island is that it is the tiny remnant of a sunken continent – the legendary continent of Mu is often cited in this context. Heyerdahl was not prepared to dismiss this idea out of hand and investigated it. All over the island there are paved roads which disappear abruptly into the sea; these, sunken continent

enthusiasts suggest, lead down to the lost land beneath the waves.

Heyerdahl sent his frogman out researching. Where the roads seem to disappear abruptly underwater that is precisely what they do. Indeed that part of Polynesia offered no evidence to suggest that it had risen or sunk since man's arrival there.

In the event it was the local inhabitants who yet again supplied Heyerdahl with a clue. Their word for the roads is *apapa* – 'unload'. Heyerdahl proposes the theory that they are ramps leading to unloading bays for ancient reed boats, of which his reed boat *Kon-Tiki* was but a pale modern example.

Señor Kon-Tiki entered into the heart and life of Easter Island and in return was given to understand much that science is grateful for. Herr von Daniken, too, visited Easter Island for a brief time, but his conversation with the islanders seems to have been perfunctory; perhaps there were language difficulties, or perhaps the insular people did not quite trust him. He had read *Aku-Aku* and goes so far as to say that he was so impressed by it that he was prepared to write off Easter Island's mystery as solved. A quick visit there, however, revealed the impossibility that natives could ever have raised the stones and the self-evident truth that the red 'hats' were space helmets. His *aku-aku* must have told him so.

Readers of both accounts, or of any other explanations in between, have to decide be-

tween what is all in the mind and all in context. There is, however, one abiding and seductive mystery of Easter Island; something it shares with Stonehenge, the Pyramids and other artefacts which are grist to Spacemen cultists' mill. One may measure and calculate and photograph with infra-red and carbon date and come up with some pretty neat answers. But with all our technology we can't seem to crack the main code, the deepest secret. What really motivated the builders of these monuments, primitive astronomical computers or whatever they are thought to be? What were these people *like*? Even looking at a photograph of the blank-faced stone men of the Pacific island poses questions deeper than words, arouses vague stirrings deep in one's consciousness, a grave and undefined doubt. Somehow the mystery of Easter Island eludes us still.

AVALON AND KING ARTHUR

The legends of King Arthur and his court make attractive reading, but it is worthwhile to determine just how much of the stories are factual. Was there at any point a King Arthur, defender of Britain against the heathen invaders? Where was his base, and who were his chief lieutenants?

valon is a place that figures in stories about King Arthur and the Holy Grail. It is said to be an island. However, its insularity is more than a matter of having water round it. Avalon is elusive and 'other', not exactly a part of the normal world. Things are different there, strange events happen there, strange beings dwell there, seen or unseen. It is an abode of enchantments and immortality and of mysteries senior to Christianity, which none the less find a place in the Christian order. It is the last destination of King Arthur himself, passing from the human world after his last battle.

The meaning of 'Avalon' is uncertain. It may be derived from the name of a Celtic god or mythical hero. Usually, however, it is taken to mean 'the place of apples' – sacred or magical apples, like those in the Garden of the Hesperides in Greek mythology.

Christ and through whose man who supplied the tomb of Joseph of Arimathea, the rich community here was founded by belief that the Christian com- Abbey graveyard; from the that Arthur was buried in the pagan antiquity; from the belief the belief that this was a holy, somewhat uncanny spot in from a mixture of causes: from fact underlying fantasy – arises claim to be the original Avalon – an island, though not quite. Its hill-cluster was indeed almost Christian era Glastonbury's from the sea, and early in the north-west has been reclaimed Much of the country to the grew around an ancient abbey. small town in Somerset which of hills cradling Glastonbury, a has been given to the odd cluster longer, the name 'Isle of Avalon' centuries and perhaps much further problems. For eight it is a problem which leads to Avalon does, and for that reason appear on the modern map. Such fairylands seldom

agency, according to medieval romance, the Grail was brought to the 'vales of Avalon' in Britain.

How much truth there is in these notions, and whether Glastonbury is actually rooted in a semi-mythical past, are questions that open up a wide field of mystery. What about the semi-mythical past itself? If all the stories of it are baseless fiction, Avalon is nothing, and therefore nothing is Avalon. However, there is no short answer. It is now agreed that the great medieval saga of Arthur and his knights and the Quest of the Grail is not totally baseless. Yet it is not historical either – far from it. Avalon is only part of a complex enigma. The unravelling has gone far enough to be fascinating, but not so far as to be more than provisional.

The Arthur of legend and romance is supposed to have been King of Britain during the late fifth century AD, or the early sixth. In those days the Roman Empire still existed, but was no longer effective in western Europe. Britain's Celtic people, ancestors of the Welsh and Cornish, were still in name imperial subjects but in practice on their own, and had been so for several decades. Officially Christian, they were harassed by heathen Anglo-Saxons from across the North Sea, who had come as mercenary troops and then revolted, seizing land for themselves and massacring Britons.

Opposite: Tintagel Castle, considered by some to have been the birthplace of Arthur.
Above: Spiral carving in a neighbouring valley.

Arthur is said to have attained sovereignty while very young. He conquered the encroaching heathen and brought them under control. He also asserted Britain's independence of Rome. He founded the order of the Knights of the Round Table and reigned gloriously, his favourite city being Camelot. His queen was Guinevere, his chief counsellor and court magician was Merlin, and his knights included Lancelot, Galahad, Gawain, Tristan, Kay, Bedivere and Modred. Tristan was involved in a famous love-triangle with the lady Iseult, wife of Mark of Cornwall. Modred was a traitor who rebelled against Arthur. The knighthood perished in civil war. Arthur and Modred both fell at the battle of Camlann. After that the heathen advanced again, gradually over-running what is now England ('Angle-land'). However, they were presently converted to Christianity and became less barbaric, so that the Celtic British population survived in many places. The Britons of Cornwall remained free for a long time, the Britons of Wales retained their identity into the Middle Ages, and consequently Arthur's Britain, the memory of it, and the dream of its resurrection, never quite perished.

Up to a point this legend of Arthur and his achievement is credible. The royal and romantic trappings are medieval fantasy, but the notion at the root is sound. While historical records are scanty in the extreme, most historians accept that a powerful British rally occurred and that a real Arthur played a part in it. Some would go further than others in allowing him the paramountcy he has in legend. The oldest allusions to him suggest that his kingship, if not simply an invention of later story-tellers, was little more than a local or courtesy office. Whatever national authority he possessed came from a role which is better documented, that of commander-in-chief. For practical purposes this may have raised him above the regional kings.

He flourished, it seems, about 500AD. A few written references to him are close enough in time to make his existence almost certain, but the only surviving account of his career was written three centuries later by a Welsh monk named Nennius, copying from lost older manuscripts. Nennius calls Arthur the war-leader, *dux bellorum* in Latin, and says he campaigned alongside the kings of the Britons against the Anglo-Saxons. He won twelve victories at obscurely named places, most of them, it is thought, ranging from Lincolnshire to southern Scotland (where he could hardly have found any Anglo-Saxons but might have fought Picts or hostile Britons). The climactic twelfth battle was at 'Mount

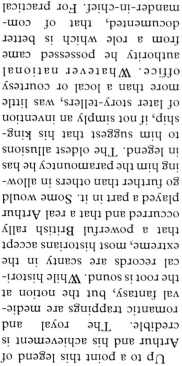

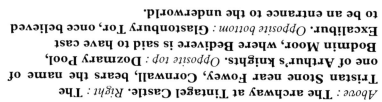

Above: **The archway at Tintagel Castle.** *Right*: **The Tristan Stone near Fowey, Cornwall, bears the name of one of Arthur's Knights.** *Opposite top*: **Dozmary Pool, Bodmin Moor, where Bedivere is said to have cast Excalibur.** *Opposite bottom*: **Glastonbury Tor, once believed to be an entrance to the underworld.**

The castle ruins now on the headland are medieval. But excavation has unearthed the remains of other buildings which may be much earlier and high-quality imported pottery that can be dated to the late fifth or sixth century, proving that a household of wealth and standing existed on the head-land about the time of Arthur. Until lately this was assumed to have been a monas-tery. Recent rethinking, how-ever, has raised the possibility of a chieftain's stronghold on a part of the site not yet fully explored, so there may be an element of truth in the tale of Ygerne and Arthur's begin-nings. Certainly the headland was an important inhabited place.

Other interesting questions overhang Cadbury Castle in Somerset, an earthwork hill-fort much more imposing than Killibury. Local legends which have been current for a long time identify it with Camelot, Arthur's capital in romance. Camelot, in that literary sense, is a dream-city and not to be looked for anywhere. But the real Arthur doubtless had a centre or headquarters of some kind, which was the 'real Came-lot' so far as anything was. If that meaning for the name is admitted, Cadbury has an im-pressive claim, indeed an un-rivalled one. Excavations during 1966–70 disclosed that the hill was refortified on a huge scale at about the time of Arthur. All around the summit enclosure – a perimeter of 1.2 km (¾ mile) – there was a stone wall 6 metres (20 feet) thick, with timber breast-works and watchtowers and a massive gatehouse. Clearly this was the work of a military leader of great resources, at least an 'Arthur-type figure', as one of the archaeologists put it. Nothing remotely like such a vast citadel, of the right period, has been found any-where else in Britain. If the legendary identification was only a guess, it was an as-toundingly lucky guess. A genuine tradition handed down

West Country where Glaston-bury is, and not round Glaston-bury alone. Here too we find – sometimes – a factual back-ground, though the evidence comes from archaeology rather than from written sources. One early belief is that Arthur had a stronghold at a place in Cornwall called Kelliwic. This can plausibly be identified as the hill-fort of Killibury near Wadebridge. Its battered earth-work ramparts date from the Iron Age before the Roman conquest, too early for Arthur. Several such forts, however, are known to have been reoccupied after Roman rule ceased in Britain, and Killibury may have been one of them. Furthermore there could be a link between the Kelliwic story and another which is far better known: the story of Arthur's birth at Tintagel, on the coast 16 km (10 miles) away. And there, archae-ology has raised serious issues.

Tintagel's main feature is an immense rocky promontory, joined to the mainland only by a narrow ridge. Legend affirms that it formerly had a castle on it belonging to Gorlois, Duke of Cornwall. The British king Uther lusted after Gorlois' wife Ygerne. Her husband kept her on the Tintagel headland. Dur-ing his absence, Merlin, by magic, made Uther look exactly like him. In that effective dis-guise Uther entered the castle and begot Arthur. The true Gorlois had conveniently died in battle a short time earlier, so the paternity was not in doubt.

Badon'. Here, Nennius tells us, Arthur slew 960 men single-handed. The flight of fancy does not invalidate his main story, and the battle of Badon was real enough. It may have happened on one of the hills round Bath or at the end of the ridgeway by the village of Badbury near Swindon.

Nennius takes us no further with the Arthur of history. But other early references show that the Badon victory did bring a spell of peace and prosperity; that Arthur did fall at a battle of 'Camlaun' or 'Camlann; and that his opponents then were British rather than foreign. While he certainly had no knights in the medieval sense, he probably had a personal army of mounted men, whose mobility gave him an advantage over enemies who went on foot. Some of the legends hover round locations in England's

from the time of Arthur seems more likely.

It is through this considera-tion of Arthurian sites and local legends that we must approach the harder problem of Glastonbury-Avalon. Nor does Cadbury Castle complete the list. The sites are not even confined to Cornwall and Somerset. They extend – dozens of them – from the Isles of Scilly through the West Country and Wales, across Cumbria and far into Scotland. Admittedly nearly all are fanci-ful. They involve things of a different date or natural features. Thus an Iron Age entrenchment becomes 'Arthur's Hunting Lodge', a cromlech becomes 'Arthur's Stone', a hill (as in Edinburgh) becomes 'Arthur's Seat'. A cave, is 'Arthur's Cairn' and a cairn, for no real reason, is 'Arthur's Cave'. While so few of these can have anything to do with the actual history of Arthur, the spread of local lore attests the spread of story-telling about him and perhaps also the range of his activities – as suggested also by Nennius' list of battles. We are concerned with a man who made a tremendous im-pression, not simply a petty chief or hero of courtly fiction. A further point of interest, and a very significant one, is that the folklore clues reinforce the more obvious hints as to Arthur's native territory. The reinforcement is easily over-looked, because it comes through silence. Certain poss-ible items do *not* occur.

Opposite : **A medieval illustration of the story of Gawain and the Green Knight.** *Above :* **Guiton takes leave of King Arthur and Guinevere.**

Neither Wales nor the north can offer, even in folklore, another birthplace to rival Tintagel or another home or headquarters like Kelliwic and Cadbury. Further, it is only in the West Country that we find places with legends of Arthur supported by archaeology. At Tintagel, Cadbury and (as we shall see) Glastonbury itself, it has been proved that a site strongly connected with him was at least occupied by people of the right sort at roughly the right time. This has not happened so far anywhere else. In the West Country the presence is more tangible.

To speak of 'people of the right sort' does not, of course, imply particular persons. British archaeology seldom gives us names. In fact only one known object bears the name of an Arthurian character – a monumental stone near Fowey in Cornwall, the memorial of someone called Drustan, who may be the Tristan of romance. Apart from this, the only answers to the question 'which of them really existed?' come not from archaeology but from early poetry, lives of Welsh saints, brief entries in annals, written summaries of lost oral traditions. Apart from Arthur himself, the best attested is 'Medraut', otherwise Modred, who figures in legend as the arch-traitor responsible for the fatal battle of Camlann. A few of the other knights can be more or less authenticated. Sir Kay and Sir Bedivere can be traced back to very early times as 'Cai' and 'Bedwyr', Arthur's chief lieutenants. There is a fair case for Gawain, a better one for Tristan and Mark of Cornwall. Of the women, Guinevere and Iseult are the likeliest. Merlin is a composite character, combining an actual bard of the late sixth century with a shadowy prophet of the fifth.

It would be unwise to lay much stress on any of them as individuals, even on Arthur himself. We really know very little about him and are unlikely ever to know much more, unless a long-lost manuscript or inscription should come to light. The essential point of it all is rather different. There is now substantial and growing knowledge of what is sometimes called the Arthurian Fact, the unique train of events in British history which Arthur came to symbolize. This, rather than the prowess of any one hero, is the key to the mythos.

Britain was alone among the lands of the Roman west in attaining *de facto* independence and putting up a fight against invading barbarians; alone in checking their settlement, repulsing their advance forces, even, it appears, in driving some of them to withdraw from the country altogether. The first part of the sixth century, after the battle of Mount Badon, was a time of triumph and fairly general peace. The rally flagged and the Anglo-Saxons pushed forward again, creating what is now England. But their success was slow, and it was neither exterminatory nor, in the upshot, complete. Wherever the British Celts and their traditions survived – in the north, in Wales, in Cornwall, over the sea in Brittany where many of them migrated – the time of triumph was looked back to as a golden age.

Arthur, as victor of Mount Badon, was the leader who had made it all possible. The achievement glorified the man. There had to be something special about him. His grave was said to be a mystery, and a belief grew up that he was not dead at all but hidden away in enchanted sleep, destined to return and lead the Welsh and their kinsfolk again. That idea came from pagan Celtic lore, and other myths and fairy-tales from the same stock became attached to him. Bardic song and story turned him into a larger-than-life figure, not only a general but a king, though the nature of his title and the extent of his domain were not very clear. His imaginary court included heroes from various periods and countries, magical beings and fairy-folk, and ancient deities in human disguise.

Thus it continued till the twelfth century, which brought a second phase of legend-making. English and French authors discovered this astonishing saga on their doorstep and made a new literature out of it. The cycle of tales of Arthur and his followers became the 'Matter of Britain', a recognized theme of medieval romance. It is the Matter of Britain that comes down to us through Malory, Tennyson, and T. H. White. The heroic golden age was turned into a chivalric Utopia, with Arthur as a courtly monarch ruling not only the whole of Britain but lands overseas. His warriors were updated as the Knights of the Round Table. Adventures were multiplied. The famous themes took shape – Lancelot and Guinevere, Tristan and Iseult, the Quest of the Holy Grail, the treachery of Modred – with antecedents of some sort in Celtic legend, even (as we have seen) in history, but largely as new creations. The cycle closed in tragedy after Arthur's last battle, when, wounded, he passed away to an Avalon which was sometimes unlocated, sometimes identified with Glastonbury. There, in the more fully mythicized versions, he remained undying as he had done in the older folk-tales. One day perhaps he would return and restore the golden age.

The making of the Matter of Britain was a long, strange process. A great deal of it is still obscure. Yet something not unlike it has happened in modern times. Much that can be said about the creation of Arthur's dream-kingdom is also true of the creation of the Wild West in novels, films and TV adven-

ture. It is not a complete fantasy. There was a period after the American Civil War, going on till about 1890, when large areas of the West actually were 'wild' by contrast with the law and order of settled territories and when ranchers, sheriffs, marshals and outlaws were prominent figures. Some of the well-known characters – Billy the Kid, Calamity Jane and others – did exist, though they seldom had much glamour. After the West ceased to be wild, its ageing inhabitants spun yarns which were taken up by authors of popular fiction – 'dime novels' – and in due course by Hollywood. The characters were glamorized, the West became a recognized realm of the imagination with its own rules.

So also with the Britain of Arthurian romance. It too is a realm of the imagination and not much like anything that ever existed . . . yet realities underlie

it. We can sometimes discern dimly what these realities were and how they were transformed.

All the same, one of the greatest themes remains one of the hardest to come to terms with or to relate to history; and it is a theme that concerns Avalon. What is meant by the Quest of the Holy Grail? There is no simple answer, if only because there are several versions and they contradict each other. In the mainstream form, the Grail is the vessel used by Christ at the Last Supper, a cup or dish in which he performed the sacrament repeated by the priest at Mass. It came into the hands of Joseph of Arimathea, who caught drops of Christ's blood in it during the crucifixion. Afterwards he assembled a group of companions, who travelled with the Grail in their midst as a supernatural source of guidance and aid. In due course it was brought to Britain, to the 'vales

of Avalon', and placed in the care of a succession of keepers. By Arthur's time no one knew what had become of the Grail. One Pentecost his knights had a simultaneous vision of it, and many rode off to seek its actual whereabouts. Most of them were unworthy. A few had glimpses and intimations. Only Galahad completed the Quest.

Behind the Grail as a

Christian object, there are pagan myths about wonder-working vessels of plenty and inspiration, magical sources of bodily and spiritual life. The earliest known version of the Quest is a cryptic Welsh poem about Arthur and his men going in search of a magic cauldron. This has nothing Christian about it. When Christian writers give a biblically-based

Vision of the Holy Grail, **detail from a tapestry by William Morris from a design by Edward Burne-Jones. The Grail story is derived partly from pagan myths and Christianity.**

account of the vessel, it is still a source of life. In Christian terms this is eternal life, to be entered through an undescribed mystical experience attained by finding the Grail. Yet relics of older and more earthy notions survive. When the knights have their vision, they are miraculously served with a literal banquet. Again, in some stories, the castle where the Grail is kept is surrounded by a waste land, and if the knight asks the right question he will not only resolve the mystery of the Grail but restore the waste land to fertility.

It has been suggested that the Grail stories give us confused traditions of a cult that actually flourished in Arthur's Britain, combining Christianity with pagan magic, in a scheme of initiation. While there is no

direct evidence for such a cult, it is a fact that the early Christianity of the British Isles was odd, different and, in the eyes of Rome, suspect. The traditions woven into the general saga of Arthur probably did include some curious religious motifs. This was realized at the time. Even when romancers presented the Grail Quest in a Christian guise, the Church frowned on it.

So now, what about Glastonbury? Is there any truth in its legends? And how far does it deserve to be called Avalon?

Glastonbury's main Christian story, that of the coming of Joseph of Arimathea, has an undoubted fact embedded in it. The most ancient building on the site of the Abbey was a small, plain, rustic church. This burned down in 1184

when the Abbey caught fire, but before then it had stood for untold ages. It was called the Old Church. We hear of many visitors through the centuries – Welsh saints, Irish scholars, Saxon kings, Danes, Normans – and always the Old Church was already on the spot. Nobody, it seems, knew who had put it there. Some said it dated from the second century AD, some from the first. The story of Joseph as its builder accounted for it by means of a figure known through the Gospels, Christian legend and, later, Grail romance. While his British mission cannot be proved fictitious, it has no support of a kind that historians would allow. Yet the Old Church, whatever its age and origin, is a fact of history. There is every reason to think that Glastonbury really was the home of the first British Christian community, already extant before the time

of Arthur, possibly long before.

Its claim to the actual name of Avalon rests partly on the reference to the 'vales of Avalon' as the divinely-appointed goal of the first Christians who came to Britain. More important, however, are two further beliefs. Glastonbury is held to have had a sacred, other-worldly aura further back still, before the Christians' advent. It is also alleged to have been Arthur's last resting-place. Either belief, if true, would justify the name after a fashion.

The case for the first is interesting but complicated, involving several factors which are not easy to assess. At least two of these are centred on the Tor, the strange hill above the town surmounted by a ruined tower, the remains of a chapel of St Michael. Around the sides of the Tor are long horizontal ridges. According to one theory they are the eroded remnants of a vast spiral maze cut in the hill thousands of years ago for ritual purposes. Less speculative is a clue in the Welsh legend of St Collen. This tells how the saint lived here for a time and encountered a being called Gwyn-ap-Nudd, who was king of the fairy-folk and lord of the underground realm of Annwn and had his palace inside the Tor. Collen exorcized him. Gwyn is known to have been a pagan Celtic god, viewed by Christians as sinister, and the legend reflects pre-Christian notions about hollow hills and entrances to another world. Excavation has revealed traces of buildings on the Tor summit dating from about 500 AD. It is not certain what they were.

In the stories of Arthur, the Avalon to which he is taken after his last battle is sometimes an enchanted island where his wounds are healed and he waits in hidden immortality till the hour for his return. As such, Avalon's location is vague. It becomes plainly Glastonbury in a more mundane version, which states that his wounds were fatal, that he died of them like anyone else, and that he was buried in the monks' graveyard near the Old Church. If 'Avalon' means 'the place where Arthur's earthly career ended', irrespective of supernatural overtones, Glastonbury on this showing has to be Avalon.

It will be clear that the belief needs to be taken in the context of other legends and theories about Somerset. There is the claim of Cadbury Castle, which is only a dozen miles away, to be Arthur's headquarters. Furthermore it has a small river near it called the Cam, which is a possible site for the fatal battle of Camlann. If Arthur fell there, a monastery a few miles off would have been a natural place to inter him. If Camlann was in the north or Wales or Cornwall, a Glastonbury grave would be less plausible. Yet the body of a West Country leader, as Arthur seemingly was, might well have been brought back to his home

territory wherever he fell.

Plausibility, however, is only a background issue. The main point is that the grave – or what purported to be the grave – was actually found towards the close of the twelfth century. Several medieval writers describe the event. They differ in detail, but not in substance.

When Henry II was travelling through Wales, a bard revealed a long-kept secret. Arthur lay in the burial plot of Glastonbury Abbey between two 'pyramids' or monumental pillars. Henry had his reasons for wishing this to be true. A grave within the borders of his own kingdom would give him a claim to the Arthurian succession. Also, if it could be proved that Arthur was dead and buried, the Welsh would be less inclined to make trouble with prophecies of his coming back to lead them.

Henry told the Abbot. The spot could be identified, to the south of the Old Church (replaced today by the Lady Chapel). For the moment nothing was done. In 1184, however, came the fire which destroyed most of the Abbey. The monks entered a phase of change, rebuilding, rethinking. Six or seven years after the fire they tested the story of the grave. They began digging between the pillars. Two metres (7 feet) down they struck a stone slab and a cross of lead, with a Latin inscription saying 'Here lies the renowned King Arthur in the Isle of Avalon'. Almost three metres (9 feet) further down they found a rough coffin made from a hollowed log. Inside were the bones of a tall man, with skull damage suggesting death through a blow on the head. Some bones which seemed not to fit the skeleton, and a scrap of fair hair which crumbled at a touch were explained as Guinevere's.

The remains were translated to a new shrine. Then, when the great Abbey church was built, a black marble tomb was constructed before the high altar, and to this they were removed again during a visit by Edward I.

Since the tomb was rifled after the Abbey's dissolution, nothing survives to show what the monks discovered. Historians used to argue that they invented the whole story, excavation and all, as a publicity stunt. They needed money to rebuild after the fire. Their claims were manifestly suspect because no one had connected Arthur with Glastonbury before. Presently, however, doubts about this extreme of unbelief began to be voiced, and the doubts remain valid. Thus, the description of the grave is too good, too suggestive of real antiquity. Medieval monks, lacking modern archaeological knowledge, would have been most unlikely to concoct it. Nor is there any proof that a fund-raising campaign based on Arthur was ever mounted; and that, after all, is central to the fraud theory. Lastly it is untrue that he was never connected with Glastonbury before. A Welsh document dating from at least several

decades earlier gives an account of his visiting the monastery.

In 1962 a distinguished archaeologist, Ralegh Radford, excavated the same site and showed that the monks had not made everything up. He found traces of their refilled hole and, at a great depth, disarranged stones which had once lined a grave. These were in a position regarded as a place of honour. The monks had dug where they said and found roughly what they said: the bones of an important man buried a long time before.

Most historians would still retort that he was not Arthur and that they merely pretended he was from the financial motive already stated. A few, however, are now willing to accept that the grave may have been authentic. The inscribed cross bearing the name ought to be a decisive clue. It has disappeared, but we have an early drawing of it. Unfortunately this fails to settle the matter.

Comment danebruy op nou

Opposite: **A medieval illustration of Gawain and the Green Knight.** *Above:* **Tristan arriving at a castle.** *Above right:* **Danebruin at a castle window.** *Below right:* **A tournament before King Arthur.**

If the style of lettering were twelfth century, we could be sure the cross was a fake, and if the cross was a fake the grave probably was – that is, as Arthur's. But the clumsy capitals look older. A scholar of high repute, Professor Kenneth Jackson, has declared that such writing might have been done as far back as the sixth century. Others have preferred the eighth or the tenth or have accused the monks of forging archaic lettering by copying from old manuscripts. The question is unresolved.

One point in Glastonbury's favour tends to be missed. When the Abbey made its announcement it was not seriously contested, even by Welshmen. No one produced a rival grave. Other prestigious claims by the Abbey were contested very hotly indeed. Glastonbury said

it had the remains of St Dunstan; Canterbury gave it the lie. The claim to the grave of Arthur went unchallenged. There was surely some reason why Celtic pride and wishful thinking, though so intense, were powerless to propose an alternative site – not perhaps a Glastonbury interment as a fact of history but at least a long-standing belief in it, a genuine bardic tradition which had been preserved in Wales though effaced by Saxon conquest in Somerset.

That is the kind of conclusion to which the legends of Avalon, Arthur and the rest often lead. To confront Britain's haunting mythology with any hope of understanding, one must learn a difficult exercise – how to take legends seriously without falling into the trap of taking them literally.

MIRACLES
AND VISIONS

THE EVIDENCE FOR MIRACLES

Throughout history there have been reports of strange events outside the scope of natural causes – miracles. Some claims are so wild they are incredible; but others have been witnessed and cannot easily be dismissed. Certainly, the evidence warrants serious consideration.

The Roman Cicero and the Scottish philosopher David Hume agreed on this point: that miracles do not happen. In the *Enquiry Concerning Human Understanding* (1748), Hume argues that no evidence could persuade him to change his mind on this. Even if all the soundest historians of the day had asserted that Elizabeth I died on 1 January 1600, was buried, then came back from the grave in February to rule for three more years, Hume would be unconvinced, he says. Such violations of the laws of nature simply cannot happen. No testimony could ever be strong or unanimous enough to substantiate a miraculous event.

A scientific outlook seems to make it more difficult to believe in marvels and miracles as anything other than misnomers for odd, inexplicable but essentially normal events. Jacob Bronowski, lecturing at Columbia University, rejected 'the view that there is a logic of another world. And that logic works in a different way and if you can only find the secret key . . . the Almighty will be on your side.' For Bronowski, the only feasible logic was the logic of science.

So we start with a fundamental challenge whether *any* evidence for miracles can be satisfactory and a rebuttal of the idea that natural laws may sometimes be overridden by supernatural powers. In Dr Bronowski's case, there is also a denial that there are powers or forces superior to those of the material world, which opens itself exclusively to the hard, regulated methods of scientific investigation. If my discussion here is to make progress, I must see whether any of the evidence for miracles, spread over thousands of years, resists such blunt dismissal.

What I mean by 'miracle' is an extraordinary and inexplicable event, beyond the scope of ordinary, natural causes, which is therefore attributed to supernatural or preternatural powers. Now, the number of events in the literature which claim to qualify runs into thousands, but many of them can be culled for one reason or another. The culling process will help to make the nature of the evidence clearer.

Let me start by throwing out unqualified nonsense, such as the transportation of the Holy House from Nazareth to Loreto in Italy, borne through the air by angels. The story is that the Holy Family's house in 'Nazareth the nursery of our Lord' fell into pagan hands during the thirteenth century. 'Therefore our Saviour meaning to take this precious prize out of the hands of Infidels, and (if we may so say) raise it from death' arranged for the 'little poore building' to be flown first to Slavonia, then 'over sea to a wood in the bounds of Recanati, belonging to a noble dame called Laureta, from whom it took its name'.

The quotations here are from three seventeenth-century works, but more recently the Vatican has nominated Loreto its patron of airmen.

Since my aim is to isolate accounts which appear to have some standing as historical records, we can continue by discarding undiluted myth and folktale. From medieval Ireland, for example, the stories tell of deer and cows that are slaughtered, cooked and eaten, yet are reassembled with full flesh and sinews next morning, perhaps appearing more handsome than they did before. Many Irish saints use the wands and bells associated with the druids and continue their practice of cursing. All Tara was desolated when King Diarmait lost a cursing match with St Ruadan. From Europe, St Eustace, out hunting, is confronted by a stag with a cross between its antlers and moral exhortations on its lips. They are re-enacting a tale whose origins may be found in ancient Buddhist texts. The role of these stories is mythological, not historical.

Certain miracle stories had no other purpose than entertainment. The Frenchman Mandeville's *Travels*, a popular book of wonderful journeys and marvels which was first published in about 1357, is enormously enjoyable but is one form of literature we can leave aside here. It makes no serious claim to factuality.

There may also be misrepre-

Miraculous spring from a watercolour by John Trinick of thirteenth-century glass in St Kunibert's, Cologne. Such springs feature in pagan and Christian traditions.

sentation. A girl committed to a nunnery by Henry Murdac, Archbishop of York, in about 1150 became pregnant; she was grossly maltreated and chained in a cell. She came near the term of her pregnancy. Ailred of Rielvaux, who wrote his report in about 1160, was consulted, so that he knew the witnesses personally and interviewed the girl. One night the dead Archbishop visited her and took her head on his knee while he performed some hidden operation. When she sat up she saw the bishop's two beautiful women attendants carrying the infant away wrapped in a white cloth. Whether this was an hysterical pregnancy or an abortion, the miracle claim is necessarily suspect.

I leave aside narratives that raise problems because of competing claims. During AD 174, the Emperor Marcus Aurelius defeated a tribe, the Quadi, in a most odd manner. The Roman army, surrounded, was being reduced by drought. Suddenly there was a great storm, which gave drinking water to the emperor's troops while – as a tempest – it beat the Quadi to the ground and made them panic. The Romans were victorious. The commemorative column in Rome shows Jupiter Pluvius flying above the scene, bringing help and victory to Marcus Aurelius. The historian Cassius Dio mentions that an Egyptian magician, Arnuphis, had called on the gods, especially Mercury, god of the air, and so had brought on the rain; but the historian Eusebius wrote in AD 324-5 that it was the prayers of the Christians which had prevailed. The life of Marcus Aurelius by Capitolinus assigns full credit to the prayers of the emperor himself.

There is also much imitation; but before looking at that I want to consider some possible meanings of biblical miracles. These are inevitably the most popular models for later writers, who frequently misunderstood the intentions of the original

Old Testament stories were often copied by Christian writers. The parting of the Red Sea (above) was the model for partings of the rivers Thames and Barrow in England and of many elsewhere. The raising of the Sultamite's son by Elijah (right) illustrates the Jewish lineage of Christ's and later Christian wonderworking.

texts. They imitated them, regardless. All that I can do here is to illustrate some details of a much larger theme.

The people for whom the Old Testament was written did not distinguish God from Nature – the 'natural' from the 'miraculous'. God was pervasive and working everywhere, always, in human history and in natural events. The stories in the books, whether they had some factual base or not, were also intended to express the development of God's relationship with His chosen people. They were signs, wonders and portents from God, and He had a reality which dimmed and qualified material realities while at the same time constituting them. His actions in the material world were also proofs to man that He was there, and to ignore His signs was purblind and culpable.

So the events in the Old Testament may not be read straightforwardly with a modern, Western prejudice. Moses' – later Aaron's – rod or serpent devouring the Egyptian rods or serpents is primarily a sign of his superiority and power, although it does also reflect historic cult rites of the region. The drama of the plagues fits into a literary tradition, signifies that God's power is with the Hebrews, yet may have echoes of recurring disasters along the Nile. Sodom and Gomorrah, which may indeed have suffered, are destroyed to manifest God's wrath against the wicked.

In the New Testament, a few major factors have changed. We are dealing with sources which, for their period, are significantly close in time to the events they describe. Staying with the miracles, there

is evidence even from the opposition, as it were, that we are dealing with facts not fabrications. For example, the Rabbinic *Tractate Sanhedrin* records that Jesus 'practised sorcery', which was a reason for his execution. Jesus is shown as a miracle-worker by Josephus, the Jewish historian (AD 37-100). This, but more potently the scriptural details of His life, suggests that Jesus' miracle-working was not an accretion. It was central to his biography.

Jesus as miracle-worker is part of a tradition. A story written in about AD 70 – not more than forty years after the crucifixion – tells how Rabbi

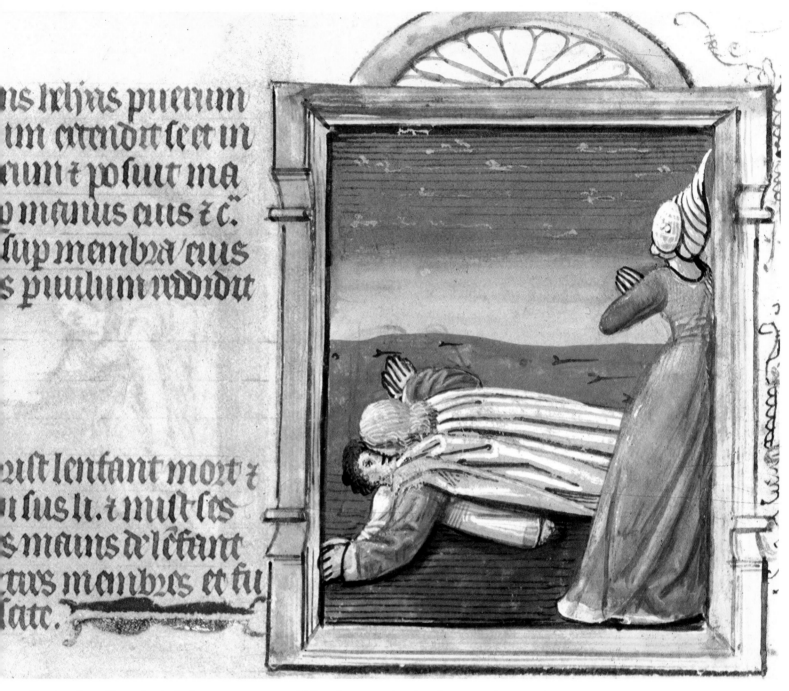

ns lelius pueum
um cundu leet in
eum t polut ma
o manus eus ?c.
fup membra/eus
s puulum reddidit

eust lenfant mort z
u sus li. z mult ses
s mains de lefant
tus membres et fu
late.

Hanina ben Dosa healed the son of Rabbi Johanan ben Zaccai, his teacher. Hanina puts his head between his knees and prays, and the boy lives. Other stories of Hanina ben Dosa's feats resemble Jesus' miracles even more closely; he prayed that Gamaliel's son should recover from a fever and, when Gamaliel's disciples got back to Jerusalem, they found that the boy had recovered at the time Hanina made his prayer. Hanina belongs within other traditions as well. As in Caxton's *St Erkenwald* and the story of a church in Dorchester, his life records that he made wooden beams grow longer when they were too short

to span a roof. That is a strand from folklore.

Jesus had to fulfil the prophecies and provide clear signs He was indeed Messiah; John the Evangelist specifically identifies Christ's miracles as 'signs' in the old sense. Some of the miracles, like the withering of the fig tree, have a teaching role, in this case complementing a parable; but this story also reflects the old theme that the Israelites are God's special vine or tree. Other miracles – the stilling of storms, walking on the waters or changing water to wine – look like Mighty Works of the kind we have seen in the Old Testament, but it does not follow

that because they conform to conventions the tales are false. For one thing, such a claim would preempt the role of prophecy. I reiterate that the sound histories of Jesus' life unequivocally characterize Him as miracle-worker, with this feature being integral to the record.

The intention here has been to make matters clearer when we look at stories that appear imitative and to see whether they can be retained for our study. Let me say at once that the repetitive actions, words and themes in some stories may simply reflect the practices and procedures that some miracle-workers have found

most effective; they need not be crude misappropriations of property. Yet it is important to eliminate some of the more misguided outbursts. We do not have to bother with the time St Peter allegedly made a camel pass through the eye of a needle (recorded in the apocryphal *Acts of Peter and Andrew*) nor with Caxton's claim that the Thames once opened 'as it dyd to moyses in the reed sea' to allow the congregation of Old St Paul's to pass through from Barking.

Outside the Bible and the Apocrypha, writers ransacked popular lives such as Athanasius' account of his friend St Anthony or Sulpicius

Above : **Christ and Peter walking on water from a fourteenth-century manuscript.** *Right :* **thirteenth-century enamel showing Namaan's leprosy being healed by heaven when he enters the Jordan, his attendants standing by.** *Opposite :* **St Dominic binds a stole from his neck round a man 'vexed with many devils'.**

Severus' *Life of St Martin of Tours*, his friend, both dating from the fourth century AD. There were two great thirteenth-century collections of tales, Jacobo a Voragine's *Golden Legends* and Caesarius of Heisterbach's *Dialogue on Miracles*. Hagiographers did not need to search far to establish the kinds of feat that might embellish a saintly life, and there was much plundering of the established sources for ideas and anecdotes. Before a story is retained here, we must be satisfied it has not been blatantly transferred from one holy life to another.

Now that such a proportion of the literature has been rejected, what is left? There will certainly still be some themes that recur in the literature, since I do not accept that they are necessarily the product of mere literary imitation. I would expect to find resemblances, for example, within some categories of healing claims and suggest that, if miracles are intended as 'signs' of sanctity, they require some common

78

characteristics if they are to work. Each account that is left must be studied according to its own evidence.

The stories I have retained will often be reported first hand or will at least be based on substantial witness. The writers are taken to be sensible, if frequently partisan, reporters of the events.

Finally let me acknowledge some proper limits to what may be claimed, following the commonsense recommendations of Bishop Robinson (author of *Honest to God*) that we should 'learn to trust the New Testament for what it is trying to say, rather than for what it is not trying to say'. Even Caesarius of Heisterbach, an enthusiast for miracles, declared that 'miracles are not the substance of sanctity, but rather its signs.' Calvin, more cautiously, wrote that the biblical miracles 'avail only to the preparation for piety or for its confirmation; they cannot by themselves bring men to worship the true God'. Despite such cautions, Benedict XIV's

De Servorum Dei Beatificatione (1738), which reformulated the role of miracles in the process of canonization, had the effect of confirming miracle as an essential element in Roman saints' lives. Because the process involves checking, validating and documenting the miracles, detailed accounts and even statistics are available. The 110 saints canonized between 1900 and 1970 worked 166 approved miracles, 102 for women (45 nuns), 36 for men and 28 for children under twelve years of age. What I want to emphasize is the range of prejudices and predispositions to be accounted for when approaching miracle tales; one writer on the subject has proposed that a capacity

for believing miracles is like a sense of humour. Nothing can be done for a person who lacks it.

It may seem my emphasis has been too Christian. The bias is corrected by looking at the personal, miraculous powers which may be attributed to the monarch, shaman, medium, adept or witch as well as to the Christian saints. A Buddhist source written early in the Christian era states that the perfect have powers like the saints to become invisible, levitate, change their shape and form, travel miraculously and walk on water. In the second century AD, the satirist Lucian made fun of claims that the Hyperboreans (exotic strangers

died, persecuted by the Soviet NKVD, in 1936.

Levitation – the spontaneous, unassisted, ecstatic raising of the body into the air – is quite disconcertingly well attested. There were several occasions in India when ten-year-old Thomas, son of the Parava Fernandes, saw Francis Xavier 'raised more than an ell above the floor' at prayer. Perhaps, in the light of my reference to the Buddhist scriptures above, this reflects an expectation that the *swami* or holy teacher should levitate, and Thomas obligingly saw what he was expected to see. Also, he gave evidence in 1616 about what he saw in 1543,

so the delay was long. It may seem more difficult to discount an event, deposed on oath in 1621, that St Bernadino Realino had such a rapture. A distinguished man, Tobias da Ponte, swore that one Saturday in April, as he was waiting outside the saint's door, he saw a bright light shining through the cracks (this too is a recurring theme). He pushed the door open and saw Bernadino kneeling before his *prie-dieu*, floating at least 750 mm ($2\frac{1}{2}$ feet) above the ground.

Joseph of Copertino (1603–63) is the saint whose flights were most frequent and apparently best observed. As

secondary evidence, it is worth noting that he was excluded from choir for many years, because his raptures so distracted the other friars. The ecclesiastical authorities moved him round the houses of his order, on account of the embarrassment he caused. The flights were spectacular. One Sunday evening, in the convent garden, contemplating the story of the Good Shepherd, he held a lamb in his arms. He suddenly threw it into the air and flew after it above the trees, hovering there more than two hours. A fellow-Dominican testified to seventy flights, and Cardinal de Laurea, a friend of St Joseph,

like those famous magicians, the Lapps) could soar through the air, pass slowly through fire and walk on the water – wearing clogs. These themes are not exclusively Christian.

None the less, such manifestations do follow the Christian saints. Stigmatization, the subject of another chapter, has specifically Christian significance and has been remarkably well testified at least since 1222, when a man with Christ's wounds in his body was shown to Stephen Langton at Canterbury. The encounter was recorded by the chronicler Mathew Paris. Walking on water is still current, for example in the life of the Russian saint Zachariah who

Above: **Joseph of Copertino who, like Buddhist adepts and several Christian saints, was said to fly.** *Right:* **mosaic of Christ healing the blind man with his spittle. An identical miracle is attributed to the Emperor Vespasian by the great Roman historian Tacitus.**

confirmed that they took place. St Joseph's process of canonization even records an occasion he was taken by the General of his order to an audience with Pope Urban VIII. Overwhelmed, the record claims, Joseph floated into the air, until ordered to land by the General.

These are by no means the oddest manifestations that have been witnessed. Bilocation – the power to be in more than one place at the same time – is also attributed to a number of saints. This has involved some holy men in being physically present in several places at once: it is claimed that St Martin of Porres was seen simultaneously in five places and (on

much older testimony) the medieval Irish saint Comgallus in three. One of the most recent practitioners was the Italian stigmatic Padre Pio, who died in 1968. According to Countess Virginia Sili, a Franciscan novice came to her once with a relic of the true cross and said: 'Last night there appeared to me in flesh and bones Padre Pio, who consigned to me this relic, bidding me bring it to the Countess. . . .' Padre Pio was at the time a day's journey away. The cardinals Gasparri and Sili were present, and the Countess a few days later confirmed what had happened with Padre Pio himself. This was not the only

occasion that involved Pio.

The theme is so established that Mario von Galli, a Jesuit opponent of Hitler's regime, exploited it against the police. Having double booked himself for lecturing, he persuaded his twin brother to impersonate him for one of the talks. Next day, he was interrogated by the Gestapo because, they said, he

had attacked the Nazi regime:
' "What we don't understand is that you were giving a completely different lecture some miles away at the same time."

"Are you a Catholic?"

"No."

"These things are always happening to Catholics." '

After death, the physical

privileges endure. In many instances, the body is preserved, not withered and strange as in the peat bogs, but fresh and supple. There is a first-hand account of this in the excellent chronicle of St Edmund's Bury by Jocelin of Brakelond. The entry for 20 November 1198 records that the Abbot Sampson, with twelve official witnesses and some eavesdroppers, opened St Edmund's coffin and found the body incorrupt. The body had been translated to the church in 903. Jocelin knew Abbot Sampson well and was a colleague of the other witnesses. The ancient corpse's feet, he wrote, were 'like the feet of a man who had died today'. The body of the sixteenth-century reformer and mystic Teresa of Ávila was inspected repeatedly after her death and was found 'in such a perfect state of preservation that nothing was wanting to it in any way' according to a panel of twenty, including a bishop, doctors, judges and other dignitaries. This phenomenon has endured long in time. St Bernadette, whose visionary experience at Lourdes we shall consider later, was exhumed in 1908, almost thirty years after she had died. It was reported that 'there was no trace of corruption. The flesh was parched but intact, and it had preserved its whiteness.' In the first century AD, to move our focus backwards, Plutarch wrote that the big toe of Pyrrhus' right foot was intact after his body had been cremated. It was by pressing his right foot on the sick that he had cured them in life, and the toe retained its 'godly power' long afterwards.

Many readers will find manifestations like these incredible, no matter how sound, sane or charming the witnesses seem to be. That is why I turn at once to healing miracles. There has been testimony for them since history and biography were first written, and the evidence is often impressive.

There is, of course, a strong Biblical tradition. Elijah brought the widow's son back to life by praying and stretching himself out on the boy three times, the threefold repetition perhaps reflecting a folklore ritual. This miracle, like most of his others, is echoed by Elisha, who raised the son of the Shunammite widow. Whatever view is taken of these stories, they clearly anticipate Christ's healing miracles. Indeed, the gospels present Christ in direct line of descent from these prophets, the very Messiah in whom the prophecies and the words of the prophets were fulfilled.

That biblical tradition is not unique, though. The Roman historian Tacitus – one of the major independent sources for the crucifixion – tells that once when Vespasian was in Alexandria a chronically blind man threw himself at the emperor's knees and begged to be cured. Another man, who had a crippled hand, asked Vespasian to tread on him – the healing method associated with Pyrrhus. The emperor laughed but was urged to work the cure. After confirming with his physicians that no normal remedy was possible, and reflecting that failure would do no harm while success would add to his fame, he cheerfully set to. He touched the blind man's cheeks with his spittle and trod on the cripple. They were both instantly healed. Another Christ-like healer in the pagan literature was Apollonius of Tyana, whose life was written by Philostratus in about AD 220.

It is characteristic of the extensive, still continuing literature that many of the accounts are narrated by an eyewitness or taken at worst at second hand from a personally known and trusted source. Augustine of Hippo, who rebuked some of his contemporaries for preferring Apollonius to Christ, gave personal testimony. Bede relates how the relics of St Cuthbert cured a young monk's tumour, the account 'being told me recently by the very brother to whom it happened'. Athanasios Parios, writing of his friend the Orthodox Saint Macarios of Corinth (1731–1805), tells of a woman healed by the saint: 'When we heard of this, we hastened to the cured woman to see and make sure with our own eyes.'

There is a problem with *all* this earlier testimony. In the last fifty years there have been unprecedented advances in medical knowledge and in the quality and equipment for diagnosis. The presuppositions of most early writers, who perhaps looked to the balance of the humours and the positions of the planets for the causes of disease, must qualify any modern interpretation of the texts. It is not possible at this distance to be sure what really happened. For these reasons I will look in greatest detail at more recent claims.

The first concerns the healing of a twenty-two-year-old Italian soldier in 1963. Vittorio Micheli, according to some who met him, is a modest, sensible and truthful man. His case was presented to an international conference on bone sarcoma in Marseilles and reported in the reputable *Journal of Orthopaedic Surgery*. It has also been the subject of a series of canonical enquiries.

Micheli became gravely ill in March 1962. The basic facts were that he suffered a viciously proliferating tumour which replaced much of his left pelvis, decalcified the femur and invaded the muscle. As a result, his left leg was shortened, hanging limply; he felt 'his leg was detached.' It was totally encased in plaster. The sarcoma of the bone was thoroughly, clinically observed and its advance recorded by X-rays.

On 26 May 1963, Micheli went to Lourdes. Immediately after going into the waters of the spring for the third time (threes recur in these tales) he felt better, regained his appetite and, for the first time in many months, succeeded in walking – by the end of June, without sticks or crutches. He later took up manual work in a textile factory, played football and, in 1967, got married.

There are no reasonable grounds for doubting the original diagnosis, and the X-rays exhibited that the entire left hip joint was obliterated. The *Journal of Orthopaedic Surgery* states that 'extensive destruction of the iliac bone ended in its reconstruction without any therapeutic intervention, except a biopsy. The histological slides, nevertheless, prove the existence of a malignant tumour, sarcoma of the pelvis.'

The American *National Enquirer* recently reported a cure at the shrine of the Madonna of Montevergine, near Naples. A forty-year-old mother of two children, who had suffered from multiple sclerosis since 1964 and was paralysed from the waist down in 1974, somewhat reluctantly made the pilgrimage. The object was to attend Mass and to visit the 5 metre (18 foot) painting of our Lady at the shrine. Mrs Rosati was staring at the picture:

' "First I saw her eyes move, then her right hand gestured as if to say, 'Come on, get up and walk to me'. Nobody else seemed to have seen her move, and I knew it was a vision."

'The figures approached her in shimmering light . . . and she heard the strange inner voice urging her to walk. She was helped to her feet by her sister, who also removed her braces and shoes.'

To summarize, she then made the first, faltering steps familiar in this literature and dropped her crutches (the walls of many healing shrines are covered with abandoned crutches as trophies): 'Then, unaided and without any pain, I walked 20 paces to the altar. I was cured.'

Mrs Rosati's own doctor declared, 'There is no question in my mind that her sudden recovery is a miracle.' Two local specialists also pronounced on the case. One said that she was not healed by any medical treatment, the other that there was no scientific explanation for the cure. At the time the article was written, Mrs Rosati was able to live with her family quite normally.

Canon Melinski, in his academic study *Healing Miracles* (1968), tells of a woman he knew who was suffering severe cancer of the womb with extensive secondary

Above : **the grotto at Lourdes where Mary appeared to Bernadette, and** *(right)* **the sick awaiting comfort and healing. There are detailed records of cures.**

growths. She was not expected to live long. In prayer, she reconciled herself to what was happening, and 'gradually with hours spent in contemplation . . . I came to this state of peace.' She believed 'that in that lay the miraculous part of it all and that everything else was secondary'. Yet the spread of the disease was stopped, the improvement being inexplicable in terms of medical science, according to her surgeon.

Here I pause to consider what may be seen as ritual, magical features in the healing stories. They are evident, for example, in the strange, verbal formulae, probably in some foreign tongue, which are sometimes used. 'Talitha cumi,'

Christ said to raise the daughter of the ruler of the synagogue; 'ephphata' to the dumb man, after spitting and touching his tongue. So also in the curing spells of the Middle Ages, runes or some little-understood tongue like Latin might be employed.

Secondly, ritual practices may be used to effect the cure. At its simplest, this involves nothing odder than the laying on of hands. This is the case with such well-witnessed healers as Leah Doctors. Or, as with Christ and Vespasian, it may require the application of spittle, mud, oil or some other agent. Whatever method is used there may be a deliberate copying of recorded practice.

You are a little bird.
You are the tern who is
dipping his beak in the water
while flying. The birth of
this bird is the sea. It is
flying low over the water
and dipping in its beak.
It is this bird that gave
you the attack.
When he gave you the
attack, you shook, because
he dug his claws into you.

Or it may be a sea turtle 'with its round form and with its arms, together with its fingers and finger nails' or simply 'the shadow that passes during the time when the sun goes over us and sets. This is what grabbed my brother's grandson. It is you who made my brother's grandson ill.' While singing, the shaman uses a rattle, and the researcher Dale Allen Olsen, writing in 1973, states that once he 'witnessed . . . an extraction by a twenty-five-year-old bahanarotu, Ramon, in which he extracted a rusty nail and a small piece of nylon rope from the patient's body'.

One of the most famous centres for healing today is Lourdes. However, in the ancient Greek world, the shrines of Asklepios were as popular, attracting large numbers of pilgrims. The most celebrated of his shrines was at Epidaurus, but the healing technique, incubation, was common to them all. The patient would sleep in the temple, expecting a dream visit from the god. Typically, Asklepios would prescribe some action, perhaps with physical remedies, behaving very much like a doctor on his rounds. Interestingly, this practice of incubation was adopted by the Christian saints Cosmas and Damien and was the healing technique associated with their church at Constantinople.

At Epidaurus, lists of cures have been preserved, inscribed on six stone columns, and the Greek Pausanias mentions such lists in the second-century narrative of his travels. The surviving records tell of some eccentric and many superficially plausible healings there.

Timon, wounded under the eye by a spear, dreamt that the god appeared with a certain herb and put something in his eye. He woke up healed. Alcetus was blind. Asklepios, in the dream, opened the sick man's eyes with his fingers. He could see the trees in the temple and went off healed the next day. Demosthenes was lame. Ordered in his dream to remain four months in the temple, he obeyed. He too was healed.

Similar lists of cures are published for Lourdes, but only a few of the healings claimed there are acknowledged as miracles by the Roman Church. The criteria applied before a miracle is declared were defined by Pope Benedict XIV in 1738: the cure must be instantaneous, without convalescence or medical treatment, it must be lasting and complete, inexplicable in scientific terms, and of course the original diagnosis that the condition was naturally incurable must be unambiguous. Three tribunals consider each case at Lourdes, two at the shrine and one in the patient's home diocese. Medical specialists are included in these tribunals. Consequently, only a tiny number of alleged cures are even considered, and the number of these finally approved totals less than 1 per cent.

The extreme form of healing is to raise the dead, and there are many stories of this as well. Bede wrote of St Fursa that when he 'had been restored to his body, he bore for the rest of his life the marks of the burns which he had suffered while a disembodied spirit . . .'. These claims have become less and less frequent over the ages, and already in the second century Irenaeus commented that, while many churches retained miraculous powers, 'they fall far short of raising the dead.'

I now return to Lourdes, but from a different point of view. It became a place of pilgrimage after a poor country girl, Bernadette, had a series of visions there. On 11 February 1858, she was crossing a tem-

For example, it is suggested that when St Peter in *Acts* kneels down to heal Tabitha he is imitating Elijah and Elisha. In an inexperienced healer, the conscious use of such a model seems unremarkable.

Finally, verbal incantations, magically potent tools and formal ritual are essential for all kinds of healing ceremony, whether in the 'faith healing' services familiar in the West or the shamanistic rituals more common in primitive societies.

Among the Indians of the Orinoco delta, there is a belief that the ancestral spirit – the *hebu* – can put itself into or take the shape of any object or animal and so inflict illness on man. To work a cure, the shaman must identify the form taken by the *hebu* and describe it precisely in the stylized song of the healer:

porarily lowered mill-canal by the Gave, towards a low cliff with caves scooped in it. Suddenly she heard a wind and saw inside the grotto 'a girl in white, no bigger than myself, who greeted me with a slight bow of the head'. Bernadette was soon suspected in the area of lunacy and hysteria, but she continued to visit the site and was repeatedly visited by the apparition.

One day, with eyewitnesses looking on unable to see or hear 'the lady', Bernadette suddenly climbed up to the grotto, and

the fourth time I was able to drink some.'

This was the origin of the spring that flows today. In 1862, Bernadette herself was apparently cured of grave pneumonia the moment she drank the waters: 'I felt as if a mountain had been lifted off my chest.'

The visionary tradition is long and puzzling. The thirteenth-century mystic St Gertrude saw images already familiar in iconography and literature: one Christmas 'she

made to a woman' so 'she must of necessity be frail and unstable, having nothing manly (which means perfect) about her'.

It is also hard to know what to make of St Teresa's claim: 'I saw an angel close to me, on my left, in bodily shape, a thing granted to me but rarely. He was not large, but small, very beautiful, his face radiant'; he then drove a lance into her heart; nor how to take a recent statement of a woman in Sacramento that Jesus visited her physically in hospital.

Even where there is an element of sharing, the impossibility of verifying the affirmation of a vision remains. Some Indian tribes regard dreams as public property. The dreamer will go around telling the dream until its proper owner claims it. Use of the hallucinogenic peyote root among North American Indians – a practice carried over into Christianity – is intended to induce 'brilliant, kaleidoscopic

visions' as part of a shared religious experience. In at least one instance, the trance has included a prophetic vision of Christ.

With the development of the charismatic movement, which stresses the activity of the Holy Spirit within Christian congregations and individuals, manifestations like these are again more commonly claimed in the West. Healings, raptures and the gift of tongues are features of the movement. David Christie-Murray has reported an encounter of four glossolalists – speakers in tongues – for an Italian television programme in December 1977. There was a Lancashire healer, Mrs Smith, who has no religious beliefs; a spiritualist healer, Mr Nokes; and Mr Morgan, a Christian reincarnationist, as well as the author himself. After their speeches in tongues, there was a conversation, entered into 'without hesitation and with complete spontaneity'; no formal, current

Visions may be prophetic and symbolic, as with Ezekiel's vision, which incorporates the four mythical figures (*right*). Some, like the appearance of Mary to Loli at Garabandel, Spain, on 11 September 1961 (*above*) are suspect. A few, like the apparition of Mary to Bernadette (*opposite*) on 25 March 1872, are tacitly approved by the Roman church and have been followed by attested healings.

started scrabbling on the ground:

'The Lady said to me: "Go and drink at the spring and wash yourself in it." Not seeing any spring I was going to drink from the Gave. She told me it was not there. She pointed with her finger to [the place of] the spring. I went there. It was merely a bit of dirty water; I put my hand in it, but I could not get hold of any. I scratched and the water came, but muddy. Three times I threw it away;

beheld all the saints standing before the throne of the King of kings, reciting matins with great devotion, for His divine honour and glory'. What can we make now of her claim that 'she saw Jesus Christ holding a Host in His hand, which he plunged in the Heart of God His Father; and when He drew it forth, it seemed as if coloured vermilion or tinged with blood'? Yet the Carthusian Lanspergius, who died in 1593, wrote a warning against the prejudice 'that these revelations were

Ezekiel Chap. 1. Ver. 1. to 28.

EZEKIEL'S VISION

language was employed. None the less, 'there were marked changes of mood which the speakers picked up and responded to instantly' without rehearsal or artificial watchfulness. This was evident to everyone making the film. A range and mixture of tongues was used. Christie-Murray speculates whether this is a form of musical or telepathic communication, while Christian glossolalists would attribute the cause to the Holy Ghost. It would certainly be perverse to dismiss all such occurrences as mere sham.

What was seen to happen at Fatima in Portugal during 1917 is more disturbing. Three peasant children claimed the Virgin had come to them in a lonely hollow near their home. After a first and second flash of lightning from a clear sky, the 'dear, pretty little lady' appeared to them, standing above a small holm oak. That was on 13 May, and more visitations followed. A large crowd gathered for the apparition predicted for 13 October. The previous day, the agnostic paper *O Seculo* wrote that some people intended to profit from a chaotic fraud. The editor – with sceptical priests, a professor from Coimbra, the hopeful devout and many curious sightseers – went along anyway.

It was raining, and photographs show a platform of raised umbrellas. A priest stood by the mutilated tree in the rain, watch in hand.

' "When will Our Lady appear?" he demanded.

"Midday," said one of the children.

After a few minutes, he said "Midday is past", and shouted to the people to go away: "You've been fooled!" '

There was a flash. One eyewitness wrote:

'There was no sun, only grey cloud and the falling rain. I saw the rain cease, suddenly, not as rain usually ends. Then the clouds were pushed back

from the sun in every direction, as if by invisible hands, and the sun appeared in colour like the blade of a knife, luminous but not dazzling.

'Then, as I looked, the sun described a swift circle, paused; described another, paused; described yet a third. And then the clouds began to sweep over it again.'

Many (but not all) the people present witnessed this, including the editor of *O Seculo*. Professor Garrett of Coimbra University saw the landscape turn purple, then yellow. Some people far away, going about their business, also witnessed it and were terrified or admiring. There was wide mass observation of the event.

It was a time of high emotion – after a child shouted 'Look at the sun!', many in the crowd cried out, 'Send back our sons from the war!' Afterwards *O Seculo* simply demanded proper investigation of a weird, rationally explicable but well-witnessed event.

Perhaps it is only where some

kind of visionary prediction takes place that doubt becomes difficult. In his second letter to the deacon Aurelius, Sulpicius Severus states that, before St Martin's death, he had a premonitory vision. He was lying in his cell when 'Suddenly it seemed to me I could see the holy Martin, dressed in a glowing toga, his face like fire, his eyes like stars. . . .' Corrie ten Boon asserts that she foresaw in a dream her own and her family's arrest by the Nazis, not vaguely but in some detail. And there is a still more dramatic, well attested occurrence from Goa in 1542. Early in June, the south-west monsoon was approaching, carrying storms. The ship *Santiago* had been separated from its convoy out of Mozambique and there was no news of it. Francis Xavier was acutely anxious, repeatedly saying 'Oh, the ship!', apparently knowing what no one could know yet – that the *Santiago* had sunk, most hands being saved, a few days before. A short enquiry, incidentally, shows that at least

two friends of mine have had witnessed, fulfilled premonitions like these.

The series of miracles I have described could be extended indefinitely, even allowing for the relatively narrow selection I have imposed. There are stories, testified by the baker who experienced the event herself, of grain and dough multiplying themselves to meet the needs of the Curé d'Ars' orphans. In a manual for witch-hunters, the late fifteenth-century *Malleus Maleficarum*, one of the two authors gives a first-hand account of multiple possession by the devil. The possessed priest gave evidence to the Inquisitor, who remarks, 'But I would not in the least have believed his words if he had not at once informed me of the facts of the case.' Prayer and fasting delivered him.

However, the evidence given must suffice. My intention has been to see, as perhaps with ghost stories, whether, after telling a range of tales, there may be a residuum which resists scepticism. It is not my argument that a cumulation of bad evidence adds up to some kind of truth. My point is that criteria applied to other claims in history and biography must let some of these stories through. There has been a continuing line of testimony to the strange, inexplicable events called miracles. It is ancient and still developing. At worst, the presence of a problem cannot be denied. If, with Bronowski, you maintain an exclusively materialist attitude, you will leave miracles there: not-yet-explained, odd physical events. My preference is to allow both for the possibility of miracles and for the impossibility of proving any single event miraculous. Belief in some miracles, like faith itself, seems more likely to be an assertion than a logical conclusion. That validates the situation of anyone who invokes divine or preternatural causality for miracles. All I ask is open-mindedness, unsettling easy certainties.

STIGMATA

The flowing of blood from the mysterious wounds of stigmatics, identical to those of Christ, is well-attested. Many Christians attribute it to God or the Devil. But is there a medical explanation?

In popular usage the word 'stigmata' refers to the wounds gained by Christ during His arrest, trial and crucifixion; in particular it applies to wounds resembling Christ's that occur on the bodies of saints and others of great piety. In the *Kirchenlexicon*, Father Pfulff defines 'stigmatization' according to the orthodox opinion of the Catholic Church: it is a 'charisma or supernatural gift' to the stigmatic who 'participates in the Passion of Christ in a way that is shown outwardly by marks on those parts of the body where Christ bore His wounds'. The Church distinguishes two components of 'true stigmata': the bodily marks or wounds, which are in turn only the outward and visible signs of an inner state of grace based on an identification with the sufferings of Christ.

Genuine stigmata have some very interesting physiological characteristics which differentiate them from pathological wounds. The blood that flows from them is clean arterial blood free of the discharges of disease; those which rupture the skin to form fissures or holes that on occasion completely pierce the hand or foot show little or no sign of the inflammation normally expected on the edges of wounds, nor are any of the normal healing processes activated in the region of the wound. More often than not 'true stigmata' appear spontaneously, coinciding with a special state of consciousness related to trance, in which the stigmatic experiences a vision which 'explains' what is happening to his or her body.

Usually, but not always, the vision is of Christ Himself who offers a share of His suffering to the stigmatic-to-be whose body, if he or she accepts, is then pierced by rays at the sites of the wounds. In some cases the wounds in the hands and feet and the 'ferita' (lance wound) in the chest appear simultaneously in that first overwhelming ecstasy; but again, as in the case of Lukardis of Oberweimar, the initial vision may simply inform the stigmatic that he or she is to become a living representation of the crucified Christ, after which the stigmata appear, still during ecstasies, but spaced weeks or years apart. Also, unlike any other wounds, except some of psychosomatic origin, most stigmatics suffer periodic bleeding, either during the traditional period of Lent, especially Easter Friday, or often regularly on Fridays. Some have borne the stigmata for most of their lives continuously, while others have suffered the spontaneous appearance of the wounds each Friday, which then regularly diminish and heal by Sunday night.

Stigmatization is popularly categorized among the miracles and is thus associated by most people with special sanctity. But the Church, whose corporate experience of extraordinary phenomena goes back centuries, immediately advises caution, followed by lengthy, painstaking and prudent investigation during which the case for and against a claim for special states of grace is assembled and deliberated; the result, if it is favourable, may be beatification

Fifteenth-century stained glass: many stigmatics have been persecuted, claiming that devils are responsible.

87

and later canonization. To the great disappointment of the multitudes who adored some stigmatics (such as Teresa Neumann or Father Pio) while they were alive, the Church's policy is not to canonize the living. The argument is simple and reasonable and also applies to stigmatization: the Devil, it is said, is never more dangerous than when he imitates the phenomena of holiness in order to mislead the credulous faithful. 'True stigmata', as hinted at in Father Pfulff's definition, originate in the inner state of grace whose central mystical elements are faith, piety, obedience and humility; all else, especially those stigmata which are only on the surface and not rooted in the spirit, is of the Devil, in the Church's judgment. There are well authenticated cases of stigmata, among many other forms of strange phenomena such as levitation, bilocation, healing and clairvoyance, being suffered by people who were not especially pious, and there have even been a few genuine stigmatics who dared to use their awe-inspiring marks for personal gain (Rose Tamiser, for instance, who in 1851, after a distinctly hasty investigation by a hostile archbishop, was prosecuted in a civil court in France for fraud and offending both public morals and religion). The process of formal recognition by the Church accepts evidence of 'miracles' not on their own merits but only in so far as they support a heroically virtuous and humble life, and any stigmata that fail the rigorous criteria of heroic virtue are automatically classified as 'diabolical'; that includes, the Church apologists say, such stigmata as may arise out of peculiar illnesses, psychoneurotic conditions and experiments by psychologists to induce the marks by hypnotism. This arbitrary and dogmatic division may be satisfying to those same apologists and to the faithful, but it hardly helps us to understand why certain people should suffer this con-

88

dition and just what happens to them.

From my own study of the considerable body of published evidence about stigmata and stigmatization and related material it is abundantly clear that the behavioural phenomena in the lives of so many stigmatics, canonized or not, are morphologically similar, if not identical, to the psychogenic symptoms of hysterical conditions and are instantly recognizable as such by any psychiatrist today. In saying this I stress that I do not preclude divine initiation but merely observe the mechanism common to both 'true' and 'diabolical' stigmata, though such comparisons, according to the Church apologists, are odious and specious. These positions will be better delineated if we first give some examples of 'true' and 'diabolical' stigmata to illustrate the range of the phenomenon.

It is a remarkable fact that for about eleven centuries after the Apostles, until the time of St Francis of Assisi, there was little reference to stigmatization and an absence of authentic cases. In Galatians 6:17 (Vulgate), St Paul wrote: 'For I bear the stigmata of Jesus in my body,' thought it is difficult to be precise about his meaning across the gulf of time. Then the hiatus, until one French and several English medieval chroniclers mention the arraignment of several apostates before the Oxford Council of Archbishop Stephen Langton in 1222. One was a woman who claimed to be the Virgin Mary, another a young man who had himself crucified in the belief that he was Christ and must bear the signs. It was judged a case of collective insanity and the unfortunates ended their lives in prison. Other than this scanty information, even the thorough and devoted researches of the Bollandists can date no cases before the death of St Francis in 1226, after which there is a veritable torrent of stigmatic blood that still shows no sign of abating today.

In 1224, only two years before his death, St Francis undertook a forty-day retreat on Mount Alvernia in the Apennines, during which, on 14 September, he was struck by a vivid vision while praying fervently outside his cave. According to St Bonaventura's *Legenda Major*, Francis saw in the sky a winged seraphic form of Christ on the cross and at the height of his rapture was impressed in his body with the wounds. In the *Life* of St Francis ascribed to Thomas of Celano (*Vita Prima*, 1229), it is said, based on contemporary accounts, that the wounds appeared on his limbs and breast after the saint had got up and called for assistance. Celano continues: 'His hands and feet seemed pierced in the midst by nails, the heads of the nails appearing in the inner part of the hands and in the upper part of the feet and their points over against them. . . . Moreover his right side, as it had been pierced by a lance, was overlaid with a scar, and often shed forth blood so that his tunic and drawers were many times sprinkled with the sacred blood.' It is interesting to note that Celano describes not just a wound but the appearance of a nail-like formation lodged through the wound. The wounds themselves were round on the back of the hands and feet and were capped by a dome of gristle or hard dried blood, while in the palms and soles the wound was elongated; over it 'certain small pieces of flesh were seen like the ends of nails bent and driven back, projecting from the rest of the flesh.' Other writers, notably Brother Elias, a contemporary of Francis, also confirm this amazing detail and the fact that nothing like this had ever been heard of before. At Francis' death crowds flocked to view the miraculous stigmata, still visible in the saint's incorrupt body, and Celano, in the *Tractatus de Miraculis*, states clearly that pilgrims could plainly see 'in the hands and feet not the fissures of the nails but the

St Francis of Assisi, seen left with St Andrew, was the first authentic stigmatic in known records, being fully imprinted with the wounds of Christ during a vision of a seraph in the sky, depicted above in a fresco from Assisi by Pietro Lorenziti.

nails themselves marvellously wrought by the power of God, indeed implanted in the flesh itself in such wise that if they were pressed in on either side they straightway, as if they were one piece of sinew, projected on the other'. Whether or not these details are later embellishments of the legend of St Francis (as is the opinion of some historians), the essential details of the story were noted within a few years of their occurrence.

The extreme form of this dramatic event obviously made a quick, deep and lasting impression upon the religious imagination of Europe, because there were a few more well-attested stigmatizations before the thirteenth century was over.

The most extensive listing of cases, by Dr A Imbert-Gourbeyre (*La Stigmatisation*, 1894), mentions 321. A more recent authority, Father Herbert Thurston (*The Physical Phenomena of Mysticism*, 1952), disputes this figure on several counts. First, there are a number of cases, ancient and modern, which Imbert-Gourbeyre does not include; second, not all those mentioned

were fully stigmatized, some simply suffering the pain without the visible wound; and, third, a great many pious and humble stigmatics have successfully kept their charismatic gift a secret known only to their closest associates and their confessors. In these latter cases the phenomena have often been thoroughly documented by depositions made under oath, sealed and locked away for assessment after the deaths of all involved. Another curious statistic is the extremely high proportion of female stigmatics. Dr Imbert-Gourbeyre's figures reflect this imbalance well enough (bearing in mind Thurston's reservations): out of 321 stigmatics, only forty-one are male and only one of these was fully stigmatized, St Francis himself. Both Father Thurston and Montague Summers (*The Physical Phenomena of Mysticism*, 1950) discuss other male stigmatics, but these lack either the full complement of marks, the periodic bleeding or proper authentification. The only other fully stigmatized male is Father Pio Forgione, in our own time.

One of the first stigmatics after St Francis was Elizabeth of the Cistercian nunnery at Herkenrode, Belgium, who lived in the latter half of the thirteenth century. In her case we find another major theme of stigmatization, not just identification with the crucifixion but visionary participation in the whole Passion from arrest to resurrection. We are told that she lived most of her (probably short) life in an almost continuous state of trance and marked with the stigmata and that every twenty-four hours she re-enacted each stage of the Passion, often portraying Christ and several of His tormentors in rapid succession. Fortunately we have the fairly detailed account of Abbot Philip of Clairvaux, written in 1275. I quote from Father Thurston's paraphrasing:

'When Elizabeth was contemplating some stage of our Lord's ignominious progress from one tribunal to another, catching hold of the bosom of her own dress with her right hand she would pull herself to the right and then with the left hand she would drag herself in the opposite direction. At another time, stretching out her arm and raising her fist threateningly, she would strike herself a violent blow on the jaw so that her whole body seemed to reel and totter under the impact; or again, while her feet remained planted motionless, she would pull herself fiercely by the hair until her head struck the ground; similarly bending back all her fingers except an outstretched forefinger she would aim it at her eyes as if she meant to gouge them out, while at other stages writhing, as it seemed, in agony on the floor, she beat her head against the ground over and over again. But the most frequently recurring feature in this ill-usage of herself was the shower of blows which, when lying on her back in the trance state, she rained upon her breast with extraordinary force and violence.'

It is difficult to see anything edifying in such a spectacle. Nevertheless, Elizabeth exhibited genuine stigmata which activated 'spurting blood' at the appropriate place in her vision-cycle.

The early religious life of St Mary Magdalen de' Pazzi, a revered Carmelite mystic who died in 1607, was a torment of inner and outer trials, although there is substantial evidence for believing, along with Dr E. J. Dingwall (*Very Peculiar People*, 1950), that she was a classic example of the ascetic female flagellant and masochistic exhibitionist with a sadistic streak. Her divine raptures were punctuated with periods in which she felt the burdens and temptations of her body and would resort to rolling in thorn bushes or whipping with nettles, rods or whips. Not unexpectedly these passages developed into the hallucination that she was being physically attacked and even sexually assaulted, and she would swipe about her, throw stones at her invisible assailants or convulse on the ground reacting to unseen blows. It was also natural for the Church at that time to explain these attacks as the actions of the Devil, who had been outraged at the sanctity of the woman. In 1585 Mary Magdalen had a vision in which St Augustine of Hippo appeared to her and wrote upon her heart in letters of gold and crimson *Verbum caro factum est* ('The Word was made flesh'). Eight days later, in a rapture so ineffable that it inspired her writings for the rest of her life, she accepted a crown of thorns offered her by Christ and exchanged hearts with him. Thereafter her stigmata pained her almost beyond endurance so that she constantly swooned or else was in a trance.

The stigmata received by St Mary Francis of the Five Wounds (d. 1791) were remarkable for completely perforating her hands. Father Thurston quotes the deposition made by her confessor under oath for her process. He had often examined the wounds closely and added:

'As the apostle St Thomas did, I have put my finger into the wounds of her hands and I have seen that the hole extended right through, for in inserting my first finger into the wound, it met my thumb which I held underneath on the other side of the hand. And this experiment I have made in many Lents, and on many Fridays in March, because it was on such days that the said wounds were most fully developed.'

Nearer our own time we find a greater number of cases which have received detailed attention from scientific investigators, including doctors and psychologists. One of the first to be thoroughly observed was St Gemma Galgani (d. 1903) who, like St Francis, was stigmatized two years before her death. Orphaned at nineteen, she was fervently devout, but spinal tuberculosis prevented her becoming a Passionist nun and she had to take up domestic work in Lucca, Italy. She continued her devotions and was frequently seen before an image of the scourged Christ praying to share in and alleviate His suffering. There was such intense admiration for her after her death that she was canonized within thirty-seven years; it must be emphasized that this was because of her heroic virtue and not her wonderful phenomena. One Friday in March 1901, alternating between agony and ecstasy, she experienced every imagined lashing of Christ, and when she was found in her room by her adopted mother her arms and back were covered with weals and her underclothing was soaked in blood. From that day on her stigmata regularly appeared each Thursday at about 8 pm, lasting until 3 pm the next day. In his *Life of Gemma Galgani* (1914) her confessor, Father Germano di S. Stanislao, notes the genesis of her wounds; apart from a 'recollection of spirit' there was

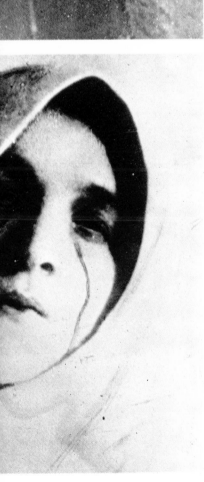

Teresa Neumann regularly enacted Christ's passion between each Friday and Sunday. She demonstrated the full range of stigmata, including weeping blood *(left)* **and lived all her life in the small village of Konnersreuth** *(above left)*. **Padre Pio** *(above)* **also bore the five wounds in great pain for fifty years and had to endure continual observation and adulation.**

little sign of the impending trauma, 'no sense of pain or impression in those parts of the body affected by it'; then, 'red marks showed themselves on the backs and palms of both hands; and under the epidermis a rent in the flesh was seen to open by degrees . . . after a little the membrane burst and on those innocent hands were seen the marks of flesh wounds.' In size and shape they closely resembled those of St Francis, and Father Germano says that they were very deep, seeming to pass completely through the

hand. 'I say seemed to pass, because those cavities were full of blood, partly flowing and partly congealed, and when the blood ceased to flow they closed immediately, so that it was not easy to sound them with a probe'. . . . This instrument was never used, both because of the reverential delicacy inspired by the Ecstatic in her mysterious state, and because the violence of the pain made her keep her hands convulsively closed. On Friday the wounds closed very quickly, and by Sunday only 'whitish marks'

could be faintly seen in the normal-looking skin. Father Germano adds that the phenomena varied from week to week, sometimes appearing only in the palms or the feet, sometimes bleeding through the skin without any sign of rupture. At other times, though rarely, the appearances of nails could be seen in the wounds, like those of St Francis, formed out of mounds and ridges of very hard and dark flesh.

The stigmata of the Belgian girl Louise Lateau were less severe than Gemma's, being bright red oval marks in the palms and backs of the hands through which, every Friday, the blood oozed, the skin remaining unbroken. Louise was stigmatized in a vision in January 1868, at the age of eighteen, and she felt the pain of their presence although they did not become manifest until later that April, remaining visible for fifteen years until she died in 1883. In that time she was subjected to every kind of test imaginable by doctors from the Belgian Royal Academy of Medicine and was attended for long periods by Dr Imbert-Gourbeyre and others. For example, Dr Lefebvre, of the University of Louvain, taking advantage of her insensibility during a trance, sealed her hand and arm inside a glass tube to preclude conscious or unconscious fakery. But Louise's honesty and piety impressed many who arrived sceptical and they went away convinced that her phenomena were inexplicable by the normal notions of medicine and biology. Like many other mystics Louise ate little or nothing for this entire period, except the consecrated Host during Communion; also, during trance, she spoke in several languages not known to her conscious self and accurately predicted the First World War. Louise was never strong, and several of her biographies overlook a series of illnesses before her stigmatization, some of which were spontaneously cured.

Teresa Neumann (d. 1962), like Louise, came from a very poor family and took up work as a domestic on local farms – and like both Louise and St Gemma she suffered mysterious illnesses in the years before her stigmatization whose spontaneous cure she, again like them, attributed to the intercession of her patron saint. During Lent 1926, aged twenty-eight, Teresa experienced overwhelming visions of the Passion during which she was stig-

matized in the hands, feet and side and later in the shoulder and forehead. During each Lent she regularly suffered this ordeal. If while in vision she saw Christ's torment her body responded appropriately: the scourging opened weals on her own back, the binding caused bleeding from her nails, the 'crown of thorns' bled from tiny punctures appearing on her forehead, the clothes torn from Christ before the actual crucifixion brought a torrent of blood from her shoulder and back as though from wounds reopened, her hands and feet reacted to the hammering of the nails, and finally her ferita gushed as Christ's side was pierced. For the thirty-two years she bore the stigmata, most of them bedridden, Teresa was under close observation by the Bishop of Ratisbon, as well as by eminent medical investigators who frequently took advantage of her trances to examine her wounds closely without her conscious knowledge. As news spread of this wonder, her village of Konnersreuth, Bavaria, became so deluged with pilgrims, curiosity-seekers and the sick that the Bishop kept Teresa under strict curfew. The stigmata were also active outside Lent, but erratically; on ordinary Fridays she wept tears of blood or bled from the forehead punctures only, and on the first Friday in each month these were joined by issues from the ferita, the rest of the grim repertoire usually being reserved for Lent. Statements of doctor after doctor could be quoted in support of her phenomena, particularly the strong resemblance of the limb-wounds to those of St Francis; these gave the impression of a forged iron nail piercing and protruding from the hands. Ritter von Lama, one of Teresa's many biographers, noted that the hand wounds originally formed only on the backs, not in the palms. Gradually they developed in

Padre Pio, who died in 1968, was the most celebrated stigmatic since the death of St Francis in 1226.

the palms 'and became covered by a scab and surrounded by scarring . . . outside the Friday ecstasies they are absolutely dry. They are new growths, hard and horny, around which lies an elastic, delicate membrane which breaks and bleeds during the Passion ecstasy and at the end of it closes again.' In 1931 he recorded a further development: ' a sort of nail forms in the wounds and seems to consist of firm. grisly flesh . . . the end of which appears to have been bent round by a hammer blow'. This formation had been examined earlier by a Dr Louis of Versailles who described the nail-head as rectangular, 'admirably regular . . . its edges delicately adorned with zig-zag borders . . . and sharp like the edges of a nail forged with a hammer'. Teresa was also clairvoyant, and according to a recent work (*Teresa Neumann* by Johannes Steiner, 1967, which includes photographs of the rectangular stigmata) no food or water, except the consecrated Host and wine during Communion, passed her lips for the last thirty-five years of her life. Indeed her total fast was well underway when in the 1920s and 1930s she was subjected to long periods of close medical scrutiny with the blessing of the Church. To test this abstinence she was once observed for several weeks without taking the least nourishment, at the same time being subjected to painful personal examinations in which all her eliminations were measured and examined. The experiment confirmed that she remained healthy with no need of nourishment, and her excreta, which had progressively diminished since 1926, apparently ceased entirely after 1930.

In 1968 the most famous stigmatic of recent years died. Padre Pio Forgione was a Capuchin friar who lived most of his life in great humility in the Italian monastery of San Giovanni Rotondo at Foggia. During his youth and early priesthood he had a delicate constitution which was seriously affected by rigorous fasts and disciplines. He developed tuberculosis, began to see apparitions of hideous monsters and was subject to 'diabolical attacks', which closely resemble poltergeist outbreaks in which furniture moves 'on its own', items are smashed, blankets pulled off beds and so on. In 1915, aged twenty-eight he emerged from a long period of meditation with stinging sensations in his hands. Nothing much was thought of it at the time, but three years later, when he was alone in the choir after celebrating the Feast of the Stigmata of St Francis, his piercing cry brought his brothers running to his aid. They found him unconscious and bleeding profusely from all five wounds. Later he begged his brothers to keep this secret – but, of course, word spread and, like Teresa Neumann, he had to endure not only the dispassionate scrutiny of his superiors but constant examinations by doctors and the open adulation of the peasants of the surrounding countryside and of other pilgrims. In fact the situation became so out of hand that the Church issued repeated exhortations to the public to stop their pilgrimages, petitions and adulations, stressing that no censure of Father Pio himself was implied. Nevertheless his cult grew, and many hundreds have testified to his stigmata, clairvoyance, bilocation, healing and other 'miracles'. His wounds consisted of large circular depressions in his palms which at times seemed to pierce them completely. The Reverend Charles M. Carty (*Padre Pio – Stigmatist*, 1963) was told by the Provincial Superior, who examined the wounds shortly after their appearance, that he would swear solemnly that he had seen clear through the holes well enough to have read print held on the other side. In another booklet by Carty (*The Stigmata and Modern Science*, 1974) confirmation of the depth comes from Dr Romanelli, who said: 'By pressing [the wounds] with my fingers I have felt a void . . . if I pressed further strongly my fingers would meet. . . . I have submitted him to this painful experience several times morning and night'. The wound in his left side was formed of two intersecting fissures like an inverted cross. It looked shallow but was covered by a scab and was very painful, bleeding as much as a cupful of blood and serum a day. Father Pio bore the pain of these wounds with true humility for fifty years, the longest of any recorded stigmatic.

Any examination of the phenomena of shamanism, spiritualism, occultism, parapsychology and paraphysics will uncover genuine events which in the Christian (and mainly Catholic) context parallel the recognized 'true' miracles; and in the Church's deliberated opinion, since 'true' miracles must have their origin in piety, humility, obedience and faith in official dogma, any such phenomena, especially those which so closely resemble Christian miracles, must automatically be the work of the Devil. As Cardinal Bona observed long ago (*De Discretione Spiritum*, 1672) the Devil seems to regard stigmata, and stigmatics for that matter, fair game.

We have already mentioned Rose Tamiser, who fell foul of civil and Church authorities for using her stigmata to obtain a degree of local fame and power. We might mention the altogether more interesting case of Palma Matarelli, who lived and died (1888) in the small town of Oria, Italy, and to whom Dr Imbert-Gourbeyre (*Les Stigmatisées*, 1873) devotes many pages, her phenomena being the most extraordinary of the four stigmatics he had personally had the good fortune to examine. Palma was an illiterate peasant girl who by the age of twenty-eight found herself widowed, her three daughters also dead. Dr

Gourbeyre says that her manifestations began when she was quite young, and she must have realised the attention these brought her. In 1857, a few years after her bereavement, she was stigmatized, her wounds appearing later, and then erratically from 1865 (except for the permanent side wound) until 1872, after which they seemed vestigial, not even bleeding. Dr Gourbeyre records testimony of many genuine and puzzling phenomena: Hosts would appear on her tongue both during Communion and outside it; cloth applied to her wounds, including her 'crown of thorns', would afterward be found imprinted with 'inflamed hearts, nails and swords' and other emblems of the

alone for a while. She would speak in patronizing tones about Louise Lateau, as though she were a rival, sometimes rather obviously fishing for information about the other contemporary stigmatics, and she was not backward in displaying her marks. 'On the other hand,' wondered Father Thurston, 'if her manifestations were diabolical in origin, one would have expected Satan to produce something less crude than childish patterns of flames, hearts, etc.' As the documents Father Thurston cites prove, Pope Pius IX believed Palma to be a puppet of the Devil; yet, despite official condemnation, she continued to be adored by the local people and great crowds came to her burial.

tinguished critic and historian of psychic phenomena as Dr Dingwall (*Some Human Oddities*, 1947), reviewing the two most famous cases of 'diabolical stigmata', is forced to observe 'that it is possible for Catholics to be totally unable to distinguish the divine from the diabolic in a number of instances'.

These 'instances' centred on two sixteenth-century Spanish nuns. Magdalena de la Cruz (d. 1560) entered a Franciscan convent in 1504, aged seventeen, and for thirty-nine years she bore stigmata, levitated, had ecstasies and gave prophecies. Her piety and miracles were widely admired and respected, even as far as the court of Empress Isabella and even within the Church. But not all were convinced; some noted that she delighted in showing off her marks, for example, or that in a vision she claimed to have conceived and brought forth the infant Jesus, but they kept quiet while the world believed in Magdalena's sanctity. In 1543 she suffered a serious illness and, close to death, made a shocking confession: since the age of twelve, she said, she had feigned everything, holiness, stigmata and all, with the aid of a pact with two demons. The confession is far from convincing, and we know very little of her mental or physical condition at the time. We do know that she had envious enemies who seized upon her confession almost gleefully, and after a public recital of her crimes, real or imagined (lasting ten hours!), she spent the remainder of her life in strict obedience in a monastery of another order, and nothing more was heard of her phenomena.

The Dominican nun Maria de la Visitacion was twelve when she entered her convent in 1568, where she quickly acquired a reputation for great virtue and was elected prioress when only twenty-six. There is some suggestion that this promotion was helped because she came from a rich family –

she certainly seemed to be well favoured by God and Mammon and was no doubt the envy of not a few of her sisters. In time, she became very influential and her blessings were sought by the military as the armada was marshalled against England. In 1587 a rumour that her stigmata were spurious was scotched by doctors sent by King Philip II. Later her enemies, angry no doubt by her championing of the independence of Portugal, accused her again; this time alleging that she faked stigmata expressly to obtain favours with the King. She was tried, sentenced by the Inquisition to perpetual seclusion and died, like Magdalena, 'a most blessed death'.

With the historical perspective we possess today we might justifiably question confessions obtained by the Inquisition, especially after the shameful pogroms against the Cathars and many other 'heretical' sects and the terrifying witch-hunt throughout Europe, in which confessions extracted under extreme mental and physical torture featured prominently in the prosecutions. Maria's confessions indeed seem full of the sort of improbable statements a desperate woman would make when asked to explain how miracles were performed – her levitations, she said, were accomplished with the aid of high-heeled shoes or blocks of wood; and her brilliant haloes by concealed candles and mirrors. It is difficult to believe that such naive tricks could have fooled anyone for long, let alone the close and frequent scrutiny of which we have some record (including a deposition by the then Dominican General). Like Father Thurston, some writers have suggested that she may have been deluded or full of pride and ambition, but her phenomena could still be genuine. It is said that Maria's stigmata came off with soap and water, as though they were painted on, and yet I cannot help but compare this with the experience of St Gemma Galgani's confessor,

One curious aspect is the way in which the marks on the stigmatics' bodies correspond more to artistic images of the crucified Christ (*above and opposite*) **than to the known physiological effects of crucifixion.**

Passion; after her death her body remained flexible up to the time of burial; and so on. On the evidence it seems that Palma herself drew attention to her teleported hosts and again that her wounds were found bleeding after she had been

There is no doubt that some of her phenomena were genuine, and she seems to have done some good, including healing. Papal secrecy, as in this case, only confuses further an already confused issue – especially when such a dis-

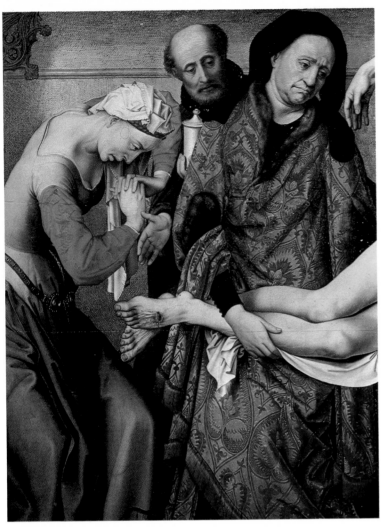

who saw a doctor wipe away the blood from Gemma's hands and forehead; almost instantly the flow stopped and the wound healed, leaving no sign of laceration. However, one thing is certain: if Maria and Magdalena had not admitted fraud (however improbable), insisting their charisms came from God, they would have suffered the same fate as St Joan of Arc, and for precisely the same reasons.

Before giving some examples of other kinds of stigmata than the basic limb and side wounds, we must take a brief look at the so-called 'invisible stigmata'. The best known of these happened to St Catherine of Siena (d. 1380), who promised herself to God at the age of seven and resisted strong family pressure to marry. After eleven years she became a Dominican nun and spent three years in strict silence and discipline in her own house. At twenty-eight she attended a Mass held by the Blessed

Raymond of Capua and passed into ecstasy before a crucifix. On coming to, she told Raymond that she bore the marks of Christ; although nothing could be seen there was no doubt about her agony. Her own account, given in many biographies (eg her *Life*, by Mother Francis Raphael, 1887), says that she swooned because of a vision of the crucified Christ, aureoled in glory. Then

'Five brilliant crimson rays darted from the five wounds, and sharp as a spear, they severally pierced my hands, my feet and my side. . . . I cried aloud, "My God . . . I beseech thee that these wounds of mine betray me not, and show that I have been found worthy in some sort to share Thy Passion." At my words the rays changed from crimson to a golden glow, and these five golden rays of lucent light transpierced my hands, my feet and my side . . . so great is the agony that unless our Lord

sustain me I shall surely die.'

At her death the marks became visible, and many impeccable witnesses testified that they had seen them in her still incorrupt body, even after her limbs were cut off as relics and scattered throughout Europe.

Less well known is Clare de Bugny (d. 1514), an Italian nun of exceptional holiness, who first received the side-wound from which gurgled such quantities of blood that doctors from the School of Medicine at Padua were amazed. Sometime later she was completely stigmatized, but the marks disappeared upon her earnest prayer, only to re-appear on her corpse, shining with strange light, when she died a year later (*Annales Minorum*, 1647). The simultaneous appearance of all kinds of stigmata (eg St Francis and Father Pio) is relatively rare; more often they arrive in distinct stages like those of Elizabeth of Herkenrode or Clare de Bugny.

One of the commonest forms of supplementary stigmata is the 'crown of thorns' bleeding from holes circling the forehead. It is often given first during a vision. Anne Catherine Emmerich (d. 1824) was born to miserably poor parents and from an early age was absorbed in visions of the lives of Christ and the saints. It was an unhappy time in Germany and after a spell with some unsympathetic and equally undernourished Augustinian nuns she found a wretched but welcome lodging with a poor widow in Dülmen, Westphalia. In August 1812 Anne Catherine awoke from an ecstasy to find a cross marked on her breast, which on certain days issued a very hot and clear lymph in quantities to soak her bedclothes and sheets. She became bedridden with mysterious maladies and that December again encountered Jesus in a vision. His wounds 'shone like furnaces of light' and triple rays impressed them upon her body. Her 'crown of

thorns' appeared in 1798, four years before she entered a convent, and she successfully hid the bleeding for several years.

Blessed Catherine of Racconigi (d. 1547), like Anne Catherine and St Catherine of Siena, was offered the choice between a garland of flowers or the thorny crown by Christ Himself and had her choice placed by him on her brow. Unlike them, Catherine of Racconigi was told by Jesus that, at ten, she was too young to bear the pain and that he would defer the wound until she was ready. In 1510, aged twenty-four, she was impressed with the full stigmata. Her 'crown' was described by the philosopher Pico della Mirandola (in the *Compendio . . . mirabile della B. Catherine da Racconigi*, 1858): 'She had, encircling her head, a depression large and deep enough for a child to have put its little finger into it, and this was punctured . . . and clotted with blood. She told me these indents often shed copious blood. I myself saw her suffering agony from this Crown, and her poor eyes even seemed full of blood.'

Sometimes the crucial vision takes the form of a mystical marriage to Christ, in which hearts are exchanged, the crown is placed on the nun's head, or a ring is given to the stigmatic. This ring is included among the stigmatic phenomena and receives considerable attention from Father Thurston and Dr Gourbeyre. The form of these rings has varied enormously, ranging from simple reddened hoops of skin around the ring finger of the right hand to the bizarre constructions of flesh exhibited by Celestine Fenouil. She was stigmatized at seventeen in 1866, received the crown of thorns three years later; in 1874 the ring appeared. According to Dr Gourbeyre (*La Stigmatisation*) it was a vivid red line around the finger, with tiny crosses and a bezel with a design of a heart pierced by three swords and was formed by a thickening and reddening of the epidermis. Another doctor quoted insisted that the ring, normally invisible, developed every Sunday. Similarly, the Blessed Raymond of Capua, in his biography of St Catherine of Siena (*Acta Sanctorum* vol III, April), tells us that she experienced a mystical espousal in 1367 in which Jesus placed on her hand a golden ring set with four precious stones and a blazing diamond. It was always with her, she said, and she never tired of looking at it – but it was invisible to all other eyes.

Frequent mention is made by hagiographers of a deformed shoulder in some stigmatics, said to represent Christ's hurt from carrying the heavy beam of his cross. St Catherine of Ricci (d. 1590), though not strictly a stigmatic, bore both the mystical ring and a wound on her shoulder during her weekly ecstatic experience of the Passion. Blessed Catherine of Racconigi and St Gemma Galgani both felt such pain and crushing weight upon their shoulders in that phase of the Passion that their shoulders seemed visibly deformed and they were obliged to walk leaning to one side.

St Gemma, with Anne Catherine Emmerich, also bore savage weals and bruises corresponding to a vision of Christ bound to a pillar and whipped.

Dominicaness Helena Brumsin, who died in Germany in 1285, only fifty-nine years after St Francis, bore only the scourging stigmata. Summers contrasts her with an Italian Franciscan nun, Archangela Tardera, who was fully stigmatized and endured painful ecstasies most of her life. In 1608, a few years before her death, during a period of mysterious blindness, she fell in a swoon and was found covered with contusions and weals. Years after her death, according to the Heuber *Menologium* (19 September), her tomb was opened and the stigmata as well as these comparatively recent scourge-marks were clearly visible on her still supple and undecayed body.

By far the strangest of the supplementary and hidden stigmata are the extensions of the ferita which leave their marks on the internal organs, especially the heart, and are discovered only during the post-mortem examination. The most complete and authentic example is that of St Veronica Guiliani. Her life was a long series of ecstasies, yet under the direction of Bishop Eustachi she was treated by her superiors as though she was insane or an imposter and was virtually imprisoned in the strict walled monastery at Citta di Castello – even her ten-volume *Diario* was carefully scrutinized for the slightest tell-tale slip. Her humility and obedience won her through all the tests, examinations and constant observation (calculated no doubt to break the most obstinate hoax or impiety). In 1697, during a long rapture, Christ told her that she would bear the marks for three years – and thus, in 1770, three years to the day, they vanished, leaving only the mystic ring and the ferita which bled periodically. A post-mortem conducted shortly after her death in 1727 at the age of eighty-seven found coherent images formed in the interior cavities of her heart. The notable ecclesiastics and doctors present signed formal depositions that they had seen clear representations of a crucifix, a crown of thorns, initial letters of some virtues, three nails, seven swords and other emblems of the Passion. What makes her case doubly interesting is that when her stigmata vanished in 1700 she was certain that they had merely moved internally to avoid further problems with her superiors. Twelve years before her death she drew a diagram of the forms and arrangement of these symbols in her *Diario*. Several times she felt their locations shift; each time she made a new drawing (in 1718, 1719, 1720), and the final one, made in the year of her death, was found to correspond impressively with the discoveries of the post-mortem. St Veronica's marked heart is often compared with that of St Clare of Montefalco, extracted and bisected on the evening of her death in 1308. The same range of symbols can still be seen in her relics, incorrupt after more than six centuries, delineated by filaments, muscles, nerves and hardened flesh.

Simple forms of markings were found on the hearts of St Teresa of Avila (d. 1582), Soeur Marie de Jésus Crucifié (d. 1879) and Blessed Charles of Sezze (d. 1671), to mention just a few. It seems that they were as well aware of these changes in their interior as they were of the surface stigmata. Sister Marie, a Carmelite nun in Bethlehem, was thirty-three when she died. Dr Carpani, the eminent surgeon, who conducted the post-mortem, could hardly fail to notice the deep triangular lesion in her heart, which had all the character of a wound of great age. It was believed to date back to a moment eleven years earlier when during an ecstasy she cried out to St Teresa: 'O Mother Teresa! Jesus has pierced my heart!' (see her *Life* by Abbé Buzy, 1927). St Teresa's own 'transverberation' has been established in the calendar of Catholic feasts, and her heart, bearing a wide horizontal fissure, is preserved at her shrine at Alba de Tormes, Spain. In her autobiography she wrote of beholding an angel of fire. 'In his hands I saw a great golden spear, and at the iron tip there appeared to be a point of fire. This he plunged into my heart several times so that it penetrated to my entrails. When he pulled it out I felt that he took them with it, and left me utterly consumed by the great love of God.' Few men have shared this form of rapture, but one, Leonardo da Lettere (d. 1621, and mentioned by Summers) seems to have experienced a vision almost identical to St Teresa's. The heart of Blessed Charles was found to be com-pletely pierced, so that doctors were amazed that it had functioned normally in life. It also contained the image of a crucifix and the 'exact facsimile' of a four-inch nail lodged in its tissues.

Debate about stigmata tends to be conducted from extreme and dogmatic points of view. Apart from obvious fraud and delusion, the Church will admit only two kinds of miraculous stigmata: 'true' stigmata, which originate in and promote 'holy virtue' and 'diabolical' stigmata, which may be just as mysterious but are flawed in some respect, lacking one or all the virtues valued by the Church. On the other side, we have the sceptical scientists who dismiss the subject as the product of hoax, delusion or wishful thinking, if not of disturbed personalities and 'unhealthy' brooding upon morbid themes. Both camps are irreconcilably divided as to whether the 'stigmatic complex' (if we may call it that) corresponds to certain psychoneurotic conditions, particularly hysteria. In the past much of the argument has hinged upon misunderstandings, by the Church and other apologists of the nature of hysteria and by psychiatrists, who tend to be sceptical about the Church's arbitrary division of stigmata into acceptable and unacceptable forms. Writing in 1952, Father Thurston, a Jesuit and author of the most widely accepted study of the physical phenomena of mysticism, admitted that he found it hard to replace the common usage of the word 'hysteria' (implying highly excitable and excited neuropaths, the weak-minded, the emotionally unstable and pathological liars) with the more exact definition developed by the medical profession after psychiatric studies of the effects of the two World Wars which is less disparaging to the patient. In previous centuries hysteria (Greek: 'wandering womb') was believed to be a woman's complaint whereas observations of men under extreme emotional stress showed clearly that it was not confined to women. Nevertheless females with hysterical symptoms greatly outnumber their male counterparts, and this may be one reason why there are significantly more female stigmatics than male.

Psychiatrists today differentiate between hysterical symptoms and the hysterical personality. The latter conforms more to the popular idea of hysterical behaviour, while the basis of the former is that conflicts between the conscious and unconscious parts of the mind are suppressed and become converted into a range of spontaneous symptoms that mimic the symptoms of nearly the whole range of conventionally originated illnesses. Thus in 'conversion hysteria' a repressed fear, anxiety, revulsion or sexual arousal, for example, may become converted into blindness, tremors and fits, anaesthesia or paralysis of any part of the body or particular movement, black-outs and amnesia, hypochondria, sensations of pain with or without any corresponding spontaneous lesion, anorexia nervosa (compulsive starvation), somnambulism, trances, deliriums and the development of supplementary personalities and hallucinations. A sort of calm disinterest, which Janet called 'la belle indifférence' is typical of the dissociative mechanism of hysteria, and with it comes a greater susceptibility to suggestion. Certain diseases (eg tuberculosis) have been found to predispose subjects to hysterical disorders, as have factors in early training or education (eg implicit obedience) which may put the subject into an interior conflict. Some emphasis must be placed too on the fact that many hysterical symptoms are often turned around to the subject's benefit (thus a paralysis may obviate a disagreeable obligation, providing a perfect excuse and even inviting sympathy). Anyone predisposed toward hys-

Many stigmatics claim to know the exact moment of their 'transverberation'. As in the case of St Teresa, depicted here by Bernini, it is usually during an ecstatic vision.

terical disorders would have this condition exacerbated by the rigorous discipline, the fasts and penances, of many holy orders, especially the monastic or discalced (barefooted) ones, designed as they are to sublimate the rule of the flesh. It is a fact that most stigmatics seem to have been delicate or weak, through constitution or illness, before their initiating vision. In contrast with this 'stigmatic type', we cannot find any stigmatics among the physically vigorous saints.

It is dangerous to generalize of course, and some element of all these factors, rather than any single one, may have to be present before stigmatization is precipitated. Mary Magdalen de' Pazzi was undoubtedly motivated by the mystical union with God that she felt during her raptures, yet the relish with which she whipped her novices and with which she exhorted her superiors to whip herself (while on all fours tied to a post) is hardly edifying. On this point Father Thurston admits that 'there are many instances of stigmatization where imposture is out of the question but in which many of the details recorded are suggestive rather of disease than of that showing forth of the divine attributes which we associate with the idea of a miracle'. These diseases are in fact the pseudo-diseases whose symptoms arise from conversion- and suggestion-hysteria. The opposing argument usually claims that the quiet, humble, unimaginative and unexcited lives of St Gemma Galgani, St Teresa or Father Pio are quite obviously not hysterical. This involves a misunderstanding of the term; there is no implication of insanity or of the transparent faking present in some mental conditions, nor should the term be incompatible with lives of the highest sanctity or preclude the possibility of divine initiation. On a closer look one finds that in their early lives these 'non-hysterical' stigmatics were physically delicate and subject to a range of maladies (including tuberculosis), most of which had the transience typical of conversion-hysteria symptoms (the sudden disappearance of these symptoms attributed to a healing intercession by a patron saint). The work of William Sargant (*The Mind Possessed*, 1973) shows that, far from being an abnormal taint, a basic level of suggestibility is a major constituent of the glue that binds society together and is fundamental to the religious experiences of normal people. But stigmatics can hardly be said to be normal; in their case this suggestibility has become exaggerated by an innate tendency towards conversion-hysteria (the product of a delicate constitution, illness or a natural inclination to meditate

upon the sufferings of Christ) triggered by some profound conflict between bodily 'weakness' and the ideals of religious life (perhaps anxiety over sexual feelings or the body's inability to keep pace with the spirit's demand for an ascetic life etc).

Lukardis of Oberweimar (d. 1309) was twenty-two when she was stigmatized, but although she felt the agony the wounds themselves remained invisible for two years, appearing one by one in a series of ecstasies. Her biographer (*Annalecta Bollandia* vol 18) tells us an interesting detail. 'Before the stigmata appeared [she] endeavoured, out of her great longing, to open the places of the wounds in her feet by boring them, as it were, with her big toe.' Partly, it seems, to relieve the pain, and partly in concert with her vision of the hammering in of the nails, she
98

would also strike her palms vigorously with the rigid middle finger of the other hand, drawing back the finger several feet and striking the same spot again and again. If this was an attempt to open the wounds it was feeble because it went on for two years between the vision and the appearance of the series of marks.

Another possible hysteric would be Teresa Higginson (d. 1905), a schoolteacher from Liverpool, stigmatized with a crown of thorns, who, in visions of Christ's trial, would beat herself mercilessly like Elizabeth of Herkenrode. Some of these beatings, she believed, were by the Devil himself; but the frightened onlooker can be forgiven for thinking them indistinguishable. Her biographer, Lady Cecil Kerr (*Teresa Higginson*, 1928), mentions other phenomena which, thought saintly at the time, also have their hysterical parallels: an ability to do without sleep for long periods; the aversion to food (which in so many cases begins as a minor dietary peculiarity and ends up as anorexia nervosa or even a total fast); and frequent trance states or fugues which sometimes caught her in the street or in the middle of some action and during which two different personalities manifested.

The phenomenon of multiple personalities is met with in a number of stigmatics. Teresa Neumann, for example, frequently slipped into a state in which an immature child-like personality described scenes from the lives of the Virgin Mary and the saints as though they happened before her eyes. This personality was sometimes interrupted by another – a deep, distant, masculine voice – which some of her champions said was Christ Himself. Teresa, like all others with trance personalities, knew nothing of these when she awoke, this amnesia also being typical of hysterical fugues. Father Thurston compares such phenomena with several obscure stigmatics – Mother

Beatrice Mary of Jesus (d. 1702) and Costante Mary Castreca – who he acknowledges were clear cases of conversion-hysteria. They both suffered trances during which several personalities, each oblivious of the others, emerged, followed by amnesia, paralysis, hyper-aesthesia, vomitings and anorexia, plus the strange

poltergeist-like phenomena attributed to 'diabolical attack' (and which Dr Nandor Fodor interestingly argues to be 'bundles of projected repressions' – see his *On the Trail of the Poltergeist*, 1958).

Perhaps one of the best examples of the hysterical structure of stigmatism is Domenica Lazarri (d. 1848). She was as religious as any other hard-working serious Catholic girl, but not obsessively so. At the age of thirteen, the death of her father, a miller at Capriana, Italy, brought on a series of nervous disorders and convulsions. In June 1833, aged eighteen, she was stranded in a mill all night on her own and suffered a severe trauma which precipitated cataleptic seizures only days later as she worked in the fields. From then on, for the remaining fifteen years of her life, she was bedridden and for most of this time was attended by Dr Leonardo dei Cloche, who studied and noted every development of her condition. She showed an extraordinary degree of hyperaesthesia in all senses: ordinary light hurt her eyes, the slightest touch caused intense pain,

nearby sounds stunned her, while the smell of cooking revolted her. In fact her aversion to food was almost complete – one crystal of sugar placed by Dr Cloche on her tongue caused a vomiting fit lasting twenty minutes. When he took up her case shortly after her trauma, she had not eaten for weeks, and continued observation confirmed that in the remaining fourteen years of her life she neither ate nor drank at all. Domenica's stigmata developed in 1834; in her hands were solid nail-like forms that resembled the description of St Francis' wounds, her crown of thorns bled on Fridays, while the wound in her side gushed fresh arterial blood and serum. Periodically she suffered convulsing fits, striking herself fiercely with her fists; at other times her ecstasies were so serene they profoundly affected all who were present. A full description of the remarkable range of Domenica's phenomena was published by Dr Cloche in the *Annali Universali di Medicina*, November 1837. In a strictly religious context they would undoubtedly have been seen as miracles, so exactly do they conform to the phenomena of mysticism, yet Domenica appeared so ordinary. The Reverend T. W. Allies, who spent some time with her, expressed the unanimous opinion of her visitors: 'The impression conveyed to me . . . was more one of great suffering and resignation than of any extraordinary tokens of grace . . . nothing that I saw led me to suppose the lofty religious abstraction, the spiritual fervour, or superhuman yearning of the soul for God, which one looks for in a female saint' (*Journal in France*, 1849).

Because of the relationship between hysterical suggestibility and the suggestibility of good hypnotic subjects, there have been many attempts to prove that stigmata are the products of autosuggestion by experimentally reproducing the marks upon hypnotic subjects.

In general these experiments have failed since they could only produce sporadic and transient reddenings of the skin or insignificant bleeding, and only then with the strenuous urgings of the hypnotist.

And yet even the genuine stigmata involve a powerful subjective component which resembles the subliminal suggestibility of psychoneurosis. As a few quick examples, I should mention that the wounds of St Veronica Giuliani opened and bled at the command of her confessor, just as Louise Lateau and others could be instantly recalled from the deepest rapture by their superiors; the ferita of Anne Catherine Emmerich resembled the Y-shaped crucifix in the church at Coesfield

where she meditated as a child; and the scourge-marks of St Gemma Galgani were said to reproduce exactly the stripes on her favourite crucifix. Besides this, any comparison of cases soon shows up an endless variety of stigmata: the nail-wounds range from simple red spots to slash- or cross-shaped fissures to round, oval, square or oblong holes; 'nail-heads' have been in palms or on the backs of hands, on either left or right feet and even in the soles; feritas have similar variations and like the shoulder wound appear on the right or left side; and so on. As far as I know, no one has yet

attempted an analysis of the phenomena of stigmatism from the point of view of suggestibility and the kinds of initiating trauma (this would certainly be difficult since considerable biographical data on many of the stigmatics we have mentioned is either not re-

corded or has not yet been made available by the Vatican, and may never be), and studies of the hysterical aspects of stigmata have generally been sceptical to the point of uselessness or heavily biased toward hypnotic experiments. We need to define the 'stigmatic syndrome' more exactly and to be precise about the susceptibility of certain physical and personality types; about how the process of stigmatization is set in motion and how it is regulated and triggered. It certainly seems to conform more towards a personal idea of the Passion of Christ than to any historical event. And I have yet to see any account by the Church apologists of

In recent years the blind and heretical Spanish Archbishop, Clemente Dominguez, has manifested the major stigmata during ecstatic visions. These pictures show an ecstasy, the 'crown of thorns' and the ferita.

the great variety in form and location of stigmata. This is especially needed since these eccentric phenomena are held in dogma to be divinely impressed from the one original model.

It cannot be overlooked that there is a high morphological

correlation between the histories and phenomena of stigmatics and those of clinical hysteria; the differences are merely of degree and context. If the classical form of the stigmata is a motif derived from the crucifixion, one would look in vain for it outside the Christian influence. Freed from the necessity of direct comparison with the wounds of Christ, however, we do find that spontaneous surface lesions and other hysterical symptoms appear within other contexts in different cultures; for example the Buddhist and Hindu saints who are characterized by certain 'signs' and 'marks' which are foretold and which appear at birth or upon illumination; then

again we have the phenomena of the 'poltergeist girls', like Elenore Zugan, studied by Harry Price in the 1920s, whose skin showed weals, bites and even lettering when she believed she was being attacked by the devil. And what of the almost universal shamanistic practice of trance self-mutilation, in which bleeding, inflammation and infection are usually absent, the wound healing rapidly afterwards? The topic may be opened up far beyond our scope or space here, once we realize that the word 'hysteria' does not (as the Churchmen believe) 'explain away' stigmata, that it does not insult nor imply low- or weak-mindedness and that it is not incompatible with the greatest sanctity. And we still have to account for the well-documented phenomenon of stigmata remaining visible in incorrupt bodies, sometimes for centuries, and for the enigma of statues and icons that have been witnessed, photographed and analysed as they wept tears or bled from the traditional stigmata sites.

Stigmata continue to be recorded. Two recent examples are of special interest. Ten-year-old Cloretta Robinson, a black, non-Catholic American, was stigmatized in her hands for nineteen days in 1972. Two psychiatrists observed blood collecting under, then oozing through, a defined patch in her palms. Then there was Teresa Musco, who died aged thirty-three in 1976. She was a poor Italian seamstress who accurately predicted that she would die at the same age as Christ. She was stigmatized in a vision in 1969 and though normally illiterate, in her trances she would speak in Aramaic (usually to the Virgin Mary) or write out whole passages from the Bible. Her wounds pierced her hands. In her presence a statue of the Madonna was seen to weep blood; and after her death her body remained without rigor mortis for almost a week. A movement is under way to make her a saint.

THE TURIN SHROUD

All relics exert a mysterious spell. But one, the Holy Shroud of Turin, is a real mystery going back nearly 2000 years. It poses intriguing questions that are on the point of being answered.

A passionate interest in relics is common to all cultures and all ages. Only time separates the pious cannibal who consumes a dead hero's heart and the medieval bishop who tried to eat a relic of St Mary Magdalene. Only circumstances divide the crowds of pilgrims who roamed through the Middle Ages from the modern queues that form for the lying-in-state of a spiritual or temporal grandee.

True, the pilgrim's faith was a central part of his life, whereas our interest in a dead celebrity is, in most cases, only marginal. But we still, as we shuffle into crypt or cathedral, have a misty expectation of gaining something – some sort of emotional or spiritual renewal, however slight – from the process. Put another way, we expect some form of magic exercised by the revered remains to work; and, interestingly enough, it often seems to.

Interestingly, too, the magic appears to operate even in such secularly-orientated societies as communist China. A Peking wall-poster appeared recently that appealed for the removal of Chairman Mao's body from its much-honoured resting-place in Tien An Men Square. 'The people demand', the poster read, 'that we root out superstition and idol worship. Take away the crystal coffin and change the mausoleum into a memorial hall.' Again, only time and circumstances separate this appeal from those made by the church and state in history to congregations who persisted in honouring the wrong sort of saint.

Idol worship, holy cult, rank superstition: the belief in what could be called 'beneficent contagion' has gained some emotive labels since it first inserted itself into the human mind several millennia ago. It is a belief with enormous implications; but, for all that, it rests on an extremely simple premise. Its basis is the idea that a man's virtue, or holiness, or protective or healing powers, do not die with him; they continue to reside in his body and can be tapped by any believer who in some way makes contact with this corporeal shrine. Mere proximity is enough: the medieval pilgrim was satisfied if he could but gaze on the tomb of his cult-object.

If the body is dismembered, so the belief goes on, the power within it is not diminished; on the contrary, each part will be as full of potency as the whole. The same thing applies to anything that the cult-object touched while alive or, indeed, to anything that touches him after he is dead. All these inanimate containers of a supposedly-animate force – whole bodies, bones, hair and teeth, clothes, books, furniture, instruments of martyrdom, winding-sheets, coffins and (if the body is cremated) the ashes that are left – are dignified by the name of 'relics' and credited with the grace that once resided in their owners.

Crowds of pilgrims wait patiently in front of Turin Cathedral, final home of the much-travelled Holy Shroud.

Nor does the process of beneficient contagion stop there. Anything that has touched the relic or has been in its presence immediately takes on some of its power. Indeed, it may become a wonder-worker in its own right. When, for example, the Byzantine empress Constantina wrote to Pope Gregory the Great in the sixth century AD and asked him for the head of St Paul, the Pope refused. However, he softened the effect of his reply by enclosing a cloth that had touched the saintly head and that had now taken on a miraculous status of its own. When it was cut, observers had seen blood flowing from it.

At the time that this correspondence took place, Europe was in the grip of one of the greatest outbreaks of relics fever that the world has ever known. The eastern wing of the Christian Church was more fervent in its devotions than its western sister; but the West was soon to catch up. Before long, every Christian priest aimed to have a relic of some sort under his church's altar, and with good reason. Whether he liked it or not, a belief in relics and in their alleged power to work miracles formed the core of religion as experienced by the majority of his congregation – many of whom still carried memories of pagan temples and sacred groves in their blood. Holy bones and the like were venerated in every town and village and, unsurprisingly, a wholesale business in fakes arose to meet this explosion of demand.

As the Middle Ages progressed, there seemed at times to be no limit to the worshippers' gullibility and the relic-fakers' guile. Among the more unlikely relics listed during the period are the Virgin's milk, hairs from Noah's beard, feathers from Gabriel's wings, portions of the Ark and manna. Alongside them, though, stood a list of objects that were surrounded by a much heavier aura of both holiness and credibility. First and foremost, there was the True Cross, discovered

during the fourth century in Jerusalem by Helena, mother of the Emperor Constantine. By the standards of the time, its authenticity went without question: it had performed the miracle of curing a sick man. There was, too, the Crown of Thorns; there were the Nails and the Spear. And there were no less than forty-three Holy Shrouds, each one passionately credited by its devotees with being the genuine piece of linen that Joseph of Arimathea wrapped round Christ's body late on Good Friday afternoon.

Forty-three shrouds: were they *all* fakes? With one exception, it now seems impossible to tell. Some of them were undoubtedly 'doubles'; the same objects, noted at different centres of worship at different times. Others have been deliberately destroyed, while many have simply vanished. And, even when submitted to the most advanced testing techniques, there is little that a length of plain white cloth can tell us about the identity of a body that might have been wrapped in it nearly two thousand years go.

Furthermore – and still with that single exception – it no longer seems to matter. For a Catholic, indeed, the question of a holy relic's authenticity is to a large extent doctrinally irrelevant: it is not – or should not – be the relic that is revered but the person with whom it is associated. Only proven frauds are ruled out.

As for the rest of us, the general attitude towards specifically Christian relics was summed up over four hundred years ago by the philosopher Erasmus, who visited the noted English shrine of Walsingham and was shown an enormous finger-joint allegedly belonging to St Peter. 'Peter must have been a man of very great size,' Erasmus murmured – and then, not wishing to hurt anybody's feelings, gave the attendant a tip.

Like Erasmus, we preserve an attitude of polite and temperate scepticism.

When, however, we approach the exception among those forty-three shrouds of history, everything changes. To start with, it still exists; it can be seen and touched. In addition, it is literally covered with indications of its past history, some clear to read and some intensely baffling. If it is a fake, it is the most astonishing fake of all time. If it is genuine – the True Shroud, the *sindon* of the Gospels – then it is arguably the first visible proof of the Resurrection that man has been granted since the Gospel period; for some, indeed, it is proof that Christ did not die on the cross at all.

It has caused scholars to drop politeness in a flash and has brought sceptics out in a welter of feeling that is anything but temperate. And it now engages the fascinated attention of priests, doctors, artists, pathologists, photographers, newspapermen, scientists and the general public all over the world.

The object on which their

attentions are focused is, of course, the cloth that was once venerated in the remote French village of Lirey – better known today as the Holy Shroud of Turin.

A simple description of this extraordinary relic instantly makes nonsense of the word 'simplicity'. So few of its charac-

teristics are in any way comprehensible; so many are hedged around with profoundly disturbing question-marks. In appearance, the Shroud is a strip of ivory-coloured linen twill, 4.4 metres (14 feeet 3 inches) long and 1.1 metres (3 feet 7 inches) wide. Down its length runs a twin row of patches and burns, results of a fire that nearly destroyed it in 1532.

Between the two rows are a series of fainter, subtler stains that, seen from a distance, resolve themselves into the front-and-back image of a man, represented with his hands crossed over the base of the stomach.

This image – itself a light sepia colour – is spattered with reddish marks and spots : marks

Opposite : **worshippers prostrate themselves before the saint's image enthroned in St Peter's in Rome.** *Above and right :* **holy relics were frequently housed in lavishly-decorated reliquaries like these. The gold cross once belonged to the Byzantine emperor Justinian II.**

whose placing and shape correspond to the wounds sustained by Christ during the Passion. Its other most striking feature is that, the reddish marks apart, the whole stain-system is a negative one : that is, the parts that would show up as shadows on the body itself – the eye-sockets, the gaps between the fingers, the hollows at the backs of the knees – appear as

pale areas in the image on the cloth. The positive version of the image was not seen until, in 1898, a gifted amateur photographer called Secondo Pia stared into his developing tray and watched the true likeness of a face take shape before him.

All this is certain. But, from now on, the question-marks crowd thick and fast. On the scientific front, for example, tests made a few years ago have shown that the reddish blood-stains on the Shroud contain no trace of haemoglobin; 'it's not blood as we know blood,' says the Reverend David Sox, Episcopalian general secretary of the British Society for the Turin Shroud.

Studies of the Shroud's actual material have yielded results that are only slightly less enigmatic. It is certainly linen; it is certainly a herringbone weave. Tiny cotton fibres have been found mixed with the linen threads. It is known that flax was being grown, spun and woven by the ancient Egyptians, while cotton was in use four thousand years ago in the great civilizations of the Indus Valley; the herringbone weave appears – but in silk textiles only – round about the time of Christ and is connected with Syria. In the absence of carbon

dating (a question which will be discussed later), these facts combine to give a rough – extremely rough – idea of the earliest possible period when the cloth could have been manufactured, along with its place of origin. (Many museums possess fragments of ancient Egyptian linen, so the sheer number of years involved is no bar to the Shroud's putative survival over twenty centuries.)

What about the *latest* possible period? Simply put, this is the middle of the fourteenth century AD; but, again, the Shroud makes nonsense of simplicity. All we know is that it appeared at Lirey in France under obscure circumstances in the 1350s (perhaps) and first started to draw a throng of pilgrims in 1357 (probably). The first definite, first-person account of it comes in 1389.

Its owners were a less-than-wealthy family called de Charny; further research into their background and connections may clear away some of the fog round the dates involved. But where did they get it from? And how – given the intense interest in relics that had spread through Christendom from the fourth century onwards – had it contrived to lie hidden for all those years?

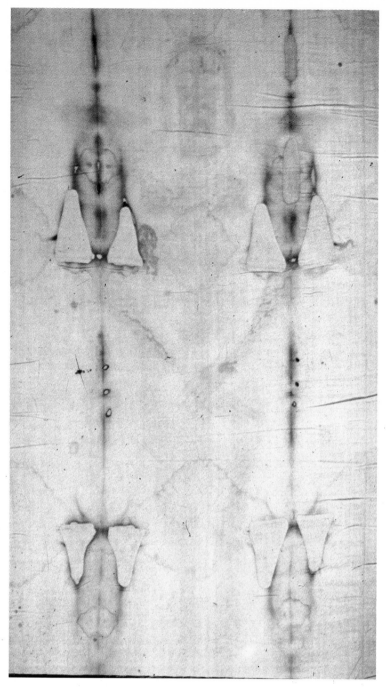

The Holy Shroud as it appears to the human eye *(above)* **and to the light-reversing eye of the camera. Like their predecessors, these recent photographs clearly show the startling change that takes place when the tone values of the negative image on the linen are reversed on the photographic negative. The expression of the Shroud face** *(right)* **remained hidden until the invention of photography.**

A partial answer to its pre-Lirey whereabouts has been provided by tests conducted by Swiss criminologist Dr Max Frei, who put fossilized pollen grains found on the Shroud under the electron microscope. But his results have posed a further question.

Analysis of the pollen has showed that, at some time during the 'missing' past of the Shroud, the ivory-coloured linen has been both in Palestine and in Turkey, notably in the Anatolian uplands. Proof of the Palestinian connection is crucial to such progress as has been made in determining the Shroud's authenticity, and the general link-up with Turkey is helpful, since a shroud that might well have been *the* Shroud attracted devotion in Constantinople at the beginning of the thirteenth century. (Our

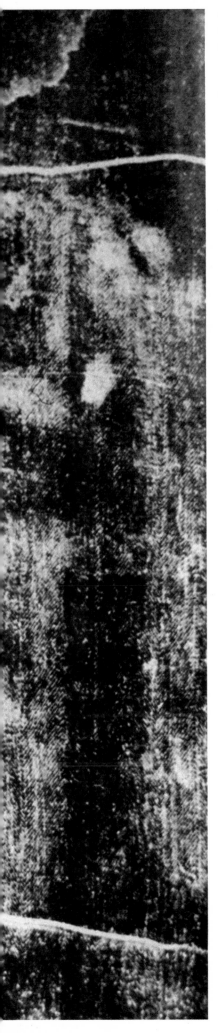

evidence for this is a report, dated 1204, from a French crusader called Robert de Clari. In Constantinople, ran his account, 'there was among others a monastery called Our Lady St Mary of Blachernae, where the shroud which had been wrapped round Our Lord was kept; every Friday, this was held up straight so that one could easily see the face [or *figure*; the text is ambiguous] of Our Lord on it.' Unhelpfully, de Clari added that no one knew what became of it after the Crusaders had taken the city.) But what was this relic of immense devotional and doctrinal importance doing in the wastelands of the Anatolian steppe?

Where, when, what . . . such answers as have been found to three of the five classic questions asked by information-seekers bring imponderables enough in their train when applied to the Shroud. But the riddles involved here seem relatively straightforward compared with those surrounding the questions of how and who. *How* was the negative image of a man – an image that, furthermore, is anatomically accurate in all its proportions – transferred to the cloth? And, if it is not the work of a forger, *whose image is it?*

Between the time of the Shroud's final transfer from France to Turin in 1578 and its public showing in 1898 – the last of no more than five during the whole of the nineteenth century – none of these momentous points arose. The Shroud was the Shroud: an object of deepest veneration on the part of clergy and laity alike and the most prized possession of the ducal house of Savoy, whose members had acquired it from the de Charny family in the mid-fifteenth century. It is, in fact, still owned by Umberto di Savoia, the former king of Italy who now lives in exile in Portugal.

From the beginning of the twentieth century, however, the Shroud's importance as an object of devotion has been almost overshadowed by the mystery of its sheer existence.

The turning-point was the moment in the exposition year when Secondo Pia, commissioned to take the first-ever photographs of the Shroud, saw what he believed to be the Holy Face appear on a photographic plate. The pattern of stains, with their light-values reversed on Pia's negative, had resolved itself not into a mere image but into a portrait: a portrait that was staggeringly lifelike.

The revelation caused intense excitement. As Pia himself had found, it was above all the face on the Shroud – the face as it really was – that attracted attention; it still is the face that attracts one's attention today. While the huge technical riddles set by the relic have been the intellectual spur to inquiry, the expression on that face has undoubtedly been the emotional one. One way or another, it is impossible to remain unmoved by it.

It was, therefore, natural that the authenticity battle should be joined almost immediately after Pia's discovery was made known. The rumour went round that the extraordinary portrait on the negative was the result of a mistake – or, worse, of discreet re-touching on Pia's part. Pia, who took pride in the fact that he never re-touched a picture, was understandably distressed; he and his work were not to be totally vindicated until 1931, when a professional photographer, Giuseppe Enrie, took a further set of pictures and got the same result.

Nor was this all. At the turn of the century, historical evidence came forward that looked likely to close the Shroud controversy before it had fairly started. Ulysse Chevalier, a French priest and historian of formidable academic reputation, unearthed the fact that the Shroud's authenticity had been queried before, back in its Lirey period. In 1389, Pierre d'Arcis, Bishop of Troyes, became concerned by the hordes of Shroud pilgrims who flocked into his diocese and by their belief that this was indeed the True Shroud of Christ. He himself was convinced that it was a fake, imposed – like so many at that time – on an unsuspecting populace for the purpose of making money. After fruitless negotiations with the de Charny family, he wrote a memorandum of strong complaint to the Pope; and it was this letter that, among a mass of other corroborating documents, Chevalier brought to light.

D'Arcis went straight to the meat of his argument. The Lirey Shroud and its reputation, he said, had worried his predecessor too:

'The Lord Henry of Poitiers, of pious memory, then Bishop of Troyes, becoming aware of this, and urged by many prudent persons to take action, as indeed was his duty, set himself earnestly to work. . . . Eventually, after diligent inquiry and examination, he discovered the fraud and how the said cloth had been cunningly painted, the truth being attested by the artist who had painted it, to wit, that it was a work of human skill and not miraculously wrought or bestowed.'

So it was a fake after all. Or was it? Had d'Arcis reported his predecessor correctly? Had Henry, for reasons of his own, invented his discovery of the fraud, the artist and the method? Or – more sinisterly – had he forced some wretched brush-wielder to 'attest the truth'? An explanation must exist. One obvious difficulty in the way of a painter-forger lies in the negative nature of the image itself: how could an artist produce such a startling positive portrait when, in the absence of the light-reversing eye of the camera, he could not see what he was doing? Much more important, however, is the fact that the Shroud has yielded no identifiable trace of paint. There are no brushstrokes, either, nor any other signs of a medieval painter at work. Whatever made the stains is still a mystery.

The first attempt at explaining how the image could have been produced naturally came when another Frenchman brought a different approach to the problem: that of science. In the same year that Chevalier published his historical evidence on the Shroud, biologist and all-but-professional artist Paul Vignon started a series of carefully-recorded Shroud experiments. The book in which he described his work and conclusions became an instant bestseller when it came out in 1902.

In the main, Vignon attacked his inquiry by trying to answer the questions 'how?' and 'what?' 'Our whole argument',

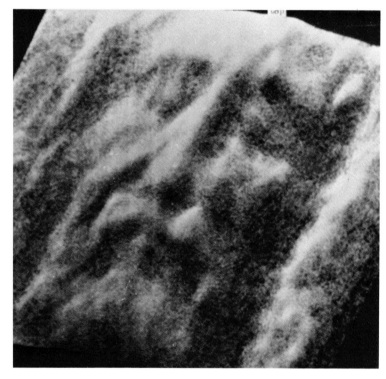

he wrote, 'hangs upon whether we are able to prove that the Impressions on the Shroud have been spontaneously produced, and that they are *not* the work of man' (Vignon's capitals and italics). To do this, he brought both artistic and scientific techniques into play.

He tried painting a picture on a cloth of about the same suppleness and delicacy as the Shroud (the Shroud's texture is, in fact, very light and fine). If he used enough pigment to achieve results, 'the paint came off at the least touch as soon as the cloth was folded.'

He experimented with the 'contact theory': he put on a

false beard, carefully smeared both his face and beard with red chalk, lay down on a laboratory table and directed his assistants to stretch a piece of linen over his face. The results, both actual and photographic, were ludicrously bad. 'One thing seems certain,' he pointed out; 'if the forger at the Abbey of Lirey had been reduced to work in the way we did, he would never have obtained a portrait which could stand photography. On the Shroud, if the features are faint in places, the proportions remain admirable; and the powerful effect they produce is mainly due to the perfect harmony which they present as a whole.' (Experiments by other researchers on these lines have pointed to exactly the same conclusion.)

Vignon then turned to another possibility: that of projection. Meticulous checking had shown him that the stains on the cloth corresponded to those parts of the body that were either in contact with it or within one centimetre ($\frac{1}{2}$ inch) of it. Their heaviness was in inverse proportion to the distance involved: when this distance rose above one centimetre ($\frac{1}{2}$ inch), the stains were absent. They seemed, therefore, to have been caused by 'some

emanation from the body'.

Vignon referred to the Bible and asked himself what was needed to make the myrrh and aloes used at the Entombment react in such a way as to produce a negative image on linen. The answer, experiment proved, was ammonia, given off by the body on to a cloth already soaked in a mixture of aloes and olive oil. And this ammonia, Vignon went on to assert, had come from sweat on the body itself: sweat which, as is usual with a person in fever or great pain, was highly charged with urea.

'We now know what name to give to these impressions, if any one seeks to coin a new word,' Vignon concluded; 'they are *vaporographic prints*' (Vignon's italics).

The vaporograph theory does not, in fact, command immense support among today's sindonologists, who tend

to query the chemistry involved. But many of Vignon's other findings – for all that they were hotly attacked on publication – have been borne out several times over by subsequent inquiries, and none more so than his deductions from the medical evidence of the Shroud. He carefully scrutinized all the 'bloodstains' shown on Pia's photographs and came to two

conclusions. The first was that they corresponded precisely to the injuries inflicted up to and even after death on a crucifixion victim. The second was that no medieval forger, steeped in Christian tradition and lacking any accurate knowledge of anatomy, would or could have been able to match such precision.

One of the Vignon findings

that has since received overwhelming backing from later researchers concerns the placing of the large nail-wound in the hand. It is not, as tradition would dictate, in the hand itself but in the wrist; Vignon pointed out that a body hanging by nails through the palms of the hands would soon have been torn off the cross by its own weight.

He also suggested the cause –

again, now generally accepted – for the mass of marks shaped like small dumb-bells that cover most parts of the image: they could only have come from the Roman *flagrum*, a two- or three-lashed whip on which each lash terminated in twin pellets of metal or bone. The instrument that had scourged Christ now had a name.

Medical investigators have since added considerably to the hideous list of connections between the Crucifixion and the clinical evidence of the Shroud. For example, the large stain made by the wound in the side has been shown to agree with both the Gospel account and with modern medical knowledge. In places, the stain has not 'taken', and the inference is that the blood was mixed with a watery fluid. St John wrote that 'one of the soldiers with a spear pierced his side, and forthwith came there out blood

Opposite, far left: **the Shroud face, as seen by computer.** *Left:* **painting of the Veronica, the cloth said to have been imprinted with Christ's face on Good Friday.** *Top:* **Good Friday itself, represented during Easter celebrations at Granada.** *Above:* **the Shroud casket in Turin.**

and water'; twentieth-century doctors, while disagreeing as to the nature of the watery fluid itself, accept that its presence in such a case would have been entirely likely.

In addition, the angle of the blood-marks on each arm is what would be expected on a body that, when living, had been suspended in the crucifixion position. And the enlargement of the chest shown on

the Shroud is consistent with the ultimate cause of death: asphyxiation.

Here, then, sindonologists appear to have another Shroud certainty to add to that somewhat meagre list: the man in the Shroud had indeed died in exactly the same way as Christ. The chances that history might contain another crucifixion victim who exhibited all the wounds of the Passion have been calculated mathematically, and the odds against such a coincidence run into the billion range. But even a probability of this order is not quite good enough – and it only answers one part of the riddle. Vignon, working on his turn-of-the-century evidence, felt that he had discovered both the method and the medium of the image's manufacture and from there proceeded via his medical deductions to come down in favour of the Shroud's authenticity. Modern authorities, though by and large convinced by the clinical evidence that has been brought forward, are uneasily aware that the questions of time and place still remain to be answered – while the mysteries of both medium and method have returned to give them difficulties of a prodigious order. They accept the near-impossibility of the Shroud's being in any way 'the work of man' – but, after that, the mists come down.

It goes without saying that firm, indisputable answers to all four questions need to be found before even a disputable answer is risked to the fifth: the crucial one of 'who?'

During the early years of the Shroud controversy, the implications of the d'Arcis memorandum seemed to give heavier firing-power to the anti-Shroud group, and it was only after the appearance of Enrie's photographs (which were much better than Pia's) that the body of evidence in favour of the relic's authenticity began to grow. At last, medical and scientific experts had a series of high-definition pictures to work on, enlargements and details.

(Experts who have gone to work on a different front – the Scriptural one – have practically argued themselves to a standstill. There is nothing in the Gospels that gives incontrovertible proof of the Shroud's authenticity or lack of it. And the argument first put forward in the d'Arcis letter – 'if it had been true, it was quite unlikely that the holy Evangelists would have omitted to record it' – remains potent.)

In Paris, a surgeon, Pierre Barbet, examined the highly-magnified picture of the wrist-wound and then experimented on an amputated arm to check whether a nail could have been driven through the tightly-interlocking mass of wristbones at that point. He found that it could: it penetrated and enlarged a minute gap known anatomically as the 'Space of Destot'. A further startling discovery was that the nail, as it went through, stimulated the median nerve in the wrist and caused the thumb to jerk inwards towards the palm. On the Shroud, the thumbs are invisible.

In Milan, Dr Giovanni Judica-Cordiglia, professor of forensic medicine, studied the Shroud wounds and produced a substantial list of facial contusions and swellings that, again, are consistent with the handling of Christ described in the Bible.

Back in France again, Vignon returned to the fray, this time working on the historical question. A close examination of hundreds of early Christian icons had shown him that they not only presented the face of Christ according to a set pattern but that this pattern included up to twenty small features that were seemingly pointless except in one context. They looked like stylized reproductions of marks on the Shroud itself.

Among them were: an 'open box' shape between the eyebrows; two V-shapes, within and below it; a short line across the forehead; another line across the throat (in reality, a double crease in the material);

a distinct fork in the beard; and a deep groove running from nose to upper lip.

The earliest icons in which this pattern occurs date back, Vignon found, to the sixth century AD and to one particular inspiration: an image known as the Holy Face of Edessa. (Edessa, now called Urfa, lies just north of the modern Syrian-Turkish border.) Significantly, the Byzantine Greeks called this image *acheiropoetos*, or 'not made by hands'. While the Holy Face – also known as the Holy Mandylion – appears to have vanished, copies of it survive to prove that it is the Edessan image that seems to have introduced those artists' memories of the Shroud into the iconographic tradition. The inference is that the Shroud has been connected in both time and place with the lost Holy Face.

This suggestion, which got a mixed reception when it was published just before the Second World War, has since received some intense attention from Shroud specialists and, at the moment of writing, looks likely to provide the best approach that can be made to cracking the joint historical/geographical puzzle. The most recent contribution on this front comes from British sindonologist Ian Wilson, who has put forward the theory that the Shroud and the Holy Mandylion were one and the same thing; that the Mandylion was the Shroud folded and embroidered in such a way that only the face showed. After a proven sojourn in Edessan hands of at least four hundred years, the Mandylion was brought from Edessa to Constantinople in 944 AD; like the shroud noted by Robert de Clari, it vanished from sight during the Fourth Crusade in 1204.

One fact that corroborates the Mandylion theory is Dr Frei's discovery of pollen on the Shroud that had indisputably come from plants native to Anatolia. It was a fact that had been unavailable to all sindonologists working before the mid-1970s. Right up to 1969, indeed, they had nothing more concrete to work on than Shroud photographs; the actual relic itself, rolled up as it was within a heavily-barred shrine in Turin Cathedral, was not available for reference.

In 1969, however, the Shroud's custodians allowed sindonology to take a giant step forward: they permitted a group of priests and scientists (which included Professor Judica-Cordiglia) to make the first-ever physical examination of the relic. The group recommended that small samples should be taken from the cloth for further examination and, the day after the Shroud's 1973 exposition on international television, this was done.

The tests on these samples showed, among other things, that those tiny fibres of cotton were present in the material; that the 'bloodstains' did not contain haemoglobin; and that the 'blood' had not seeped into the spaces between the linen fibres – a fact that seems to rule out a liquid staining agent, whether blood, paint or anything else.

One testing technique that was not used was the well-known Carbon-14 dating method. Journalist Robert Wilcox, who was researching his book, *Shroud*, at the time of the TV showing, had the reason explained to him. 'The test,' said Monsignor José Cottino, spokesman for the Archbishop of Turin, 'involves burning a piece of the material, and too large a piece would have to be destroyed. And there is no assurance that the test would be accurate. Carbon 14 can only give you a date accurate within two hundred years, plus or minus.'

So the search for a reasonably definitive answer to the time question had been ruled out from the start. And, in spite of the 1973 Commission's work, the questions of medium and method remained as obscure as ever.

Despite this, a new 'how?' theory was soon to start attracting attention, and it is in this area that the biggest Shroud breakthroughs of the future may well lie. In essence, the theory dates back to well before the 1973 examinations, but its arrival on the Shroud scene went largely unnoticed until long afterwards. It has its origins in the kitchen of a fellow-contributor to this book, Geoffrey Ashe.

Above right: **the Holy Shroud of Besançon, a copy of the Lirey Shroud that became famous on its own account.** *Right:* **the empty shroud of Easter morning, displayed during the Granada celebrations.** *Above:* **the Holy Shroud goes on exhibition in Turin Cathedral in 1978.**

brighter parts correspond to the raised areas, where the body would have touched the cloth or been close to it. The greater the distance, the darker the corresponding bit of cloth. This gives a more or less correct gradation of light and shade. The positive – the image actually on the Shroud – is the opposite: the closer, the darker. I asked myself: how could an

Ashe – 'I am *not* a sindonologist' – was in 1961 inspired by pure curiosity to attempt to make an image similar to that on the Shroud. 'The primary reason,' he says,

'why the Shroud negative is a better picture is that the

object mark a cloth in that way?'

The answer, he felt, might lie in scorching by heat or by any other form of radiation that would darken the cloth with varying degrees of intensity according to distance. To

108

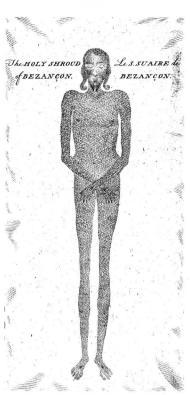

The HOLY SHROUD of BEZANÇON.   Le S. SUAIRE de BEZANÇON.

test his hypothesis, he took an ornamental horse-brass, heated it on a kitchen gas-ring and dropped a handkerchief over it. 'The result was a scorch-impression which appeared at a glance to have the main Shroud characteristics. Photography confirmed: the negative was the "good" picture of the horse-brass.'

He does not believe that the Shroud could have been faked by heat-scorching. Supposing, then, that it is authentic? 'It faces us', Ashe goes on, 'with a choice between the miraculous and the incomprehensible – the Resurrection, or total mystery.' It is conceivable, contrary though it would be to all known natural laws, that the Resurrection of the body of Christ

might have involved a burst of some sort of radiation; 'We have no means of knowing.'

Since the mid-1970s, this radiation or 'scorch-mark' theory has gained enormous ground, and it is now the main one current. 'The next chapter of the book', comments Canon Sox, 'has to be written by scientists'; and sindonology has indeed now taken off into the upper scientific stratosphere. Spectroscopy, photon energies, neutron fluxes, Kirlian photography, flash photolysis: the terms involved go way beyond the layman's ordinary vocabulary, just as the concepts behind them lie outside all but a specialist's understanding.

The equipment needed, in contrast, belongs not so much

to the stratosphere as to space itself. It was, for instance, with a VP-8 Image Analyser used in moonshot research that, in 1976, two young USAF captains produced one of the most startling facts yet known about the Shroud. Drs John Jackson and Eric Jumper put a transparency of the Shroud portrait through the analyser and instantly got an accurate three-dimensional image, shown in low relief on the instrument's screen. No photograph used on its own has ever produced such a result before.

In 1978, the quest for the truth about the Shroud moved into top scientific gear. The relic was submitted to an examination for X-ray fluorescence (which should show what chemical elements are present in the image); to infra-red and ultra-violet photography (much used in detecting art forgeries); to an X-ray radiographic test; and to a whole series of camera-calls for computer analysis. A minute sample was also taken for ion microprobe analysis; again, the hope is to detect what the stains on the Shroud are actually made of. The carbon-dating issue has again been brought up – the testing techniques used have recently been much refined – and it appears that, this time, there is a chance that permission may be given for the test.

The results of the tests that have taken place already will not be known until the end of 1979 at the earliest; 1980 is a much more likely date. What they will tell us is anyone's guess. 'It's still the scorch theory that stands more than the others,' says Canon Sox, 'but that could all collapse with the analyses that are being made.'

One thing, however, is certain. The Shroud of Turin is not going to divulge its central mystery as easily as that. 'The realm of the unknown will narrow with each step gained,' wrote Vignon in 1902. Only when it has narrowed to a single point will the secret of the Shroud be revealed.

CONTEMPORARY MYSTERIES

MONSTERS OF LAND AND SEA

The 'creature' in Loch Ness is one of many monsters persistently reported by eye-witnesses. The evidence – faked or real – for 'Nessie', Bigfoot, Yeti and the others is looked at here.

Perhaps one of the most puzzling and extraordinary of modern mysteries concerns the reports stemming from the vast mountain regions of south-central Asia and from North America, of huge, upright, hair-covered two-legged creatures; reports that are neither accepted as real by the public at large nor dismissed as fantasy. Some evidence undoubtedly exists for these unlikely beings, and there are those within the scientific community today who would go so far as to admit to their existence, even if the 'establishment' view is contrary. But if a balanced assessment is to be made, we do need to know something of the history as well as the more recent data concerning these phenomena. In short, precisely who or what are we talking about? And, where should we first look for evidence?

In the mighty Himalayas and the associated ranges that stretch for 2900 km (1800 miles) both east and west across the northern borders of Afghanistan, Pakistan, Kashmir, India and the states of Nepal, Sikkm, Bhutan and Assam, a

Left: **the mighty Himalayas, home of the 'Abominable Snowman'.** *Above:* **'Snowman' relics – a dried hand from Pangboche monastery, and a faked scalp.**

legend has existed for centuries among the local people of a huge, shaggy bipedal creature. Occasionally it makes raiding forays, killing Yaks by tearing out their throats and eating parts of them, or grubbing for moss beneath the frozen wastes. The outside world knew nothing of the mystery surrounding this somewhat unlikely creature until September 1921 when a Mount Everest expedition led by a British Army colonel spotted some dark shapes crossing a snowfield high above them. Colonel Howard Bury and his companions watched through binoculars from the 5180 metres (17000 feet) Lhapka-La Pass,

and when they climbed up to the snowfield the next day, some 1500 metres (5000 feet) above the sighting point, they found enormous footprints in the snow, about three times larger than human prints. The Sherpa porters at once stated that these had been made by the *Metoh-Kangmi*, the hairy man-like creature of legend which their people feared.

In Bury's report, which was telegraphed to his representative in India from Katmandu, it seems there was a misspelling of the word *metoh*, which was interpreted *metch*, meaning 'abominable' (*kangmi* means snowman). Eventually, when the story was published

in the *Calcutta Statesman*, the name 'Abominable Snowman' was seized on by the world's press. *Metoh-Kangmi* was the Tibetan name used by the Sherpa porters, and its romantic but cumbersome English mistranslation has now gradually come to be replaced by the native Nepalese term 'Yeti'.

Between 1921 and 1951 there were numerous reports of sightings, and of footprints made by Yetis, and interesting research was done into native history and legend. Then, in November 1951, Eric Shipton and Michael Ward, two experienced mountaineers whose word could not be doubted, made history when they pub-

Left: **photograph of a bi-pedal 'Yeti' track melting out in the snow and** *(above)*, **mystery 'Apemen' are the source of much interest and speculation. Not all are genuine, but some appear to have features which are difficult to explain away and should not be treated with disdain by scientists.** *Below:* **the legendary Himalayan peaks.**

lished photographs of footprints in the *Illustrated London News*. Exploring the Menlung Glacier at about 6000 metres (20000 feet), they had found bi-pedal tracks of footprints, quite unlike any they had ever seen before, measuring 330 mm (13 inches) by 203 mm (8 inches) and continuing for almost 1.5 km (1 mile). Such evidence could hardly be ignored.

Since then, many people have regarded the Abominable Snowman or Yeti as a real creature; there have been many reports of it, and major expeditions have taken the field to search for it. In 1954–5 the London *Daily Mail* spent thousands of pounds trying to

get to the root of the mystery. With the aid of porters, zoologists and a famous animal-collector they scoured the passes and snow-scapes but retired exhausted without any clear evidence to support their belief that the Yeti really exists.

To some extent these adventures have been confused by the discovery of dried remains of Yeti hands and arms and of a supposed scalp kept as a relic by the Buddhist monks at a monastery – which has been proved to be a rather subtle fake. There is considerable competition between monasteries in this area to own such relics, because, although the Yeti is not considered holy, its

remains carry with them a certain local prestige and on occasion, financial benefit.

Despite all the difficulties and setbacks however, and the technical pros and cons argued interminably by anthropologists and zoologists, a sparse flow of reports from this vast and rarely explored area continues to suggest that the Yeti is not entirely a figment of the imagination.

In May 1975 a press story from Nepal described an attack made on a cow and three yaks by a huge two-legged creature said to be over 2 metres (7 feet) tall. Witnessed by a local girl of seventeen, the enormously powerful hair-covered creature tore the throat out of the cow, killed the yaks by smashing their heads with its huge fists and ripped one apart, gnawing at its carcass. A police inspector confirmed the story stating, 'I'm convinced the girl saw a Yeti – no beast I know could have mutilated her animals that way.' Later he found the Yeti's footprints which measured 355 mm (14 inches) by 150 mm (6 inches) at the widest part, as well as two hand-prints; these were not human prints and were deeply impressed, suggesting an animal of great weight.

In 1977 the London *Sunday Express* published another strange account of an intruder which rummaged through a food rucksack outside the small tent of two Himalayan mountaineers, pitched on a slope at 5180 metres (17000 feet). Both men were in their sleeping bags and huddled down petrified with fright – not daring to venture out when they heard the scuffling and growling sounds outside. At first light they found two sets of huge 305 mm (12-inch) footprints in the snow, one approaching, the other leaving. The only food missing was a single carton of thirty-six bars of chocolate, which had been removed complete with plastic bag. There were no signs of paper or plastic debris – which ruled out a bear as the culprit, because a bear would have at once ripped the pack to shreds to get at the food inside. Furthermore, the tracks they photographed bore a marked resemblance to those previously catalogued as the Yeti's.

Again, both witnesses were men of repute in the climbing world. Their testimony and photographs did no more than add another tantalizing question-mark to the whole controversy.

In comparison with the mists and mystery of the Himalayas, the North American continent seems at first glance to be an unlikely hiding-place for a giant unknown two-legged species of primate. Yet, if the facts and fables are analysed, it appears that there is a case for supposing that certain wilderness areas of both Canada and the United States do contain exactly that. Like the Yeti, however, the more human North American monsters have been known about by local Indian tribes for a very long time and have been given Indian names. The two best known are 'Sasquatch', from Canada's west coast mountain regions of British Columbia, and 'Omah', just over the American border to the south.

Descriptions again indicate the presence of a giant hair-covered upright bi-pedal creature, generally man-like in appearance but far more massive, standing 2.5 metres (8–9 feet) tall and leaving huge striding footprints up to 500 mm (20 inches) long and 250 mm (10 inches) across, and walking flat-footed, with evidence of a very big toe and four regular smaller toes. The anatomy of the footprint is not truly human, however. These creatures are popularly known in America as 'Bigfoot' – which is apt. Many thousands of prints have been found and hundreds of sightings have been reported over the last hundred and fifty years, again by reliable people.

The truly 'impossible' nature

of Bigfoot, both anthropologically and zoologically, tends, as in the case of the Yeti, to make scientists wary of getting too close to the 'phenomenon' and the evidence which supports it. However, there are a few exceptions, and some splendid analytical work has been published by Dr Grover Krantz, in particular on a dramatic set of prints known as the 'Bossburg prints', found in October 1969 in Washington. These numbered over a thousand in all and included the prints of a deformed left foot which Dr Krantz found had subtle characteristics in keeping with those of a classic club-foot deformity. In his notes he makes the balanced statement that 'all good quality bigfoot prints must have been made by one or the other of two possible agencies. Either they are real footprints of a gigantic sub-human primate, or else they are faked as a hoax. (Only very vague prints could be confused with those of bears.)'

Another scientist who has written on the subject is Dr John Napier, an acknowledged expert on primate biology, anatomy and anthropology, who has held posts at the Smithsonian Institute and the British Museum. His book *Bigfoot, the Yeti and Sasquatch in myth and reality*, presents a mass of evidence, information and some conclusions which leave the reader 'sitting on the fence' – in the same position, in fact, as the author who, like other investigators, found himself on the horns of a dilemma when assessing the physical evidence of the footprints. As Dr Napier says in his book:

'The dilemma is simple enough. Either some of the footprints are real, or all are fakes. If they are fakes then an explanation invoking legend and folklore memory is adequate to explain the mystery. But if any one of them is real then as scientists we have a lot to explain. Among

A 2.3 metre (7½ foot) tall female Bigfoot filmed in colour at Bluff Creek, California, in 1967 by Roger Patterson.

other things we shall have to re-write the story of human evolution . . .'

With rare exceptions Bigfoot has managed to evade the camera – and the few photographs that exist are usually so blurred as to be almost useless. However, there is one startling exception, the now famous Patterson Film, shot on 16-mm colour movie film by Roger Patterson while out Bigfoot searching on horseback in the remote northern Californian forest, with his associate Bob Gimlin in autumn 1967. The two men surprised a huge female Bigfoot crouching by a stream in the dried-up Bluff Creek Valley. The horses reared, unsaddling both men, but Patterson recovered from his fall and grabbing a 16-mm Bolex movie camera ran towards the creature, which had risen to stride off through the forest, swinging a mighty pair of arms as it twisted its huge shoulders and body trunk to look squarely at the intruders. In seconds it disappeared among the trees but not before about 6 metres (20 feet) of film had been exposed. Subsequent study showed the film to be clear, if a little jerky – and it portrayed for all to see a massive upright two-legged creature, with fur-covered pendulous breasts, pronounced buttocks, a somewhat conically shaped head set on great shoulders without any visible neck, obviously alive and immensely powerful. Later analysis has suggested a height of up to 2 metres (7 feet) and a weight of perhaps 225 kg (500 lbs) or more. Footprints left behind in the silt were 380 mm (14½ inches) long with 1 metre (41 inch) stride – modest by Bigfoot standards. Arguments about whether the Patterson film is of a man in a monkey suit or the real thing go on to this day. If it is the former, then it is a very, very cleverly executed hoax; if the latter, a uniquely important photographic proof of a tremendous natural discovery, yet to be accepted by science.

Reports of Bigfoot in other parts of the United States and Canada have been recorded – which, if they are true, suggest that groups of the creatures have wandered across the continent at some time in the past, to live in different areas of wilderness. A case in point is Everglades, in Florida, an area of over two and a half thousand square kilometres (a thousand square miles) of primeval swampland, crawling with wildlife. It is a perfect hiding-place, and more than a hundred reports have been recorded here, with footprints. There have been stories of actual encounters with Bigfoot too, that are hard to dismiss, like the *Miami News* account of a man who hit the 'Skunk Ape' (as it is known locally) with his car, putting a dent in the fender. He called the police who sent up a helicopter, and three hours later a patrolman saw 'a large shadowy figure, maybe 2·5 metres (8 feet) tall run off the road and into the Glades by the canal'. The policeman was understandably shaken and decided 'I wasn't going in there after him'. Local Seminole Indian tribes know of the Skunk Ape, which they call 'Sandman', and some of their older people still regard him as sacred.

One thing common to all the Bigfoot stories – including the Yeti – is that it really does smell abominable. It is also said to make high-pitched whistling calls, to be non-aggressive and omnivorous. Family groups have been seen, and it may be that Bigfoot has already been shot and his body concealed by the shooter, fearing a charge of murder; for at close quarters the creatures seem more human than animal, although they live like animals out of doors, foraging for food.

The greatest contribution to the search for Bigfoot, to the arduous fieldwork on the mystery and to disseminating new information is undoubtedly made by the Bigfoot Information Center at Hood River, Oregon. It issues a monthly bulletin, *Bigfoot News*, which has a growing circulation of several thousand copies. The editors, Peter Byrne and Celia Kileen, are true explorers, dedicated to the full-time pursuit of Bigfoot, with the aim of establishing him as an endangered legally protected species of primate of near-human character. They spend nine months of each year in the Pacific north-west, where Bigfoot reports are most numerous, and three months or so leading 'white water' safaris down virtually unexplored mountain rivers in Nepal, home of the elusive Yeti. Peter Byrne's book, *The Search for BIG FOOT – Monster, Myth or Man,* is a definitive study.

An overall view of Bigfoot leads the impartial observer to believe in the existence of these primates and to conclude that the evidence for them is more detailed and extensive than that for the Yeti in the Himalayas. At the same time, however, it would be wise to regard all the evidence critically; false foot-prints, men in monkey suits and other ingenious hoaxes have from time to time confused the researchers and searchers in the field, and although it is generally quite easy to spot false evidence, the garbled accounts of it which so often find an outlet in the 'nonsense press' create an atmosphere of incredulity. Despite these problems, and indeed the truly incredible nature of the real evidence, it seems likely that both the Yeti and the Bigfoot will continue to occupy the minds of certain *bona fide* scientists and the more general interest of the public.

Perhaps the most controversial, and certainly the best documented and researched, aquatic mystery is the fabled Loch Ness Monster, beloved by millions around the world.

View looking westward down Loch Ness from a boat stationed half-way along its 38 km (24 mile) length.

The fabulous beast – nick-named 'Nessie' – lives, so we are told, in the deep black waters of Loch Ness in the Scottish Highlands. The Loch is a giant puddle of fresh water which has formed in the trough of the Great Glen Fault, which stretches across the face of the Highlands, linking the western and eastern seaboards through the line of the Caledonian Ship Canal and a chain of three lakes, or lochs, as they are known in Scotland.

Loch Ness is by far the deepest of the three and extends in a narrow and straight line for 38 km (24 miles). More than a third of it goes down to over 200 metres (700 feet), more than twice the depth of the North Sea, and in places it

is deeper than that; the maximum depth recorded on sonar is 290 metres (975 feet). Six rivers flow into it, but only one flows out – the River Ness, which winds its way through a luxuriant valley to Inverness, the ancient capital city of the Highlands, and so on into the tidal salty waters of the Moray Firth.

Loch Ness has a surface area of 5260 hectares (13000 acres) and contains three times as much water as any other lake in Great Britain – fresh water from valleys, tributary lochs and rivers and countless 'burns', cascading precipitous gutters which flood in stormy weather lacing the mountain slopes with white wisps of feathery water looking for all the world like

strands of 'witches hair'. It is a strange place, a place of contrasts forever changing its face and mood, from the sombre and sinister to colour and light, from glass calm waterscape to white-capped wavetops blown by winds down the funnel of the Great Glen Fault. A colourful flow of visitors in their cars enjoy its majesty during the brief tourist season then leave it all but abandoned for nine months of the year.

Sparsely populated today, Loch Ness is steeped in history. For centuries it has marked the ebb and flow of human settlement, internecine strife, rebellion, piracy and invasion. In folklore it has made a home for the 'Great Water Horse' of ancient Highland legend, the

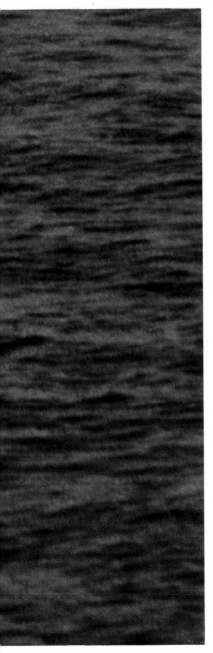

dreaded 'Kelpie' or 'Eigh-Uisge' in the Gaelic language, known today as the 'Loch Ness Monster' by practically everyone.

Surprisingly enough this title was only acquired fairly recently, in the early 1930s, when a new 'A' class road was constructed from one end of the loch to the other. Before that there had only been an inadequate, winding single-track road along which 'motor-cars' made a perilous journey. When workmen arrived in numbers, they felled the trees at the lochside and blasted a terrace from the rockface on which the new road perched. The blasting and the cascades of rock that plunged to the bottom of the loch revealed a unique view of the water and gave rise to numerous reports of something

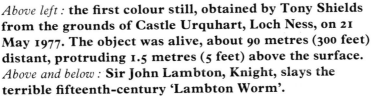

Above left: **the first colour still, obtained by Tony Shields from the grounds of Castle Urquhart, Loch Ness, on 21 May 1977. The object was alive, about 90 metres (300 feet) distant, protruding 1.5 metres (5 feet) above the surface.** *Above and below:* **Sir John Lambton, Knight, slays the terrible fifteenth-century 'Lambton Worm'.**

large moving on the surface, something which had no right to be there at all, for, with the exception of the occasional stag swimming across from one side to the other, the largest living species was salmon. But the reports described something that did not look like a stag, a salmon or any other known animal for that matter – a creature with a small head, a long serpentine neck, a long and flexible body with a tail, and two pairs of limbs or paddles.

This animal, or these animals (for on occasion more than one was seen, suggesting a breeding colony) looked disturbingly like one of the species of extinct marine saurians, known as Plesiosaurs, which were supposed to have died out seventy million years ago, during the Cretacious Period.

On occasion witnesses described long and narrow V wakes, with nothing visible at the apex and no boat in sight. Sometimes the small head and neck was seen, with no sign of a body, and on other occasions a huge back like an upturned boat which moved across the surface at speed. Sometimes curious humps were reported; water separated them, but they appeared to be part of the same animal.

These reports were not always clear, and they varied according to the nature of the 'monster' parts exposed, their movement, distance, the light and water conditions, the powers of observation of the witnesses and their ability to express themselves and make sketches.

In one respect they were consistent, however: most witnesses expressed surprise at what they had seen and in some cases absolute astonishment. From the relatively few reports recorded from people in boats,

fear was evident too, for no one wished to be tipped out into the freezing water by a rising hump or by an accidental collision with a monstrous unknown animal swimming at speeds of up to 36 km/h (20 knots).

Before the excitement of the early 1930s, the Monster had been seen and reported by local people but had no generally accepted title other than the names bestowed on it by tradition and by folklore. The world outside knew nothing of it. Modern researchers have found local accounts of sightings going back to the mid-nineteenth century and apocryphal references centuries older still which, if they are to be taken seriously, describe strange animals in Loch Ness and in some other Highland lochs as well. From as far back as the sixth century comes a Latin text describing an event which occurred at Loch Ness. The text, translated by Father J. A. Carruth, a member of the Benedictine community of monks at Fort Augustus, is described as being from the 'trustworthy life of the great St Columba, the Abbot of Iona, written by St Adamnan, who later himself became Abbot of Iona'; it is in Book 2, chapter 27, of Adamnan's Book and the occurrence is roughly dated 565 AD.

'OF THE DRIVING AWAY OF A CERTAIN MONSTER BY VIRTUE OF PRAYER OF THE HOLY MAN

"At another time, again when the blessed man was staying for some days in the province of the Picts, he found it necessary to cross the river Ness; and when he came to the bank thereof, he sees some of the inhabitants burying a poor unfortunate man, whom, as those who were burying him themselves reported, some water monster had, a little before, snatched at as he was swimming and bitten with a most savage bite, and whose hapless corpse some men who came in a boat to give assistance, though too late, caught hold of by putting out hooks . . ." '

The translation goes on at some length to tell that Columba asks Lugne, one of his followers, to swim across to the burial party, but when he entered the water the Monster surfaced again and approached the swimmer rapidly with an open mouth. The watchers were terrified, but Columba raised his hand, made the sign of the cross, invoked the name of God and shouted to the beast not to touch the man and to go back – 'Then the beast on hearing the voice of the saint was terrified and fled backwards more rapidly than he came, as if dragged by cords, although it had come so near to Lugne as he swam, that there was not more than the length of a punt pole between the man and the beast. . . .'

This encounter, if it is true, may have taken place at the 'Bonar Narrows' at the eastern extremity of Loch Ness, leading into little Loch Dochfour, which in turn trickles into the shallow headwaters of the River Ness. The monster has been seen here recently, and it could be that the ancients regarded Loch Dochfour as part of the River Ness. Whatever precisely happened, this is the first known

event involving a 'monster' in or near Loch Ness. Perhaps this is why modern researchers and monster-hunters tend to regard St Columba as something of a patron saint!

But let us return to our own times, in particular to 1934, when the late Commander Rupert Gould published the first original book on the topic, *The Loch Ness Monster and Others*. He researched the phenomenon at first hand, talked to a fair number of witnesses and drew some startling conclusions. He believed that by and large the evidence was genuine and that, in spite of hoaxes, genuine mistakes and over-credulous witnesses, a body remained of valid verbal testimony to the presence of large unknown aquatic animals which had originally come in from the sea since the last Ice Age, when the loch was an arm of the sea. With the passage of centuries, the land gradually rose, separating the loch from the sea, at first with a sand bar and later with a plug of land through which a river cut a path, spilling off the rainwater which flowed down it from the Ness. Over centuries of time, the salt in the loch was washed out, and the animals adapted to their new environment and continued to live and breed, right up to the present.

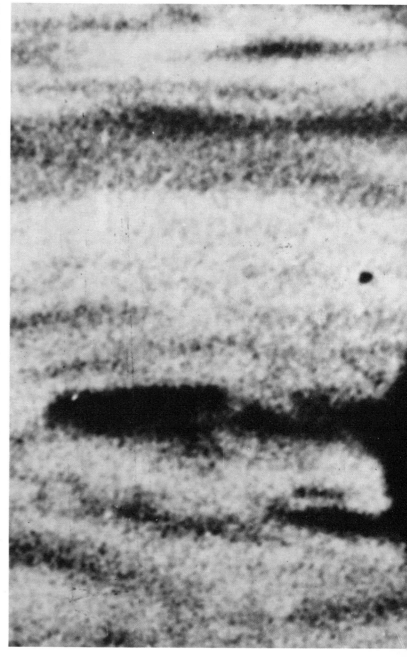

Left : **searching for the monster opposite Tor Pint, Loch Ness.** *Above :* **taken in 1934 by Dr Kenneth Wilson using a waterplate camera.** *Opposite :* **'Morgawr', the Cornish sea monster taken by the mysterious 'Marie M' in February 1976 at Rosemullion Head, Falmouth, Cornwall.**

This hypothesis was not impossible, and although Gould's work was at first received with scepticism some people found his conclusions stimulating and exciting. He was logical, erudite and methodical in eliminating known species as contenders for the 'what is it?' title. Although the 'evolved form of Plesiosaur' theory was popular at the time (and has remained so), Gould eventually veered away from it, preferring the 'giant unknown amphibian' theory, thus changing from the

'pro reptile' camp to the 'pro amphibian' camp. Although both reptiles and amphibians (like newts and frogs) are cold-blooded he did not seem to think that the very cold water in Loch Ness would prove an absolute bar to them. This tends to be the view of scientists too, because cold-blooded animals become lethargic and even comatose when their body temperature goes down, but there are some notable exceptions, of which Gould must have been aware.

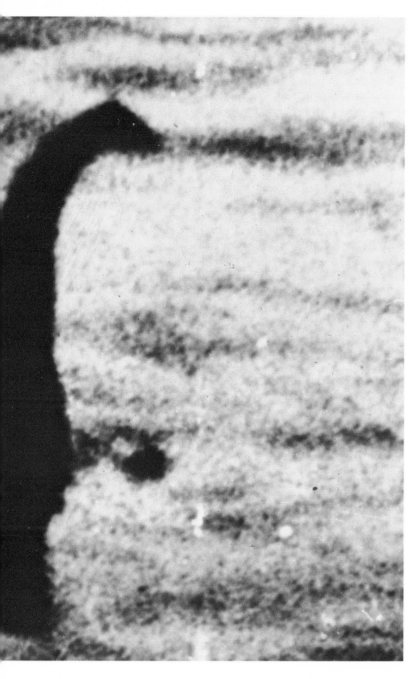

perpetrated and some still photographs and scraps of black and white movie film showed wakes, humps and bumps, a head and long serpentine neck. On more than one occasion the 'Beastie', as it was sometimes called by local people, was actually reported out of the water! Some of these stories were so bizarre that music-hall jokes were made about them and cartoonists inevitably had a field-day. Though serious interest had been roused at first, as time passed and expeditions failed to secure any tangible evidence the scientific community tended to adopt an attitude of frosty indifference to the verbal testimony which continued to come in every year, right up to the outbreak of World War II. In the war itself, Loch Ness was enveloped by a cloak of military security.

Somewhat irritatingly, the Monster was not so easily disposed of. It was watched and reported by a Royal Observer Corps station on the mountainside and was struck by a Royal Navy Auxiliary vessel passing through the loch, a collision which, according to the young naval officer aboard at the time (who still remembers the incident vividly today), caused a dent in the bow. A signal was sent to the Lords of the Admiralty in London to the effect that the ship had been damaged as a result of striking the 'Loch Ness Monster'. History records that these gentlemen were not overly amused.

After the war, life gradually began to return to normal but many years passed before large numbers of visitors made the circuit of the loch, stopping in their cars to munch sandwiches and to peer into the distance, hoping secretly that they would spot something interesting. Outwardly the Monster had almost ceased to exist; so many years had passed without any material proof in the form of carcasses or bones that, with the exception of local people and visitors who actually claimed a sighting, the vast majority of ordinary people no longer believed in it. Even the jokes had stopped.

In 1957, however, something happened which in time proved to be of the utmost consequence. This was the publication of *More Than a Legend*, a book by Mrs Constance Whyte, a local resident. Her husband had for a long time been the Chief Engineer on the Caledonian Canal system. After years of research, she put the facts together, the innumerable interviews with witnesses, the delvings into folklore and history, and brought the Monster

Perhaps more important, Gould's wide knowledge of the marine environment, both as a naval officer and hydrographer and as a student of the great body of evidence for unknown marine animals (in 1930 he published a book *The Case for the Sea Serpent*, about them) made him an expert on the subject.

After the publication of Gould's book, the fabled 'Loch Ness Monster' became far more real to many people. Once discovered, the Monster regularly made international news. Questions were asked in Parliament about it, huge prizes for its capture were offered, private expeditions began to take the field, hoaxes were

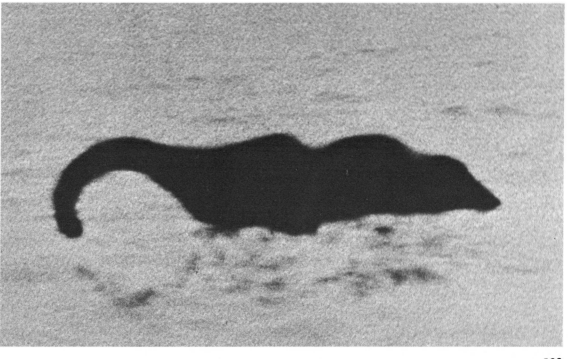

Above : **Dr Robert Rines, President of the Academy of Applied Science, Boston, USA, servicing 'Old Faithful', the Edgerton underwater flash camera which obtained pictures in 1972 and 1975 at Loch Ness.** *Right :* **Tim Dinsdale's 'Water Horse', used as a floating observation post since 1969. Two sightings have been made from it.**

up to date and into the modern era. Her conclusion was that a small colony of unknown aquatic animals really did exist in the loch, that they were breeding there and that they had originally come from the sea.

More Than a Legend was a turning-point, for after its publication, individuals and groups of seriously-minded people began to search for new and better evidence and to lecture on the subject. One was Torquil MacLeod, a much travelled and educated Highlander, who spent the last year and a half of his life at Loch Ness observing and researching, with his Australian wife. In 1960 MacLeod claimed that he had seen the Monster lying partly out of water on the shore across the loch from where he was standing. He

viewed it through binoculars with graticulated lenses and, as he knew within 45 metres (150 feet) or so how far off it was, he was able to measure it with a fair degree of accuracy. He estimated that the parts out of the water were some 15 metres (45 to 50 feet) long. And it was *alive*. The animal had a long neck, a great body, two sets of limbs (the rearmost he described as being paddles 'as big as table-tops'). He was alone at the time and was unable to photograph the creature as he had no long lens equipment. After some nine minutes the Monster – for monster it certainly was – heaved its great bulk round and re-entered the water, which was deep at that place.

That year proved a milestone in photography, for in April the author of this chapter, an

aero-engineer who had spent the previous year reading and analysing the subject, came to Loch Ness armed with a borrowed 16-mm Bolex movie camera and a telephoto lens. After a week of rising with the dawn each day to watch, he saw and filmed the humped back of one of these strange animals as it swam across the water, submerged, turned and moved parallel to the far shore, throwing up a big wash. Later he measured the length and beam of a rowing boat and sent it out with a 5 hp outboard motor, clocking its speed along the foreshore with his car speedometer. The boat was filmed where the Monster had been seen. The film was developed under control by Kodak and later shown on television. The programme had a profound effect on popular thinking. In May a close-up flashlight photo showing a great bulbous back and a pole-like neck a mere 23 metres (75 feet) offshore, was claimed to have been taken by a professional fireman, Peter O'Connor, when the Monster paddled by his campsite. But the controversy that subsequently raged round the picture did not help to establish credibility, although the original contained some interesting detail lost in the gross black and white newsprint enlargements made of it.

In mid-summer 1960 the 15-metre (48-foot) yacht *Finola* proceeding up the Loch under motor power was overtaken by a huge animal swimming just below the surface. It threw up a wake and paddle splashes, and three separate rounded humps were seen. It passed the yacht, then submerged, to resurface on a collision course. This caused anxiety on board, and *Finola* altered direction 'to avoid close contact' – which fact was recorded in the log. Some photographs were taken with an old camera, the best of which showed the long V wake on calm water. This was one of the best documented sightings, for the episode was watched by independent people

on both shores, including Liz and Torquil MacLeod, who made careful sketches showing the manoeuvring of the yacht and the Monster.

As a result of these and other excitements, monster-hunting became a real and absorbing task for many different people during the next decade. In 1960 the first scientifically-orientated sonar expedition took the field. A small group of undergraduates from Oxford and Cambridge universities and a handful of staff members watched from a campsite and 'pinged' with an echo-sounding fishfinder from a boat. A brief surfacing was also witnessed. The echo traces showed strange 'crescents' which did not appear to be caused by fish, but rather by a bigger target, diving rapidly. The team returned two years later with better equipment, and on one occasion a sonar machine produced a huge, dense target response from within the water.

In 1962 too, a surface watch

from a sailboat was organized over a two-month period by Lieutenant-Colonel G. G. Hasler. A team of fifty-six watched in shifts and listened with hydrophones. From shore the first of the newly formed Loch Ness Phenomena Investigation Bureau expeditions took the field with a pair of army searchlights, hoping to film the 'Beastie' down the beam at night. Instead they filmed a daylight sighting of a large shadowy shape moving sub-surface against wind and ripple.

None of these teams obtained conclusive evidence, rather just enough to whet the appetite. The Bureau expeditions continued until 1972, involving hundreds of volunteers trained to operate the very-long-range camera equipment built for the purpose. But with 35,000 hours of watching only a handful of the exposed films showed wakes and distant objects, none of which was truly adequate. However, in 1966, as a result of a study made by

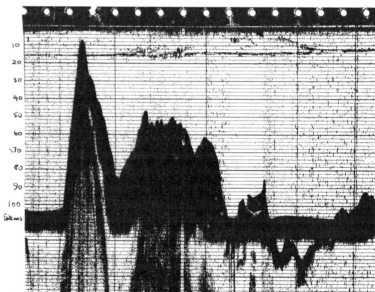

the RAF long-range photo experts of *twin* wakes recorded on film, David James, executive director of the Bureau, invited Tim Dinsdale to submit his original 1960 film for similar analysis. This he did, with an interesting result, for the Joint Air Reconnaissance Intelligence Centre published a report on it, vindicating the film. The object, while moving at 3–4

metres per sec. (7–10 mph) was 1.8 metres (6 feet) wide and 1.5 metres (5 feet) deep, and was, they said, neither a surface vessel nor a submarine. It was therefore 'probably animate'. On publication of the JARIC report the Monster began to don a cloak of near-respectability.

The expeditionary arm of the 'Bureau' had now come

Opposite top : **early expedition at Loch Ness.** *Opposite below :* **a 1960 sonar chart showing precipitous rock walls underwater and shoals of fish at 15 fathoms.** *Left :* **Colonel H. G. Hasler's searchboat 'Jester' which in 1962 used cameras and** *(below)* **a 'look-box'.** *Above :* **hydrophones produced a record of low-frequency tapping sounds.**

to be known as the LNI – the Loch Ness Investigation – and based its operations at Achnahannet, a field high up on the northern shore, east of Urquhart Castle. In 1964 a summer-long watch had been kept from the castle battlements with special photographic equipment. In 1965 Achnahannet came into use and grew with each successive season into a cluster of caravans, observation platform, information centre, workshop, cookhouse and mess, residential caravans, car park, flag poles etc. It was an immensely popular and busy place, crews of young volunteers coming for two-week stints of training

and observation under the leadership of a group commander, the resident technical staff and a photographic director. Achnahannet today is but a memory – but a unique one in the minds of many people. In 1971 it had some 54,000 visitors, and more than eighty volunteers were trained to operate the cameras and the 'mobiles', old motor vans with roof-top camera platforms.

In 1968, with the help of the LNI, Professor D. Gordon Tucker and Dr Hugh Braithwaite of Birmingham University, set up a new type of 'digital' sonar screen in Urquhart Bay which sent out a ten-second pulse of sound, day and night for two weeks, photographing the sonar-scope return on movie-film. Several targets were recorded which seemed to rule out fish. This dramatic sonar result was reported in the *New Scientist* and caused so much interest that in 1969 the 'Great Monster Hunt' with considerable individual sponsorship, was born. *Pisces*, a deep-diving submarine, spent more than 250 hours underwater on explorations, and a tiny one-man fibreglass submarine, *Viperfish*,

dived to depths of 45 metres (150 feet) over a two-month period. A special sonar boat, *Rangitea*, equipped with a mobile sonar unit, and another long-range sonar boat, *Jessie Ellen*, also searched the depths. In addition, two film companies worked from Urquhart Bay; Walt Disney, making a semi-serious documentary with animation and Mirisch Films, who introduced a 5 tonnes (5–ton) model monster – which promptly sank in a storm! Altogether 1969 was a colourful episode but added little to the record, other than the new sonar results obtained by the American Robert Love in *Rangitea* and by the crew of *Pisces* underwater. *Viperfish* too had an odd experience with turbulence that seemed to be created by something monstrous swimming past at a depth of 36 metres (120 feet).

In 1970 Dr Robert Rines and his team from the US Academy of Applied Science, arrived. They had a decisive success with a Klein side-scan sonar and have, since then, returned each year with better high-technology equipment. In 1972 they obtained the now famous 'flipper' photograph underwater. This showed a huge diamond-shaped limb-like structure and coincided with a sonar trace which showed the intrusion of a moving object 6–9 metres (20–30 feet) long. From then, despite the closing down of the LNI at Achnahannet after a decade of fieldwork, operations continued largely on an individual or small group basis, with more and more underwater equipment. In 1975 the Academy obtained a colour flash picture in Urquhart Bay with the same reliable Edgerton strobe-set that had shot the 'flipper' picture.

These pictures, and some new surface long-range 'hump' photographs obtained by an Englishman, Alan Wilkins, caused great press interest. This culminated in a private debate held at the House of Commons in December 1975, at which both sides of the argument for the Monster's existence were given a hearing.

In 1976, expeditions to Loch Ness included a week of night-time sonar-searches by an Englishman, Roger Parker, assisted by Dr James Buchanan of Stirling University. They used a boat-full of electronic equipment which recorded colour film of two large mid-water moving sonar targets. A *New York Times* sponsored Academy expedition to Urquhart Bay also scored with sonar. In May 1977, two high-quality colour pictures reputedly showing the head and neck of the Monster were taken in May by a private watcher, Tony 'Doc' Shiels, using a telephoto 35 mm camera. Later, in August, a short sequence of super-8 colour movie film was exposed from the south shore on a head-and-neck-like object which extended vertically out of the water and then submerged. The still pictures were the subject of an affidavit sworn by Mr Shiels. The best of them was analysed by Dr Vernon Harrison, a recent President of the Royal Photographic Society, who said it had not been retouched and showed subtle detail – though he could

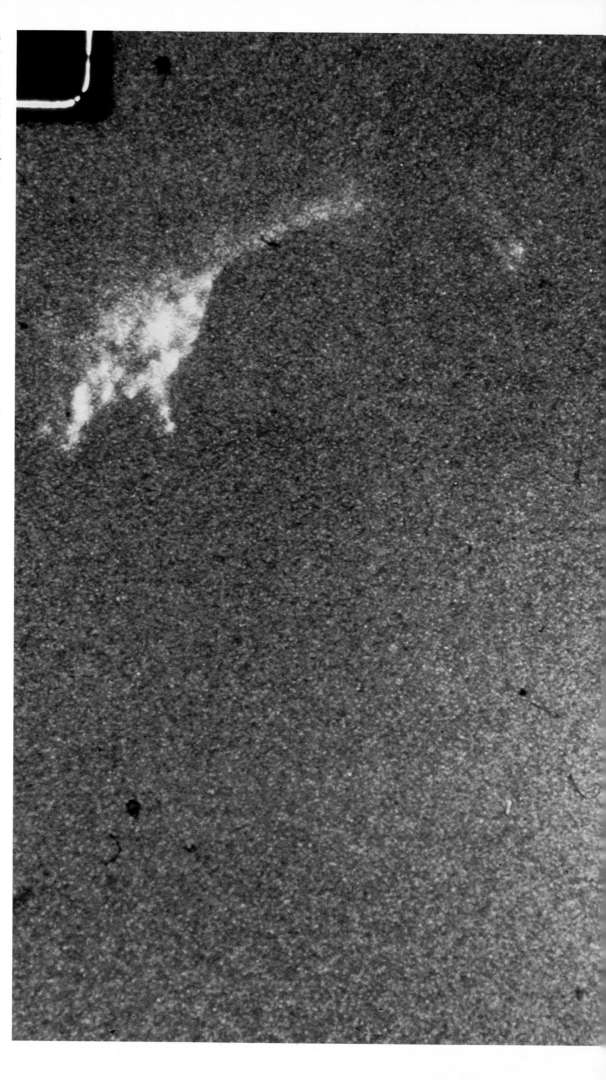

Opposite : **an underwater picture obtained by the Academy of Applied Sciences in 1975 showing a large 'long-necked' object.** *Above :* **in 1974 an automatic sonar camera rig was lowered from a barge, but the experiment was spoiled when it tipped over on the bottom.** *Left :* **diver going in.**

not say of what precisely, even if it did resemble the head and neck of a Plesiosaur! The super-8 movie film remained confidential for a long time until the RAF was able to report on it briefly in August 1978. They too could not say what the object was but noted a diameter of 230 mm (9 inches) and an extension of 760 mm (30 inches) rising from below the surface on three occasions. Side movement was no more than 610 mm (24 inches), but as the object was stable in rough water the report concluded that it must be 'heavy and mostly submerged'. The question of a hoax could not of course be ignored, but when examined carefully, the facts of both case histories seemed to rule it out.

In the future, with better high-technology underwater equipment and with the ever-ready cameras and watchful eyes of the surface photographers, more information is likely to be gleaned. Whether this will be sufficient to tip the weighing-scales of science in favour of the Monster's existence is a matter of conjecture.

However, for individuals well informed about the subject (including the writer) the question of 'reality' has already been resolved, for it is a case of 'seeing is believing'. No one who actually sees a Loch Ness Monster surface, or those parts of it that break surface, is ever likely to forget the experience, or to confuse those parts with parts of other known aquatic animals common to the British Isles.

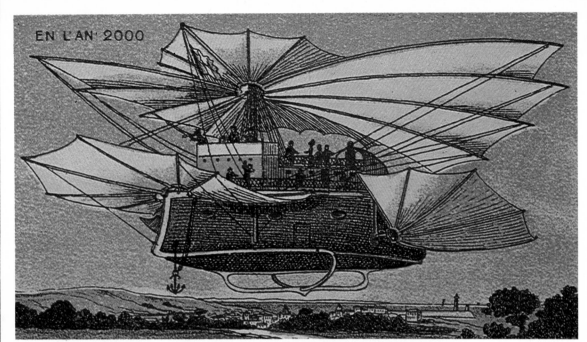

EN L'AN 2000

UNIDENTIFIED FLYING OBJECTS

For over thirty years UFOs have been a source of controversy and a subject of speculation. But, have researchers been looking in the right direction? Do UFOs provide a glimpse into an alien world or do they relate to the equally mysterious realm of the tricks of man's mind?

Socorro, New Mexico, is a small town whose name is enshrined in UFO lore. On the afternoon of 24 April 1964, one of the town's policemen, Lonnie Zamora, came on duty and began his regular patrol-car beat. At ten to six that evening a series of events began that had a profound effect on his life and fixed the image of the UFO indelibly for millions of people.

Zamora had been chasing a speeding car and was heading south out of town when he heard a roaring sound and noticed a brilliant blue flash of light from across the desert. Breaking off from pursuit of the speedster he headed out towards the light. He knew that an explosives store was nearby and feared it had exploded. Driving over the crest of a hill, Zamora

glimpsed, half-hidden in a ravine ahead of him, a white object and two overalled figures. Not knowing what to make of the scene confronting him, he radioed a '10–40' (accident) report back to his base. Then he got out of the car and walked forward to investigate. From a vantage point Zamora saw, about 45 metres (50 yards) ahead of him, a white, egg-shaped object supported on three legs. As he watched there was a tremendous roar, flame spurted from under the object, and Zamora flung himself to the ground. Slowly the object rose into the sky, and Zamora scrambled back to the cover of his car. The roaring noise stopped, and the policeman twisted round in time to see the mystery craft disappearing away to the south-west.

When Zamora's report was filed, all hell let loose. Investigators from military establishments, the US Air Force's notorious 'Blue Book' UFO unit and private amateur UFO societies descended on the town, bringing world-wide fame both to Lonnie Zamora and to this remote desert corner of the USA. In fact it was this rapid rise to celebrity which led some debunkers to suggest that the whole episode was an elaborate hoax by the little town's civic leaders to put Socorro on the map.

Although the events witnessed by the officer are by no means unique (far stranger events are reported almost weekly in the UFO specialist press), this particular event was taken up at once by the major news media. It had a lot

From the fantasies of nineteenth-century authors *(above)* **to modern movies** *(opposite)* **science-fiction writers see the future as an extension of their own level of technology.**

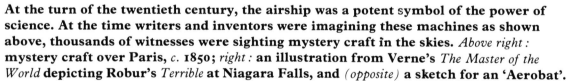

At the turn of the twentieth century, the airship was a potent symbol of the power of science. At the time writers and inventors were imagining these machines as shown above, thousands of witnesses were sighting mystery craft in the skies. *Above right :* **mystery craft over Paris,** *c.* **1850;** *right :* **an illustration from Verne's** *The Master of the World* **depicting Robur's** *Terrible* **at Niagara Falls, and** *(opposite)* **a sketch for an 'Aerobat'.**

going for it. For one, the witness was a reliable police officer, well regarded in the community. And the events themselves were not *too* outrageous; after all, to land a strange craft, get two crewmen to leave it to look around and then blast off again was exactly what the United States' NASA team was planning to do on the moon just a few years later. The time was right for Socorro.

Socorro was one of the first UFO reports to be taken seriously by the media and not to be subjected to the sort of wink-and-nudge treatment that many similar stories had been given in the past. It was a solid-sounding nuts-and-bolts account of a strange craft landing on Earth. And as such it confirmed the public image of UFOs as alien spacecraft conducting some sort of explora-

tory survey of Planet Earth and its inhabitants.

This concept, known to UFO buffs as the 'Extraterrestrial Hypothesis' (ETH for short), began to emerge in the 1940s. Throughout history there have been innumerable tales of strange objects in the sky and strange beings on the ground. Many of these are chronicled in the hundreds of UFO books and magazines that have been

mediately before the outbreak of the First World War, there came reports of strange airships sailing through the skies of many countries around the globe. The biggest of these 'airship flaps' was in the USA in 1897. Communities across the continent were visited by large dirigibles with noisy engines, apparently able to out-race and out-manoeuvre anything produced by the primitive airship technology of the time.

But at the turn of the century the explanation for these mysteries was not interplanetary spaceships but mystery inventors. This was the time when Edison and other pioneers were at their prime, and the public waited breathlessly for a stream of wonder inventions, from the electric light to the phonograph.

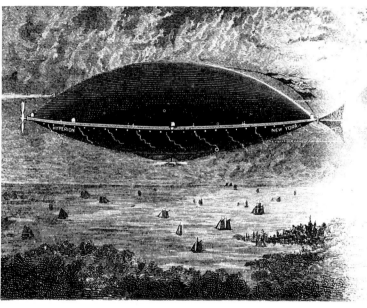

produced over the past thirty years. Here they are firmly brought into the ETH fold and explained as sightings of otherworldly craft, described in terms familiar to the era in which they were seen.

But in fact, when witnesses of aerial anomalies in past centuries have described what they have seen, their descriptions have usually been quite clear and precise, and in most cases it takes a considerable effort of manipulation to turn their descriptions into blueprints for strange spacecraft.

From about the 1880s through to the period im-

Later, the scene of the airship visitations shifted to Europe, and Great Britain was plagued by these baffling ships in 1909 and 1913. But by now the phantom inventor was a figure of the past, and the new culprits were foreign spies and imperial Germany's growing military might.

It was another policeman, Constable Kettle of the Peterborough force, who was one of the first to encounter the airship of 1909. On duty in this ancient city at 5.15 on the morning of 23 March, he was startled by a buzzing sound like 'a high powered engine'.

Suddenly a powerful light beamed down from the sky, and he saw the outline of a strange airship, *without* the characteristic gas-bag. It was travelling at a 'tremendous' pace and disappeared to the north-west, the sound of its engines gradually fading. Throughout the next three months similar sightings all over Britain produced an atmosphere of near-panic, as the public feared a German invasion.

In earlier centuries strange aerial sights were regarded as frankly supernatural and were often considered as portents of major events and disasters. Ancient tomes are full of accounts of strange lights, double suns, phantom armies, visions and such. While some of these almost certainly were misrepresentations of natural

phenomena, others are described in such detail as to be incapable of any such interpretation. In July 1662, for instance, the people of Chillington, Somerset, in the west of England, saw giant figures of horsemen fighting in the sky above their town.

These aerial visitations began to enter the space age in 1946, when Scandinavia, especially Sweden, was haunted by 'ghost rockets'. At first these were thought to be Soviet secret weapons designed by captured German scientists from Peenemünde. However it soon became obvious that there

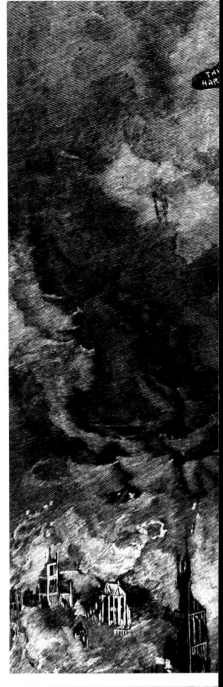

Mystery airships inspired writers such as Jules Verne; in turn, their writings and drawings seem to have helped along the airship scares. These illustrations are typical of the thousands that appeared in magazines in the years about 1900. *Above left and right :* **scenes from Verne's** *Clipper of the Clouds; opposite top :* **a scene from Fred Jane's** *Hartmann the Anarchist* **(1902) and** *(opposite below)* **an illustration from** *Cassells Family Magazine* **captioned 'We perceived the cars of the Mercurians floating in space'.**

was something very strange about the rocket-like shapes crossing the northern skies. Although over two thousand reports of these ghost rockets reached the Swedish military, none ever appeared to land or crash, and they seemed to originate from all points of the compass, not just from the east.

This scare was rapidly overshadowed by the great 'flying saucer' flap which broke in the USA next year. Kenneth Arnold's sighting of flying discs over Mount Rainier in the north-western state of Washington was destined to become legend in the UFO world.

On 24 June 1947, Kenneth Arnold was flying his private plane over the Cascade Range when he saw half a dozen flat, disc-like shapes skimming at a fantastic speed among the mountain peaks. Arnold described their progress as 'like a saucer skimming over water'. This phrase got transformed

into 'flying saucer', and a new name, a new mystery and even a new science was born.

The world of the 1940s was a different, more complicated, place than the America of the 1890s. The 'great inventor' had been replaced by more sinister forces. The world was still reeling from the shock of the atom bomb, cold war tensions were at their height. The UFOs of these years began to attract the attention of military brasshats, and the US Air Force began an involvement with the UFO enigma that has continued to the present day.

The government of any country will naturally be concerned about reports of strange craft flying over its territory. When the UFO reports began to come in, military establishments across the world began to investigate them to see if they represented any defence threat. The US Air Force set up a small investigating panel with the code-name 'Project Grudge'. Despite a rather

rushed report in the early days which seemed to give some credence to the ETH, the official investigators soon found that, despite the often spectacular eyewitness testimony they were receiving, they were never able to pin down any clear evidence of the reality of actual nuts-and-bolts craft. This did not satisfy the UFO enthusiasts (or 'ufologists' as they began to all themselves), who feared a major government cover-up. In fact a number of inept bureaucratic moves and some less than honest dismissals of well-attested cases lent some justifiable impetus to this idea. However, many ufologists became convinced that the US government knew about the extra-terrestrial origin of the saucers and was even in contact with them. A number of UFO organizations sprang up to try to wrest this 'truth' out of the government. One of them, NICAP, led by an ex-Air Force major, is still operating today.

Despite lurid rumours of

crashed UFOs in Air Force bases, there seems to be no evidence that any government agency does have final proof of the origin of UFOs, and in recent years the US military have shown increasing signs that they want to get out of the whole subject altogether.

The late 1940s and early 1950s saw a whole series of UFO 'waves', large numbers of reports emerging from a particular area over a short time. One such wave hit the USA in 1952, and the reports from this era began to set the popular image of the UFO as an interplanetary visitor.

In August 1952, William Squyres, a musician working for a local radio station, was on his way to an early morning performance – this was still the days of live radio! At about 5.30 he was driving through a wooded area near Frontenac, Kansas. His attention was suddenly caught by a strange object at the side of the road and he stopped to take a closer look. Later he described it as 'like two turtle shells glued together'. It was about 18 metres (60 feet) long and 4.5 metres (15 feet) high and hovering about 3 metres (10 feet) off the ground. There were rows of brightly illuminated windows through which the startled witness saw moving shapes. At one end of this strange craft there was a window in which he could see the head and shoulders of a figure. Suddenly the object shot upwards, leaving only some marks in the vegetation to show it had been there.

This encounter is typical of many thousands that have been reported since then, all of them seemingly reports of people meeting a strange otherworldly craft. Inevitably there soon came reports of people meeting and talking to the occupants of these objects and even of people taking a ride in them themselves. And here we come to what is possibly the key to the whole mystery, though not in the way the ufologists suspected.

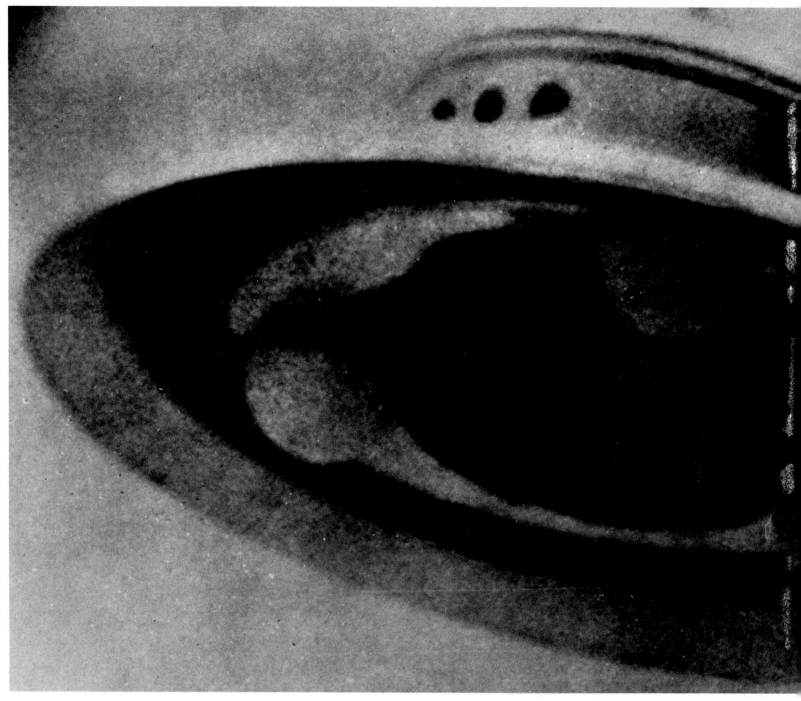

Investigators have tried to capture positive proof of the nature of UFOs, such as John Shepherd, owner and project director of 'Project Strata', but despite batteries of sophisticated electronics *(opposite below)* that proof has been elusive. Similarly, photographs ranging from Adanski's highly dubious contraptions *(above)* to well attested but extremely unclear pictures taken by Italian police officers in 1978 *(opposite top)* all fall short of final proof. Photographs and drawings by English schoolboy Stephen Darbishire *(right)* have sparked claim and counter-claim.

The question of 'contact' soon divided the UFO world. The nuts-and-bolts ufologists were more interested in the scientific hardware that they sought and were uncomfortable with the reports of people meeting occupants and communicating with them. A circus-like atmosphere surrounded many of these cases and this, they felt, detracted from the scienti-

fic respectability they were trying to create. And it is undoubtedly true that many of the early 'contactees' (people who claimed to communicate with the UFO beings) were either mentally unbalanced, extremely over-imaginative or just plain frauds.

The most notorious of these people was George Adamski, and his story appears in many

UFO books. After alleged meetings with tall, beautiful 'Venusians' in Arizona and California, he wrote a string of pseudo-philosophical books on his experiences and spent most of the rest of his life travelling and lecturing on UFOs and the kindly 'space brothers'. Other contactees set up quasi-religious sects, some of which still flourish.

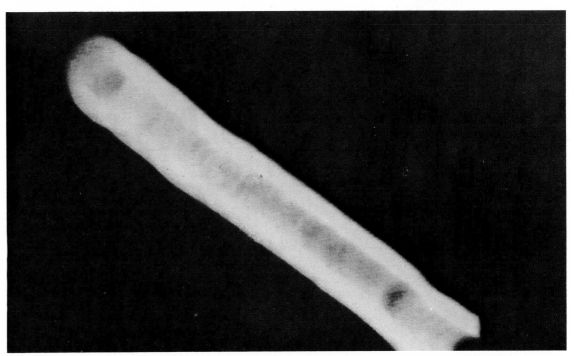

Some contactees, however, did not try to cash in on their alleged exploits. Cynthia Appleton didn't even write a book about the strange happenings that shattered her quiet life in the Aston district of Birmingham, England. She had no knowledge of UFOs and had no inkling of what was to happen as she put her three-year-old daughter to bed on the afternoon of 18 November 1957. She heard a cry from the front room of her house, where her younger daughter, baby Janet, was sleeping. As she rushed into the room to see what was wrong she was struck by what she described to investigators as an 'oppressive atmosphere', as if there were about to be a thunderstorm. Then, with a feeling of terror, she saw the figure of a man materialize before her, gradually coming into focus. A noise 'like a radio being tuned' filled the room and she felt a gentle, calming influence and was able to take

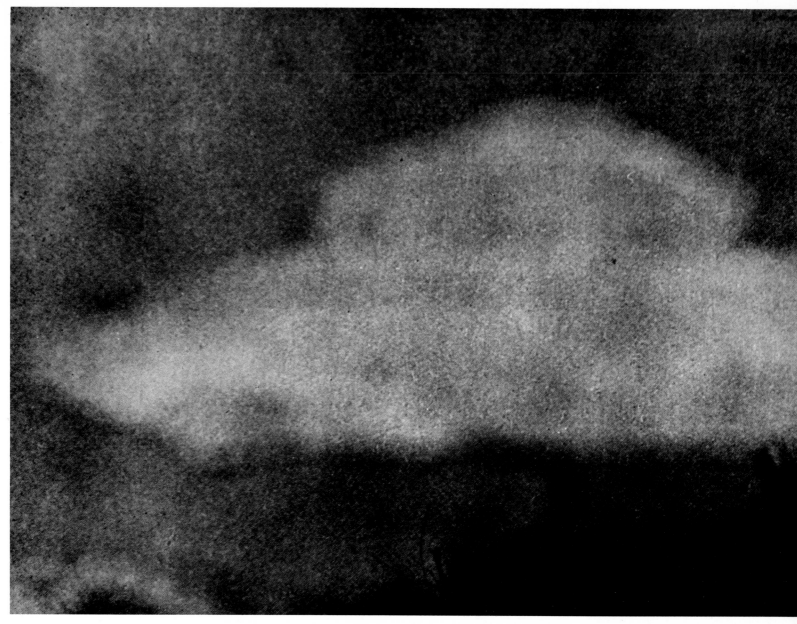

stock of the incredible apparition.

Her visitor was tall and fair, wearing a tight-fitting silverlike suit with a high, 'Elizabethan', collar. The man's lips began to move, but soundlessly. Instead his voice reached the perplexed woman by a form of telepathy. He told her a vague tale about mining titanium from the sea-bed and generalizations about mankind approaching space travel 'the wrong way'. As he moved his hands a circular craft seemed to appear from a transparent dome, on which were peering several similar figures.

After 'speaking' for a few more moments the figure and his saucer vanished. Or, in a curious phrase used by Mrs Appleton, 'he didn't disappear, he just wasn't there any more',

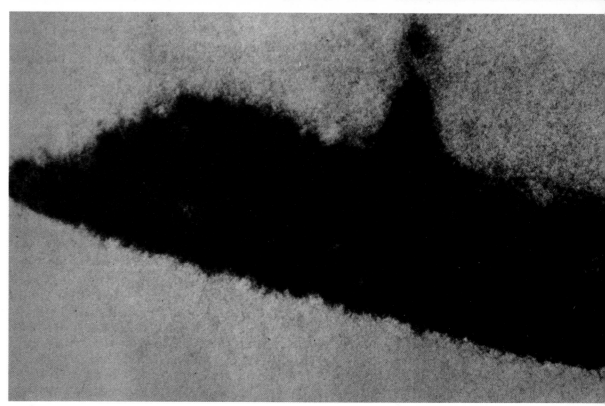

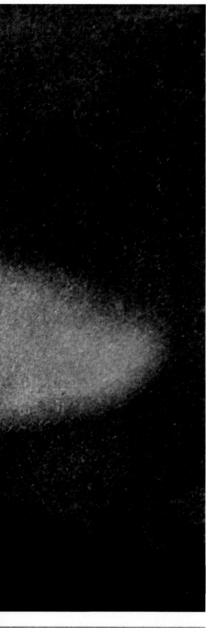

The photograph taken by Paul Trent at McMinnville, Oregon *(opposite below)* **is perhaps the one that has stood up best to continued investigation. Even the ultra-sceptical Condon Report gives it guarded approval. Other photos – shown here is a picture taken by Stephen Darbishire** *(opposite top)* **and a photograph of a sighting in Yorkshire** *(above)* **– have been more contentious.**

a phrase which gives a considerable clue to the nature of our mysterious visitors. Mrs Appleton had six subsequent contacts over the next year, in which beings materialized and arrived at her home in a more normal manner.

Cases like this put the ufologist on the spot. Although there are obvious superficial similarities with the Adamski-type 'man from Venus', the incident obviously has much in common with more traditional apparitions – ghosts or the various angelic creatures who have appeared to the pious from time to time with enigmatic messages and warnings. Could our modern spacemen be this generation's version of a phenomenon that has been with us for a very long time?

Another incident which puts new light on the origins of these mysterious visitors happened in 1976, in the village of Fence Houses in Tyne and Wear. It was about 9.00 p.m. on a September evening when two women

friends, aged sixty-three and eighteen, were walking home from a visit to a neighbour. They were passing a piece of derelict land when they noticed a peculiar object and claimed that they were 'strangely attracted' towards it. It proved to be a small oval thing, about one and a half metres (5 feet) long and one metre (3½ feet) high, resting on ski-like metal runners.

As they crossed the empty site towards the object the ladies noticed a strange thing. The noise of the wind in surrounding buildings and trees seemed to stop, and they could hear no traffic noises from nearby streets. Suddenly two creatures appeared in a glass-like section of the strange machine. They were tiny beings 'as big as a doll' with long white hair, huge eyes and claw-like hands. This apparition terrified the women, who hurried away. As they ran all the noises of the surrounding area returned. They turned just in time to see the object

rise quickly and shoot off, making a humming noise.

Cases abound in the UFO literature in which witnesses approaching a grounded saucer suddenly notice that 'all the noises stopped, even the animals' or, a frequent comment, 'it was a busy road, but all the time I was there no other cars passed us'.

Beit Bridge is one of the main border crossing-points between Rhodesia and South Africa. The road from this town to Salisbury is the main international highway and is usually crowded with cars and trucks heading to Rhodesia's only trading neighbour. On the night of 30 May 1974, a young couple, identified as Peter and Frances by the investigators who studied their incredible experience, took the road from Salisbury, aiming for Durban. It was when they passed the town of Umvuma that their strange journey began. At first a UFO appeared and began to pace the car. It was a bright light, quite near the witnesses, which turned on and off in a regular pattern. Then as often happens in UFO close approaches to cars, the headlights began to fade. Now the car grew cold, and the passengers had to wrap up and turn the heater on to keep warm. Then Peter took his foot off the accelerator – but the car kept moving! Throughout the night UFOs kept company with the car, seemingly wresting control from its terrified driver. After a series of weird adventures the two travellers at last arrived at Beit Bridge, and control was returned to an exhausted Peter.

But throughout the journey of almost 400 km (250 miles) the witnesses had not seen one other car or lorry, except for an empty bus parked in a lay-by. Even stranger, at one point in their drive they had passed through an unfamiliar landscape that they knew did not exist along that stretch of road. And during the whole journey they heard nothing but their car radio, no sound of traffic, none of the night sounds of the bush, not even the sound of their own engine.

The picture these incidents paint is rather different from our image of the UFO as a machine from outer space. It looks more and more as if there is something that is happening here on earth, something to do with people, not spaceships. And shorn of its surface veneer of interplanetary travel and technology, the UFO mystery begins to look like part of a far broader pattern.

People who have looked closely at the UFO phenomenon have described a spectrum of 'strangeness' in UFO reports. At one extreme there are descriptions of unidentified lights moving across the night sky. Most ufologists consider these of little significance, as there are so many possible explanations. Besides such natural objects as meteors of ball-lightning, there are orbiting satellites, space debris re-entry, even conventional aircraft seen under unusual conditions. More notice is taken of day-time sightings of metallic-looking discs, especially when, as has sometimes happened, these are seemingly confirmed by radar or photographic records. But even here, proof of a genuine strange phenomenon is hard to come by. Even by daylight, natural objects and aircraft can look very strange in unfamiliar circumstances or particular meteorological conditions.

As we pass through this spectrum of 'strangeness' we start to come to those reports which cannot be considered misinterpretations – the close encounters.

It is when we start to examine closely some of the very strange close encounters, such as the case of Mrs Appleton or the Rhodesian couple, that we seem to be going beyond any possible consideration of interplanetary visitors. Some UFO encounters seem to veer from the reasonable, even explicable, to the sort of high strangeness of the event we have just been looking at.

In the late spring of 1963 a woman and her two children were walking near their home in Phoenix, Arizona, when the woman's attention was caught by an object hovering a few yards away over a lawn. It consisted of three concentric rings and was shining brilliantly. At first this report looked as if it might be a 'plasma' or ball-lightning, a rare but well-authenticated form of atmospheric electricity – interesting but not too mysterious.

However the witness's reactions to this event *are* strange. She finds she cannot speak, a neighbour hosing his garden seems to take no notice of this spectacular vision. As we might now expect, she hears no sounds from the numerous animals in the vicinity. Later she described how she 'lost all track of time',

'it seemed as if all life had stopped . . . as if we were somehow frozen in time.' On walking away she felt a sudden euphoria.

So what is happening here? The simple ETH seems inadequate to explain events and reactions such as these. Are we moving into the field of psychic phenomena, of ghosts and religious visions? Far from being from outer space, is the UFO phenomenon something that is deep within man himself?

There is a well-known psychological phenomenon called a 'false awakening' – most people have experienced one. They wake up in the morning, get washed and dressed, then start for work . . . and then they wake up! An interesting experience, and extremely annoying especially on a cold and wet morning

when it is difficult enough to get up once! Now there seems to be some evidence that many UFO experiences are a variant of this strange type of 'dream' or 'hypnogogic hallucination', as it is called in technical jargon.

There are literally hundreds of cases on record in which the witness claims that he was awakened by a strange noise. In a case investigated by this writer in 1973, a girl living in a town near Manchester woke early one morning when she heard a mystery humming noise. She found she could not move, and as she looked about the bedroom she saw a 'bell-like' object in the corner of the room and three silver-clad, faceless beings standing at the foot of her bed. As she watched, they turned and entered the object,

Photographs taken by a pilot over Venezuela, 1963: sightings and photos by air crews are often considered to have a higher credibility as they are more experienced observers.

which then rose and disappeared out of her view.

Now if this had happened in the open air, or if the girl had gone to the window and witnessed these strange events in the backyard, this could have been a classic UFO landing. But what are we presented with now? UFOs that can fly through brick walls? Ghosts? Or a strange and vivid waking dream?

But if all this is a dream, it is a strange and disturbing one. It is a dream that is being experienced by people throughout the world. With only slight variations it turns up from Buenos Aires to Bradford, from

Wimbledon to Wisconsin. It was in Wisconsin, early on the morning of 15 October 1973, that another unsuspecting witness woke to a scene that could have come from a science fiction B-movie. Again, it was a high-pitched sound which woke our sleeper and a bright orange-red glow that first indicated that something strange was happening. Three weird wrinkled figures, one to one and a half metres (4–5 feet) tall, materialized, and perhaps understandably the witness passed out. When he came to again he was on the floor, and the creatures were examining him with a strange instrument

that showed the bones of his leg as they passed it over him. Again he passed out and woke again at dawn.

It certainly looks as though there could be some connection between false awakenings and *some* UFO experiences. But can this explain those cases where the witness was wide awake throughout the whole event or where there is some physical evidence such as footprints, marks of 'landing pads'? Can it explain why thousands of people in different parts of the world, in different societies, in different cultures, are all having apparently the same dream?

Carl Jung was one of the pioneers of psychoanalysis. His work on the way the human mind operates is rivalled only by that other controversial

genius Sigmund Freud. He was also one of the few truly great minds to turn his attention to UFOs. Other scientists and scholars who had looked at the topic were usually astronomers or physicists, because that was the frame of reference into which UFOs had been fitted. When they looked at the subject as astronomers and physicists they soon found things that didn't add up. Some of them we have already seen. They pointed out that many of the reported manoeuvres of the UFOs were physically impossible, that any inhabited planets would be too far away for their inhabitants to be visiting Earth on practically a daily basis. Many of the arguments that the astronomers used to wash their hands of the whole subject were summarized in the *Condon Report*, commissioned by the US government, supposedly as the last word on the subject. With one or two notable exceptions the astronomers gave up on the subject.

But Jung was not an astronomer. He brought a new viewpoint to the mystery. What, he asked, if the UFOs came from inner space, from that space within the human mind and subconscious which is just as unknown and infinite as the light-years of outer space?

Jung claimed that through millennia of shared experience, mankind had come to develop an elaborate system of shared symbols. In all cultures the same sorts of images produce similar emotional responses and hold the same meaning at a deep level of the mind which Jung called the 'collective subconscious'. Using this concept, he analysed the phenomenon of the flying saucer, claiming that it represented a 'mandala', a circular symbol of wholeness and unity.

In recent years some ufologists have begun to examine the symbolic content of some UFO experiences. They have asked whether certain common elements of these stories have any significance in

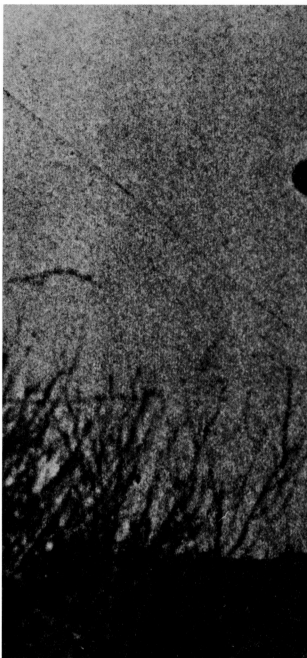

Opposite below : **taken by military personnel off Brazil, another classic which has stood up well to investigation, although not all recognize its genuineness.** *Above and above right :* **photographs by Daniel Fry, one of many contactees who followed Adanski's example and published accounts of meetings with visitors from other planets.**

terms of Jung's shared symbols.

People who claim to have met and communicated with the occupants of UFOs have reported that these mystery visitors claim to come from a remarkable variety of planets – from the ones we know such as Mars and Venus, where we can be sure there is no chance of intelligent life, to mythical and unknown ones such as Clarion (allegedly on the far side of the sun), Shomdic, Antir, Aenstria and dozens of others. But when we look at the descriptions of these creatures we see that they

fall into two major groups. There are first the tall, beautiful beings like those described by Mrs Appleton or George Adamski and then smaller, more unpleasant folk like those seen in the mini-UFO by the two ladies in Tyne and Wear or the big-eared, goblin-like entities that terrorized a family in Kentucky in 1957. If we are looking for symbols, could these two types of 'ufonaut' be symbolic of good and evil? And if so, what disturbing conclusions can we draw from the fact that over the thirty years that the

UFO phenomenon has taken its present form the 'good guys' seem to be losing out to the 'baddies' in numbers of reported contacts?

In briefly reviewing the history of visions in the sky we saw how they reflected the society that viewed them. At the turn of the century the UFOs mirrored terrestrial preoccupations with the marvels of the developing technology of powered flight. In seventeenth-century England, riven with Civil War and political strife, the signs in the heavens were of armies and

horsemen, swords and blood. In neutral Sweden after the Second World War people saw missiles like the V2 rocket.

And it looks as if our 'interplanetary' UFOs are a reflection of the space age that dawned in the 1950s. In the early years of the decade, when space flight was familiar only from the world of the science fiction writer our 'occupants' were handsome, helpful people, eager to teach and guide us. Some of the contactees even referred to them as 'space brothers'. Later, in the 1960s, space travel (or at least moon landings) was a familiar reality. Now the saucer occupants seemed more like practical scientists from some other planet. Like our own astronauts they got on busily with their task of collecting rock samples or tinkering with strange devices. The Socorro incident is typical of this period.

But when science features in today's headlines it is probably not on the hopeful, up-beat note of the 1960s, when the space projects really did seem to be presenting us with a new frontier. Today the science news is more likely to be scare stories on sinister computer surveillance, the potential horrors of genetic engineering or the untold social upheavals that may be brought about by the silicon-chip micropro-

cessor. Science today, to many people, is something rather scary. People feel trapped in a world they cannot understand, alienated from an impersonal world that has little room for the individual. The psychologist Skinner has compared man's future with a laboratory rat, programmed for survival in a world it cannot understand or control.

And out of these dark preoccupations has come the latest and most sinister manifestation of the UFO phenomenon – the abduction stories.

One of the earliest and best-known abductions was that of Betty and Barney Hill, an American couple who found that after seeing a UFO at close range several hours seemed to be missing from their lives. Hypnotic regression brought out a strange story of being taken aboard a spacecraft and being given a peculiar medical examination. In independent accounts, which compare well, they describe their captors as treating them well, but impersonally, and actually compare themselves with experimental animals.

In their hypnotic state, they reported being taken aboard a huge, circular craft, where they were separated from each other and given their strange 'medical'. Betty testified that they collected skin and nail parings and plunged a long needle into her abdomen. The beings, humanoid creatures with broad, flat faces and 'mongoloid' eyes, showed considerable interest in Barney's false teeth and even tried to remove Betty's real ones! A cup-like object was placed over Barney Hill's genitals, producing a freezing sensation, where later a ring of warts developed.

On being released from the craft, the couple were told by the humanoids that they had been hypnotically programmed to forget the whole incident, which did indeed happen until they were re-hypnotized by the investigators. The Betty and Barney Hill affair has become a *cause célèbre* in the world of

ufology, and many writers have discussed it at length. At least one full-length book has been written about it. Some investigators, looking at the psychological side, have suggested that the fact that the couple were racially mixed (Barney was black, Betty white) may have been significant, producing feelings of exclusion from the society in which they lived.

Since 1961, when the Hills had their alarming experience, the number of UFO abductions has grown steadily. Although some doubts have been expressed about the value of the hypnotic regression techniques which have been used to reveal these cases (it has been suggested that the investigators may unthinkingly ask leading questions which themselves suggest the type of answer the investigator is hoping for), there still remain dozens of reports which demonstrate that the abduction scenario has now become one of the most significant aspects of the UFO mystery.

The implications of the human abductee as a helpless laboratory specimen being experimented upon by unknown forces, perhaps representing 'science' in the abstract, can hardly be better demonstrated than in the experiences of Lee Parrish in January 1977, near his home in Kentucky. During hypnotic investigation of a close encounter UFO experience with a baffling 'time lapse', Lee described how he had been taken aboard a mystery 'craft', whose occupants appeared to be huge featureless machines which moved about and appeared to communicate with each other. Despite their manufactured appearance Lee was convinced that they were sentient beings. One, a black, monolithic slab almost six metres (20 feet) tall, appeared to control two other, smaller objects.

Featureless machines, talking only to each other, treating a human being as an inferior laboratory specimen. What more vivid symbol could there

be of man's fears of a runaway technology?

Carl Jung explained the potent force of our symbols. Their power lies deep within us. They can spur us to war, inspire us to peace; religious leaders, politicians, philosophers and rogues have known and exploited the power of symbols throughout history. And within each individual their power can sometimes be so great that they can distort or even replace our view of reality. Jung spoke of 'psychological projections', images produced in the hidden parts of our mind, which can sometimes break through into our conscious senses. Psychologists recognize a phenomenon which they term a 'metachoric experience', a type of hallucination in which the whole world of the percipient (the person who is having the experience) is replaced by a

psychological image. The percipient sees that he is walking through familiar scenery, where everything seems normal, when suddenly he comes face to face with some strange event – a ghost, UFO, monster of some sort – which seems an intrusion into the normal world around him. In fact, what is happening is that the *whole* of that event is a metachoric experience; the normal parts, the scenery or the buildings are just as much an illusion as the UFO or ghost. To an independent witness our 'percipient' may have been sitting in a chair at home the whole time.

There is evidence that many UFO events are a form of 'metachoric experience'. Recall the strange remark of Mrs Appleton about how her visitor didn't disappear – 'he just wasn't there any more' – or the odd changes in the environment

noticed by the Fence Houses ladies. They seem to suggest that the *whole* of their surroundings had somehow changed, a move into a different sort of reality. And doesn't Mrs Appleton's remark seem to describe the way that a dream ends? It doesn't end, it just isn't there any more!

But can all UFO cases be explained like this? We have seen one example of how an 'ordinary' fireball can have some strange features when examined more closely. Another seemingly straightforward report came from Heanor, Staffordshire, in October 1977. Awakened by a strange humming noise in the early hours of the morning, the witness got out of bed to try to discover its source. He searched the house without success. Just before getting back to bed he glanced through the window

and saw a brilliant glowing white disc. Convinced that 'they had dropped the bomb', he sprang into bed and pulled the bed-clothes over his head – without waking his wife.

Local investigators tried to attribute the light to some natural cause, but without success. But they missed important clues. There was the irrational action of the witness in the face of an apparent nuclear attack! And that humming noise was a clue, for it was the same noise heard by Cynthia Appleton or the frightened girl from the small town near Manchester, a 'humming' or 'buzzing' noise that seems to herald another incursion into the twilight world UFOs seem to inhabit. More clues to the unreal aspects of the case came in descriptions of the 'oppressive atmosphere', an unnatural silence from the wit-

Typically, UFO photographs show ill-defined shapes which do not allow detailed analysis *(opposite and top)*. **However, the picture opposite was released by the Aerial Phenomena Research Organization, after close scrutiny. The picture by Californian highway engineer Rex Heflin is detailed enough to have led to a number of complex studies, although many claim it is a hoax.**

ness's dog and many cage birds, and instead of the normal street lights in the road outside everything was 'pitch-black'.

So even this apparent 'low strangeness', light-in-the-sky case seems to belong to that same mysterious, otherworld reality as the weirder, more spectacular cases we have examined.

But does all this *explain* UFOs any better than more conventional 'extraterrestrial' theories? Can it explain cases such as Betty and Barney Hill's, in which two or more people seem to undergo the same experience? It does seem likely that people close to each other, married couples, families, close friends, even workmates, can sometimes share an excursion into the symbol-haunted 'otherworld'. Possibly a dominant personality can impress their vision on others, and there may

be an element of telepathy involved. Or maybe Jung's 'collective subconscious' is such a strong force, deep in the human psyche, that it can manifest itself to any number of people at a time.

Over the years researchers have come up with thousands of pieces of what they call 'physical evidence' – alleged footprints, landing marks, burn traces, materials supposedly jettisoned from UFOs, even pieces of the elusive machines themselves. But none of this has ever been conclusive enough to convince scientists that they have discovered what has been tagged 'genuine extraterrestrial hardware'. In fact it is probable that no one piece of physical evidence, or even a single photograph, is unanimously accepted by even ufologists themselves as absolutely convincing.

So all we seem to be left with

is the testimony of the witness. Those people, normal, sane, rational people with nothing to gain from notoriety, who consistently report the most bizarre and irrational events, events which, behind their strange façade, seem to reflect something of the world we live in rather than some other planet light-years away. Strange encounters with weird beings, sometimes beautiful, sometimes hideous, reassuring or

frightening; sometimes warning us and communicating with us, more often indifferent, occasionally hostile.

Strange encounters, maybe not from outer space; but no less real, no less of a mystery, encounters with ourselves. Encounters with the demons and devils, angels and apparitions that dwell deep within mankind.

Encounters with another reality.

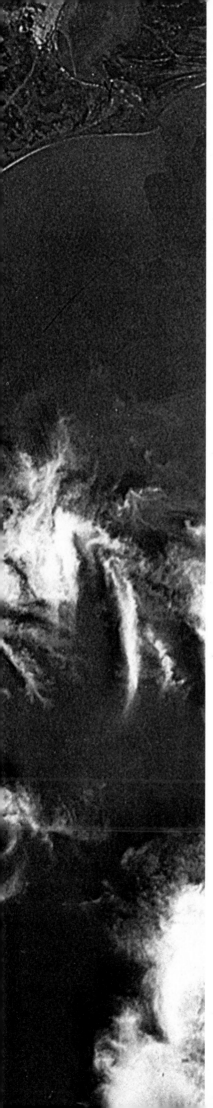

THE BERMUDA TRIANGLE

Some people believe that there are areas of the globe where the normal laws of the Earth are frequently suspended. In these regions strange happenings can occur including unaccounted disappearances and other unusual phenomena. Such an area is the Bermuda Triangle.

It has often been said that mystery is where you will find it. Everyone is intrigued by the challenge of the inexplicable, and the history of mankind itself may be seen as a continuous process of puzzle solving. Man has always felt uneasy in the face of the unknown. Where no rational explanation for phenomena has been readily evident man has devised one, giving rise in far pre-history to a pantheon of gods and a network of sentient forces responsible for the workings of the world. In this way, we assume, even before the development of cohesive religious and philosophical thought and before the stirrings of ordered scientific discovery man could cope with the mysteries of his existence. People faced with, as yet, totally unpredictable and bewildering threats to their survival (bad weather, disease and 'natural' disasters) had to take them as events that could be prevented by altered behaviour or some deference to the appropriate spirits and forces – or else they would have lived in perpetual terror and suspense.

Both experience and science have explained a great number of nature's mysteries satisfactorily, but we are far from being as complete in our mastery of the world and ourselves as many people choose to believe.

Throughout history certain places have been designated as specially sacred, evil, haunted or just plain strange. We are still finding them. And in a century that has seen astounding developments in technology, science and knowledge of the environment, people seem more determined than ever to scrutinize and understand inexplicable phenomena. The popular science and science fiction writer Isaac Asimov has suggested that nothing is really inexplicable; it only seems so as long as we are without the data necessary for the explanation.

In the realm of contemporary mysteries, the most widely popularized and sensationally reported (in addition to and association with UFOs) deal with so-called triangles, vortices, terror zones or flap areas situated around the world. These flap areas are so named because they are said to represent flaps, folds or tears in time and space – pockets in the world where known natural laws do not always apply. Flap areas, it is theorized, are characterized by a number of mysterious phenomena: strange disappearances, electrical, magnetic and gravitational anomalies, concentrated activity by UFOs and USOs (unidentified submersible objects), leaps in time, ghostly apparitions and eerie legacies from lost civilizations.

Flap area theories and the evidence for them can best be clarified by examining the case for the most popularly publicized of 'weird vortices' – the Bermuda Triangle.

The Bermuda Triangle is the name now widely understood to describe an area of the western Atlantic in which, allegedly, there is a staggeringly high incidence of baffling phenomena which require explanation. Unsolved disappearances, uncanny mechanical disorders, UFO and USO sightings and all the other earmarks of a flap area are ascribed to the area.

The specific geographical location and dimensions of the Bermuda Triangle vary according to different theorists and researchers, but the 'hard core' of the Triangle may be pictured by drawing a line from the south-eastern tip of Florida through the Bahamas to Puerto Rico, then north up to Bermuda and then back south-west to Florida. This is how Vincent Gaddis, the writer usually credited with coining the term 'Bermuda Triangle' in the 1960s, saw it. Others use the name but consider Triangle a misnomer, arguing that the area concerned is a lozenge or ellipse covering a far more extensive sector of the Atlantic.

In the twentieth century the lovely islands and turquoise waters of the Bermuda Triangle have made the area a mecca for tourists and a place with a strong fantasy image. Romance and hints of mystery have surrounded it from the very first chronicled voyage of discovery to the New World from Europe.

In 1492, shortly before making land in the West Indies, Christopher Columbus recorded in his ship's log that he and his crew had observed a

Many investigators have reported that areas such as this, off the coast of the USA, have mysteriously claimed people, aircraft and ships. One theory, put forward in the 1960s, is that there are as many as twelve 'flap' areas around the world.

angle – is one of the few places on earth where a compass needle does indicate both magnetic north and true north.

Since the time of Columbus, the Bermuda Triangle has experienced disproportionately heavy sea traffic compared with most of the planet's waters. The first explorers, conquering armies and adventurers made the journey to the rich New World via the West Indies. Colonists, merchants and slave traders followed. The sector is still much traversed, by trade vessels as well as by air traffic, a busy spot for island hopping private planes and small pleasure craft and a convenient site for US and British Naval and Air Force exercises.

An area with so many people constantly on the move can be expected to have more accidents, wrecks, crashes and losses than a more remote region. But according to the growing legend of the Bermuda Triangle too many disasters of a strange and unnatural kind have occurred there to be dismissed easily. Certainly there have been undeniably dramatic occurrences among these numerous tragedies, among them cases which even

large ball of fire fall into the sea. On 11 October, the eve of their historic landfall, Columbus and one other man saw a light over the water which vanished abruptly.

Within hours land was sighted. While these incidents have been cited as the first known indications that the Bermuda Triangle is fraught with bizarre happenings, Columbus himself was not apparently disturbed by what he had seen. The ball of fire may have been a meteor. The light may have been a fire on the shore, a torch in an Indian's boat or even an hallucination. Whatever it was, Christopher Columbus unwittingly provided the Bermuda Triangle with a five-hundred-year pedigree.

Even more interesting is Columbus' observation, while in the vicinity of the Sargasso Sea, that his compass needle was beginning to deviate from north to north-west. In the following days the deviation increased, frightening the crew and reinforcing their fears that they were entering · an unnatural region.

Columbus himself believed that the compass needle did not point at the North Star, or true north, but at something else, then undefined. His intuition was quite correct; this something else was, and is, the north magnetic pole. Although Columbus was the first to note such compass deviation, it occurs to some extent almost everywhere and is automatically compensated for by navigators. Curiously, the line longitude 80° west – at the western boundary of the Bermuda Tri-

unfanciful investigative authorities still acknowledge as insoluble.

Perhaps the most famous episode in the saga of the Bermuda Triangle is that of Flight 19. On 5 December 1945 at two in the afternoon Flight 19, a squadron of five TBM Avengers under the command of Lieutenant Charles C. Taylor left Fort Lauderdale Naval Air Station on a routine training flight. Fourteen men took part in the mission. A fifteenth man, Corporal Allan Kosnar, had been relieved of flight orders that day at his request.

The squadron proceeded to a wreck fifty-six miles east of Fort Lauderdale for mock bombing runs. They were scheduled to continue on an assigned course east, then north, then west south-west, describing a triangle that would bring them back to base at 4 pm.

At 3.45 pm the radio tower at Fort Lauderdale learned that Flight 19 was in trouble. Lieutenant Robert Cox, who was leading another airborne training squadron that afternoon, had picked up Lieutenant Taylor in FT28 communicating with one of the other pilots on Flight 19. Cox heard 'I don't know where we are. We must

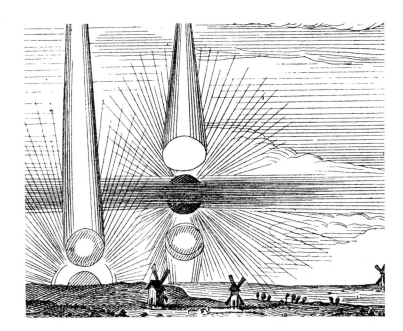

Opposite : **Christopher Columbus, who crossed the Bermuda Triangle unscathed on his historic voyage to the New World in 1492. Many natural phenomena, such as comets** *(left),* **meteors** *(above),* **and triple suns** *(top),* **that once puzzled observers have been explained by modern science; but the Bermuda Triangle is a reminder that many such mysteries still remain.**

have got lost after that last turn.' Cox alerted Fort Lauderdale, made contact with Taylor and relayed messages between them. Taylor reported that both his compasses were malfunctioning. From Taylor's description of broken land below him Cox felt sure that Flight 19 was then over the Bahamas or the Biminis. Then Cox had trouble with his transmitter, lost radio contact and had to land.

From this stage the story of what happened to Flight 19 is one of confusion and frenzy on the ground and in the air. Port Everglades, a communications base near Fort Lauderdale, had picked up Lieutenant Taylor and was able to establish two-way contact. Fort Lauderdale also picked up messages from Flight 19 but was not in direct communication with Taylor. Radio operators at each of the two bases received messages the other did not hear as Flight 19's transmissions alternately grew louder and faded out. This accounts for the contradictory reports of Taylor's messages: 'It looks like we are . . . entering white water. . . . Everything is wrong . . . even the

ocean doesn't look as it should.'

It seems certain that Lieutenant Taylor thought he had strayed over the Gulf of Mexico. The squadron changed directions several times and spotted some islands. Presumably they did not attempt crash landings because they still hoped to make base. A message – 'Don't come after me' – was received. Was it a warning or an expression of confidence?

Contrary to some accounts, the squadron had enough fuel to remain in the air until roughly 8 pm. At first, attempts to make a fix on their position by radio bearings failed. Then, at about 6 pm their position was calculated to be east of Florida and north of the Bahamas. But by that time radio contact was erratic and the fix was not communicated to Taylor. Two-way communications with him were lost at 5.30. After 6 pm their course is unknown.

It was not until just before 7.30 that the first search planes went out after Flight 19. Two Martin Mariners, Training No. 32 and Training No. 49, left Banana River Naval Air Station on separate courses. Training No. 32, carrying a crew of thirteen, was supposed to make a report at 8.30. She didn't. Now the Martin Mariner was also missing.

The last weak and garbled sounds of Flight 19 came at about 6.45, when Port Everglades heard one of the pilots trying to raise Lieutenant Taylor. After that, nothing. Just before 10 pm operators heard a weak 'FT . . . FT . . .'.

Meanwhile the pilot of the second Mariner reported heavy air turbulence and very rough seas. The area had been completely dark since 6 pm.

Coast guard vessels looked for survivors through the night. At first light the most intensive air-sea search in the area's history commenced. Hundreds of planes and vessels including destroyers and submarines combed nearly 1 million square kilometres (400,000 square miles). No trace of either Flight 19 or of the Martin Mariner was ever found – no debris, no life jackets and not even an oil slick.

The Navy Board of Investigation came up with a number of opinions about the fate of Flight 19. The favoured belief was that on running out of fuel the planes made forced landings in 'unfavourable conditions'. As for the Martin Mariner, a large explosion observed by a ship at 7.50 off the east coast of Florida was believed to have been the end of the plane, a type sometimes described as a 'flying gas tank'.

Nevertheless, a member of the Naval Board confessed that the evidence did not provide any real conclusions. 'They vanished as completely as if they had flown to Mars.'

Another case that commonly figures in accounts of the Bermuda Triangle is that of the *USS Cyclops*, which disappeared in March 1918 *en route* to Baltimore from Barbados. The true circumstances surrounding the *Cyclops* are so bizarre that a thriller-writer would be embarrassed to concoct such a wild plot.

The ship's master was Lieutenant Commander George W. Worley, who had changed his name from Wichman and had entered the USA illegally in his youth. He was German born. He was also a notorious eccentric, who frequented the bridge wearing

Above : **a squadron of Avengers.** *Right :* **the** *Sylvia L. Ossa,* **seen here docked in New Orleans in March 1975 – a cargo ship that disappeared in the Bermuda Triangle, with all 37 crewmen.** *Opposite above :* **the** USS *Cyclops* **whose mysterious disappearance still baffles all the experts.** *Opposite :* **a** *Mariner* **aircraft, equipped for sea searches.**

long underwear and a bowler hat. Reputedly a vicious disciplinarian, he was hated by his crew, which included a number of known ruffians. On board as a passenger was the U.S. Consul General to Brazil, Alfred Gottschalk, who before the USA's entry into World War I, had been outspoken in his support of Germany. Also on board were three naval prisoners, former *Cyclops* crewmen who had been court-martialled after a murder on the ship. One of the prisoners was to be executed.

Not surprisingly, with a cast like that rumours about the *Cyclops*, its crew and passengers were rife among naval personnel in Rio de Janeiro, where the ship had lain over during January and February.

According to Brockholst Livingston, the US Consul at Barbados, where the *Cyclops* made port on 3 March, Worley requested money from him to take on large quantities of coal and food. Livingston subsequently learned that the *Cyclops* had been under orders to proceed directly to Baltimore from Rio and that the ship already carried plenty of coal and provisions for the journey.

The *Cyclops* left Barbados on 4 March heading the wrong way – south, according to eyewitnesses – but she was in radio contact with a British liner on 5 March, reporting that all was well. On 13 March the ship was declared overdue in Baltimore and a massive search unsued. Newspapers reported that naval officials refused to believe that

the largest ship in the Navy ever to disappear could have sunk in reasonably good weather without leaving any trace of either the vessel or any of the three hundred people on board.

It emerged later that Naval Intelligence had followed up the many rumours about those on board the *Cyclops*, speculating that there had been a mutiny by the crew, a conspiracy to turn the ship over to the Germans, a bloody escape bid by the prisoners or an explosion at the hands of saboteurs. Otherwise they feared the ship had been

theses. German records examined after the war established that there were no mines or German submarines in the area at the time. No evidence ever came to light to indicate that the ship had been handed over to the Germans or taken by mutineers to South America. There were no reports of weather bad enough anywhere on the ship's possible routes to disturb the cargo. If the ship had encountered any trouble she could have radioed for help. (The *Cyclops* was the first large ship

German submarine in the North Atlantic. And in late November and early December 1941 two of the *USS Cyclops's* sister ships, *Proteus* and *Nereus*, both vanished on separate runs from the Virgin Islands to the USA.

Dozens of other planes and vessels have been lost without a trace in the Bermuda Triangle over the years. Most of these have been small private planes and craft whose losses, while tragic, are not necessarily mysterious. In these cases the effect

radioed that they would shortly be arriving on schedule. On 28 December 1948 a DC-3 carrying thirty-five people from Puerto Rico radioed that it was just 80 km (50 miles) south of Miami and then disappeared. On 17 January 1949 the *Star Ariel*, sister aircraft of the *Star Tiger*, reported to its point of departure in Bermuda that weather was good and that it was switching radio frequency to notify Jamaica of its arrival. Such contact was never made and it too vanished.

torpedoed by a German submarine or struck a mine.

On top of all this, the ship was heavily loaded with a cargo of manganese ore, and there were theories that the cargo shifted and sunk the ship, that her bottom had dropped out, that she had broken in two or that she had flipped upside down, like the liner in the disaster film *The Poseidon Adventure*. Two journals even suggested that she had been dragged down by a gigantic squid.

But the Navy could not give credence to any of these hypo-

so equipped to disappear without sending a single SOS.)

The *Cyclops* is still remembered as 'the most baffling mystery in the annals of the Navy'. It is also the first link of a chain of very uncomfortable coincidences. A British ship, also called *Cyclops, was* sunk by the Germans, in the North Atlantic. In November 1928 the British liner *Vestris*, the ship that had been the last to communicate with the *Cyclops*, disappeared without a trace while bound for Barbados. In January 1941 a second British *Cyclops* was destroyed by a

of human error, mechanical failures and weather difficulties, non-professional pilots and seamen must be taken into account. Nor is the utter disappearance of small craft in a big ocean wildly remarkable.

However, there are on record major disappearances that have been followed by heavy but fruitless searches and thorough but inconclusive investigations. The aircraft *Star Tiger*, for no known reason and without sending any distress message, vanished on 30 January 1948 *en route* to Bermuda with thirty-one people after the pilot

Perhaps even more striking than the disappearances of craft, and further fuel to the Bermuda Triangle mythos, is the incidence of vessels found intact but abandoned. Yet the more peculiar cases of this phenomenon also weaken the case for the Triangle as a definable flap area. To encompass the more spectacular riddles, the area of the Bermuda Triangle must be stretched up the US coast past four states and much further east over the mid-Atlantic.

The 'star' abandoned vessel mystery of maritime history is the famous case of the *Mary Celeste*, found drifting in December 1872 minus her captain, his wife and child and eight crewmen. The lifeboat was gone and so were the navigation instruments. Her journey was from New York to Genoa, and the last position entered in the log put her a hundred miles west of the Azores. When the *Mary Celeste* was found she was nearer Portugal than Bermuda. Despite theories ranging from mutiny to fraud (perpetrated to claim the cargo) to a false fire alarm on board (the suggestion to which Lloyd's, the ship's insurers, incline) there has never been a clue to what really happened.

Among other well-documented cases is that of the *Carroll A. Deering*, found run aground on the North Carolina coast in January 1921, its sole occupants two ravenous cats. The twelve-man crew and the lifeboats were missing, but no one could understand why they abandoned ship. All her sails were set and the schooner was in first-rate condition. The most eerie part of the mystery was the table set with a partly-eaten meal. Obviously something had happened quickly.

Compounding the mystery was the complete disappearance at the same time of the steamer *Hewitt*, believed to have been in the same area. For several months the US government suspected that the *Deering* crew and possibly the *Hewitt* had been kidnapped by modern pirates, rum runners or Russian agents. There was some evidence pointing to intruders. A lightship crew who had seen the *Deering* were hailed by a red-headed man who could not be identified later as a crew member. They also observed an unidentified steamship close behind the schooner. Was it the *Hewitt*?

Soon after the *Deering* discovery a message in a bottle was found which purported to be from a crew member and read 'an oil-burning tanker or submarine has boarded us and placed our crew in irons.' Handwriting experts agreed that it was in the hand of the *Deering* engineer, but Lloyd's were contemptuous. As they pointed out, a flaw in the piracy theory was that it was the crew and not the ship that had gone missing. Why would brigands or Bolsheviks want only the men?

The insurers and the Coast Guard leaned to the theory that the crew had panicked in bad weather and bolted in the life-

boats, only to be lost at sea. Lloyd's also opined that the crew may have been rescued by the *Hewitt*, which subsequently sank.

Eventually the man who had found the message in the bottle – named, of all things, Christopher Columbus Gray – admitted that it was a hoax. Piracy, mutiny and accidental drowning all have their proponents, but each of these explanations leaves tantalizing questions about the derelict *Deering* unanswered.

No matter how bizarre such losses are, it is possible to come up with some rational explanation for their occurrence which is within the realms of nature as we know it. The US Coast Guard's official statement on the Bermuda Triangle provides a definitely no-nonsense line. 'The Gulf

Above : **the *Mary Celeste*, found drifting and crewless, one of the world's most celebrated unsolved mysteries.** *Top and right :* **two nineteenth-century illustrations of a kraken, a fabled sea monster said to inhabit the North American coast.**

Stream, with its turbulence and swiftness, can quickly erase any sign of disaster. . . . The weather in the Caribbean-Atlantic area, with its ability to change rapidly, can produce thunderstorms and waterspouts without warning, making pilots and navigators face sudden catastrophe. . . . Weather conditions, equipment failure, and human error, rather than something from the supernatural, are what have caused these

tragedies.'

Since the Coast Guard Air Station Miami currently receives about eight thousand distress calls a year and can boast that the majority of its rescue operations are successful, this opinion merits some respect.

But the argument that the Bermuda Triangle actually exists does not rest upon disappearances alone. It is the other reported incidents in the area which have given it a claim to

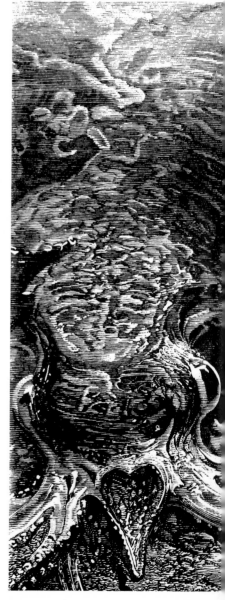

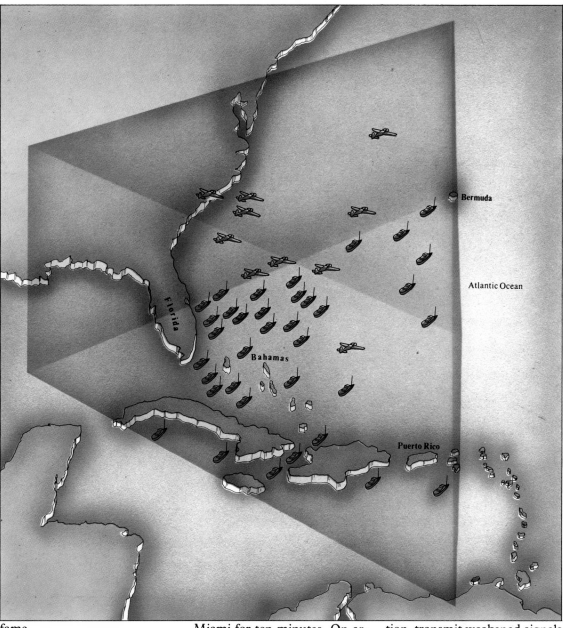

fame.

According to Triangle researchers, including Charles Berlitz (author of the most popular book on the subject, *The Bermuda Triangle*), Adi-Kent Thomas Jeffrey (*They Dared the Bermuda Triangle*) and Richard Winer (*The Devil's Triangle*), airplane pilots have told them that their compasses and instruments have become temporarily useless on some flights through the Bermuda Triangle. Others relate that strange glows appeared along their wings. Yachtsmen have attested that their electrical equipment has suddenly failed and has sometimes just as suddenly started up again.

More amazing is the case that Berlitz quotes of a National Airlines 727 passenger flight that disappeared from radar at Miami for ten minutes. On arrival the crew denied that anything odd had happened to them except that they had flown through a light fog for ten minutes. All the timepieces on the plane were ten minutes slow, although they had matched up in a time check with the airport shortly before their 'disappearance'. If it is correct, the incident suggests an aberrant energy field that creates time warps or gaps. A few pilots have related marvellous experiences of gaining impossible time on flights after flying through sudden hazes.

Particularly intriguing is an electronics-related phenomenon first noticed in 1972. All the polar-orbiting weather satellites sent up by a US government agency, the National Oceanic and Atmospheric Administra-tion, transmit weakened signals while passing over the Bermuda Triangle. A college physics professor named Wayne Meshejian, who has locked horns with NOAA over his observations, believes there must be an electromagnetic force in the area strong enough to affect the electronic pulses and erase the magnetic tape in these satellites, which are 1290 km (800 miles) overhead. Various officials have attributed the black-outs to different causes, such as unspecified 'interference' and tape rewinding. But no one has explained why they consistently start in the Triangle zone.

The mystery of the weather satellites may prove the key to the whole Bermuda Triangle controversy. So far a number of theories have been put for-

marine life either unknown to us or believed extinct, UFOs that are also aquatic or vehicles operated by either an unknown underwater civilization or inhabitants of a hollow region inside the earth.

Again there is absolutely no evidence for any of these thoughts, although they make for interesting speculation. Undoubtedly people have seen

Above: **John Fairfax, who saw two UFOs on his solo row across the Atlantic. Sea monsters were the 'vogue' mystery of the second half of the nineteenth century;** *right:* **a sea serpent attacks the** *British Banner* **and** *(above right)*, **a monstrous algae in tow behind the** *Peking. Far right:* **a phantom burning ship.**

ward concerning flap areas and the secrets they contain. Both sincere researchers and blatant sensationalists jumping on the bandwagon have presented an assortment of mind-boggling hypotheses.

According to Berlitz, Winer and other persuasive writers, there have been a number of UFO sightings in the Bermuda Triangle. John Fairfax, the Englishman who performed the amazing feat of rowing across the Atlantic solo, witnessed two UFOs on his passage to Fort Lauderdale, to name but one case. It may be pointed out that as NASA has found Florida a good location for launching space shots, so extraterrestrials may have found the area a fine entry path.

If UFOs are of extraterrestrial origin, are powered by devices and methods alien to us and do frequent the Triangle,

their presence could provide an acceptable explanation for previously unexplained disappearances and odd instrument malfunctions. If one is prepared to accept that UFO occupants are potentially 'people nappers' they could also be made to account for missing persons. The film *Close Encounters of the Third Kind* opened with the discovery in a desert of an abandoned squadron of planes missing since the 1940s and ended with the missing squadron crewmen, unaged, emerging from an alien ship – thus depicting what some people would like to believe happened to Flight 19.

But these are very big 'ifs' for UFO sceptics. There is no concrete evidence that extraterrestrials operate in the Triangle. If one accepts the official records of communications with planes and vessels in distress,

never has a pilot or boatman reported 'they look as if they are from outer space' or anything like that. Those whose mistrust of officialdom runs deep may choose to believe that governments and their scientific and military agencies are covering up UFO-related phenomena in the area. But there is no concrete evidence of that either.

USO sightings have opened up even more lines of thought, since they are variously held to be monstrous species of sub-

USOs, but like UFOs they are, by definition, unidentified. Richard Winer cites the testimony of Bruce Mounier, a commercial diver from Miami who saw two fast-moving objects he described as 18 metres (60 feet) long, grey and egg-shaped. Winer has also witnessed a gigantic something, round, purple and pulsating, ascend towards him and a companion while they were diving and then descend into the darkness. Years later he saw a lagoon full of jellyfish; the similarity of their movements to those of the USO he had seen led him to wonder if it might not have been a monstrous jellyfish. Adi-Kent Thomas Jeffrey quotes a Florida skin diver named Louis Lento who has seen dazzling lights appear out of nowhere in deep water and then vanish.

Dr J. Manson Valentine, an expert on the Mayan and Aztec cultures, has discovered what

seem to be the ruins of ancient stonework on the sea bed near Bimini. The 'Bimini Wall' and other possible constructions may be man-made remains of a sunken land mass, and the general area is one of the many proposed as the location of lost Atlantis.

Those who believe that the Atlanteans still survive underwater are in a distinct minority. More numerous is the body of firm believers in the fabled achievements of the Atlanteans. Drawing largely from the writings of the late prophet Edgar Cayce, they suppose that the Atlanteans had mastered lasers, atomic power and other wonders of our modern age. If this were so, and their sophisticated technology were ultimately the destruction of the Atlanteans, might there be some unimaginable and potentially deadly power source lying lost in the depths of the Bermuda Triangle?

The unexplained black-outs of weather satellites become particularly intriguing in relation to this notion, pre-posterous though it appears.

Something powerful is affecting sophisticated equipment over this area and there has yet to be a satisfactory explanation of what that something is from the orthodox experts.

Phantasms are the last type of phenomenon reported in the Bermuda Triangle. While legends of ghost vessels are nearly as old as navigation, a few of the apparitions in the Bermuda Triangle are fascinating.

In the late evening of 27 February 1935, guests in the Hotel Daytona Beach and sea-side strollers were horrified to see a plane heading straight towards them plunge into the water. Coast Guard vessels were called and found nothing, but separate eye-witnesses told the same story. No plane answering their descriptions was reported missing.

In autumn 1967 two stewards on the *Queen Elizabeth I*, bound for Nassau, saw a small plane heading towards them silently disappear into the water when it was nearly upon them. The ship turned back but found no signs of an accident.

Since both these experiences were shared by more than one person, there seem to be two explanations. They were either cases of joint hallucination or genuine apparitions. 'Ghost planes', if that is what they were, at first do not seem to fit into the picture of the area as an 'anomalic flap'. But a growing body of opinion on 'hauntings' has it that they are electrical energy 'imprints' of traumatic happenings. If the Bermuda Triangle is a hotbed of electro-magnetic deviation, such apparitions could be time-looped re-enactments of past tragedies.

After attention was focused on the Bermuda Triangle people started to piece together a case for similar phenomena reported in other parts of the world. Flap areas or anomalic zones have been indentified as such when the incidence of Bermuda Triangle-related phenomena is considered to have become out of proportion with those occurring in 'normal'

places.

Weird disappearances have happened all over the world – the famous American writer Ambrose Bierce went missing without a trace in 1913, a regiment of British soldiers apparently walked into oblivion in Turkey in 1915, children on bicycles have vanished in Britain in recent years. Heavy concentrations of UFO sightings have been reported in various countries – the southern USA in October 1973, and Italy and Australia in December 1978, for example. Ghost stories abound in every culture. Are there really anomalic regions where all of these things happen to a greater extent?

It was the late Ivan T. Sanderson, head of the Society for the Investigation of the Unexplained, who put forward the theory of twelve mystery lozenges or flap areas around the world in the late 1960s. These include the North and South polar regions, the Bermuda Triangle and its so-called opposite on the other side of the world, Japan's Devil's Sea.

The Devil's Sea is often referred to in accounts of the Bermuda Triangle. It is said to cover an area lying between south-east Japan, Iwo Jima in the Bonin Islands and the Mariana Islands. Coincidentally, longitude 150° east, which passes through this zone, is another spot where compass needles point to both true north and the north magnetic pole. According to flap area phenomenologists, the Devil's Sea has claimed a staggering

number of planes and boats. There were huge losses here during World War II, and the famous aviatrix Amelia Earhart may have met her unknown fate near the Marianas. For years small Japanese fishing boats have been lost in the area, but the same statement can be made about other parts of the ocean around Japan. Lawrence David Kusche, who successfully demystified several disappearances claimed to be Bermuda Triangle riddles in *The Bermuda Triangle Mystery — Solved*, made many attempts to authenticate the Devil's Sea legend and states that he had difficulty finding anyone in Japan who had heard of such a place.

The major disaster 'credited' to strange forces in the Devil's Sea is the loss of a government research ship, the *Daigo Kaiyo-maru*, in September 1952. Contrary to most accounts, the *Kaiyo-maru* was not on a mission to investigate the Devil's Sea but was inspecting the Myojin Sho Reefs, which had recently been thrust up from the ocean bed by violent underwater tremors and possible underwater volcanic activity. Japan and its surrounding regions have, of course, suffered from earthquakes and related waterspouts and tidal waves throughout recorded history.

The *Kaiyo-maru*, with thirty-one people on board, probably disappeared in a tidal wave resulting from an underwater volcano, according to Japanese meteorologists and the Coast Guard. Afterwards the Japanese government did not, as has

been claimed, declare the Devil's Sea an official danger zone. It was the Maritime Safety Agency which, in one of their periodic notices to mariners, warned boatmen to avoid the Myojinsho Reef area because of sporadic underwater volcanic disturbances. The area is still considered dangerous.

Unfortunately for the thinning plot, the long well-known violence of storms and typhoons in the western Pacific can be considered responsible for disappearances at sea – particularly since it is admitted that the scanty number of specific cases categorized as phenomena were lost mainly in winter months.

One interesting radar mystery does exist in the Devil's Sea. Dubbed 'The Galloping Ghost of Nansei Shoto', it seems to be a large, slow object picked up on radar screens near Okinawa. Richard Winer states that US planes investigated the reported object many times during World War II, but it always disappeared from radar screens as the planes approached. Since that time, however, it has not been observed enough to arouse much comment.

The absence of any other alleged phenomena makes the Devil's Sea a poor second to the Bermuda Triangle as a contemporary mystery. Using these two locales as the basis for plotting a network of equidistant anomalic regions, Ivan Sanderson arrived at his twelve lozenges, five of them north of the Equator and five south, with 72° intervals between them. Besides the poles, the Bermuda Triangle and the Devil's Sea these flap areas are sited in the middle of the Indian Ocean, east of Australia and north of New Zealand, in the North Pacific between the Devil's Sea and the Bermuda Triangle, in the middle of the South Pacific, just off the east coast of Brazil and Uruguay, at the top of north-west Africa, just off the east coast of South Africa and around Afghanistan.

As far as the poles are concerned, observed phenomena

there are scarce since these are remote uninhabited areas visited only by a few explorers and scientific expeditions. 'White blindness' has been a trial and sometimes a tragedy for explorers who have suffered extreme disorientation in the vastness of the snow and ice.

Of the other areas, few have been accredited with any detailed instances of electro-magnetic aberrations. It is merely hypothesized that they are there. A single dramatic mystery for the North Pacific zone may be found in a story recounted by the American television personality Arthur Godfrey on a national programme broadcast in the early 1970s. Godfrey, a licensed pilot, had been invited to go on a test flight of an experimental plane, the *Mars*, from Hawaii. Godfrey was delayed and missed the flight. Disappointed, he waited in the airport tower and watched the plane on radar. Suddenly the plane blinked off the screen and rescue planes and ships dispatched immediately found no trace of it.

The Indian Ocean zone has a little more in common with the Bermuda Triangle. In June 1909, the captain and crew of a Danish steamship, the *Bintang*, reported witnessing a huge, round USO which rotated and projected beams of light. Sightings of a similar mystery wheel of lights have been made in the Bermuda Triangle. As for disappearances and apparitions, the Indian Ocean can claim the most famous and spectacular of all sea legends. In 1650 a Dutch merchant ship captained by Bernard Fokke set sail from Holland for Indonesia. Her day of departure was Good Friday, which was regarded by some as blasphemous. The ship never made any of her scheduled ports, so it is unlikely that she got anywhere near the Indian Ocean. But it was in the Indian Ocean less than a year later that another Dutch vessel encountered Fokke and his ship during a storm. Drawing close the crew hailed Fokke and his men and then saw them vanish

into thin air. In the intervening three centuries the same story – sighting a seventeenth-century Dutch vessel and seeing it vanish – has been reported over and over again. Fokke and his crewmen have been immortalized as the mariners of *The Flying Dutchman*.

Mysteriously deserted ships have also been found in the Indian Ocean. In February 1953 the diesel ship *Holchu* was found drifting. As in the case of the *Deering*, a meal was laid out, the ship was in good con-

dition and there was no clue as to why the crew should have abandoned her.

As for the rest of the flap areas, there is disappointingly little to get hold of for the most avid of mystery spotters. During World War II, several planes are said to have disappeared over Afghanistan, but no other startling revelations seem to be there for the unearthing. The north African coast of the Mediterranean has seen a sorry share of maritime disasters, but not necessarily

Hurricane over the Caribbean, a possible explanation for some of the mysterious disappearances.

more than one could realistically expect in an area with a high concentration of sea traffic since the earliest days of navigation. The Cape of Good Hope has taken a horrific toll in lives, but the area is characterized by some of the most unpredictable weather and violent storms sailors have to encounter. The Brazilian coast is unremarkable in chronicles of the bizarre, as are the practically empty ex-panses of the south-eastern Pacific.

In the southern Pacific zone just north of New Zealand sudden storms are probably responsible for the disappear-ances documented there. It is only since the spate of UFO sightings in December 1978 along the east coast of Australia that the general area is begin-ning to attract second looks. Almost as if in fulfilment of expectations of doom an Australian pilot disappeared with his plane that December, and he *did* report seeing a UFO just before he went missing.

Attempts to debunk the Bermuda Triangle mystery have not met with the same popular success as the stories that continue to enlarge it. It must be said that there is little mystery for the sceptic to solve if one determines that it does not exist in the first place. There is an old proverb that decrees 'if you don't wonder at the wonderful, it ceases to be a wonder.'

Certainly when wonder has been aroused it becomes self-perpetuating. People expecting a good mystery in the Bermuda Triangle may be more sus-ceptible to finding themselves participants in unusual ex-periences. How many of the flap area phenomena there have a rational explanation? Looking again at the classic drama of the Bermuda Triangle, the loss of Flight 19, one can argue very plausibly that it is no mystery at all. A slight initial human error, compounded by the breakdown in communi-cations, the inefficiency of the direction-finder equipment and the inability of those on the ground to give the squadron firm, consistent instructions probably sent them to their doom in the dark expanse of the Atlantic. The ghostly 'FT . . .FT' picked up by a radio operator after the planes presumably ran out of fuel was almost certainly a last effort of one of the other stations in-volved to contact FT 28.

A single electrical spark could have blown apart the Martin Mariner rescue plane.

The *USS Cyclops* may well have been on a furtive course to who-knows-where when she went down too suddenly to signal for help.

The crew of the *Carroll A. Deering* may have been mur-dered for an illicit cargo of rum, which was removed.

However, so long as people claim, as they are continuing to do, that they have seen strange things and grappled with inexplicable forces in the Bermuda Triangle, they cannot all be dismissed as cranks or yarn spinners.

The number of incidents alleged to involve electro-magnetic disturbances could point to two simple expla-nations, both of which are serious matters. It is known that at various times in the earth's history the planet's magnetic field has gradually faded and then reversed itself, affecting climate and life forms to a devastating extent. Such a reversal of the magnetic poles about seventy million years ago took place in the age that saw the dinosaurs perish. It is believed that the magnetic poles have reversed at intervals of about 200,000 or 250,000 years, and it seems that we are long overdue for another magnetic upheaval, the last one having been placed at 700,000 years ago. If there really are spots on the earth where the magnetic field is unstable – and some of the Bermuda Triangle investi-gation suggests that it is – it could be the beginning of a long process leading to the world's magnetic reversal. If that is going to happen there is nothing we can do about it.

The other idea that has to be taken seriously is a growing source of concern to scientists. Massive pollution on a global scale. particularly from the burning of fuels and the dis-persal of radiation, may be having a dangerous effect on weather patterns and atmos-pheric conditions. If such changes are taking place the phenomena that vigilant Bermuda Triangle watchers could be observing may be the results of atmospheric changes unnoticed elsewhere.

That fictional master of seem-ingly insoluble mysteries, Sherlock Holmes, was fond of the dictum 'When you have eliminated the impossible what-ever remains, however improb-able, must be the truth.' Our problem is in knowing what to eliminate. How certain can we be of what is impossible?

INDEX

Page numbers in italics indicate illustrations

ACKNOWLEDGMENTS

The publishers would like to thank the following organizations and individuals for their kind permission to reproduce the photographs in this book:

Academy of Applied Science, Boston, USA: 128, 129 below; Associated Press: 106 left, 150–1 below, 151 above; Janet and Colin Bord: 32–3 below, 62–3, 65 below; Camera Press: 122 below, 127 above left and right, and below, 129 above; Tim Dinsdale: 118–9, 124–5; Robert Estall: 31 above right, 36–7 above, 38–9 above, 40–1 above left, 41 below, 44–5 below; Mary Evans Picture Library: 80 left, 84 below right, 85, 131, 132 left, 132–3 above and below, 133, 134, 148–9, 152–3, 154 below, 154–5 above, 155; Fortean Picture Library: 84 above left, 116–7, 120–1 above, 123, 124, 145 below; Sonia Halliday: 86–7, 89; Robert Harding Associates: 12–3 above, 30–1, 57 left and right, 60–1 above and below, 103 above; The John Hillelson Agency Ltd: 54–5, 56 below, 56–7; Michael Holford Photographs: 1, 22–3 below, 28–9 above, 35 left, 46–9, 52–3 above, 53, 61 above and below, 74–5, 88–9, 97; The Kobal Collection: 130–1 above and below; William McQuitty: 4–5, 18–21, 24–7 below; The National Gallery: 106 below; The Observer: 126 below; Picturepoint Ltd: 66–71 below, 76–8, 78–9, 80–1, 82–3 below, 95, 156–7; Popperfoto: 90–3, 114–5 above, 115, 122–3 above, 136–7, 137 above and below, 154 above left. Rex Features Ltd: 100–1, 104–5; Spectrum Colour Library: 2–3, 6, 10–11, 12, 13 below, 14–17, 33 centre–35 below, 39 below, 41 above right, 43, 50 below left and right, 50–1 above, 58 below, 59 above, 63–64 below, 65 above, 72–3, 79, 82–3 above, 102, 103 below, 106–7 above, 109 below, 110–1, 112–3, 113, 114–5 below, 120–1, 146–7; Stern/ Pixfeatures: 98–9; Michael J. H. Taylor: 150–1 above and below; Robert Wilcox: 108; Maureen Willis: 107; Ian Wilson: 104; Zefa Picture Library: Endpapers, 8–9, 17, 29, 35 right, 36, 36–7 below, 42–3, 46 above, 52–3 below, 58–9 above, 60 above left, 94–5.